How the other half lives

Manchester University Press

How the other half lives

Interconnecting socio-spatial inequalities

Edited by

Samuel Burgum and Katie Higgins

MANCHESTER UNIVERSITY PRESS

Published by Manchester University Press
Oxford Road, Manchester M13 9PL
www.manchesteruniversitypress.co.uk

British Library Cataloguing-in-Publication Data
A catalogue record for this book is available from the
British Library

ISBN   978 1 5261 4655 7   hardback
ISBN   978 1 5261 7675 2   paperback

First published 2022

Typeset
by New Best-set Typesetters Ltd

Contents

Figures

Contributors

Maurizio Artero, University of Milan
Maurizio's main research interests are in the field of forced migration and urban refuge. His current research deals with practices and policies of refugees' reception and integration in Italy in light of the conflict between local policies of exclusion, de-bordering initiatives by civil societies, and practices of 'citizenship from below' by asylum seekers and refugees.

Rowland Atkinson, University of Sheffield
Rowland's work crosses the boundaries of urban and housing studies, sociology, geography and criminology. Much of his research hinges on identifying hidden and sometimes invisible social problems and issues, including the ways in which social inequality drives spatial problems. His current research focuses on higher income groups and the 'alpha city'.

Samuel Burgum, Birmingham City University
Sam's recent research has been an ethnographic focus on squatting in London, as a practice of shelter, protest and culture. Going forwards, he will focus on the potential impact that proposals to criminalise trespass in England and Wales will have on vulnerable groups. Sam is also interested in the connection between history, archives and possibility.

Nigel de Noronha, University of Manchester
Based in the School of Social Sciences, Nigel's central research interests are in housing, race and migration in the UK, exploring the contradictions and struggles arising in the conflicts between national and

local state policies and the right to adequate housing. Central to this approach is understanding the historical context of social and spatial inequalities and an ambition to contribute to breaking them down.

Anthony Ellis, University of Salford

A critical criminologist, Anthony's ethnographic research focuses on violent crime amongst men in economically deprived communities in the north of England. Recently, Anthony's work has focused on recorded increases in higher harm violence, particularly homicide and weapon-enabled violence, in England and Wales.

Katie Higgins, University of Sheffield

Katie's research engages with social and spatial inequalities through a focus on the everyday experience and reproduction of power. In particular, her work with privileged migrants explores themes of nation, colonialism and 'race', while her more recent research with ultra-wealthy elites and their professional intermediaries examines dynastic wealth, the production of elite business subjects and fraternity for capitalist owners and executives.

Sarah Kunz, University of Bristol

Sarah's research interests include privileged and investment migration, the politics of migration categories, the relationship between mobility, coloniality and racism, and the study of elites and their intermediaries. Her chapter is part of a project that draws on ethnographic and archival research to examine the postcolonial history and politics of the category expatriate across multiple sites.

Gaja Maestri, Aston University

A political sociologist, Gaja's research addresses questions of migration and civil society organisations, with specific attention to urbanism. Her wider research interests include ethnicity and migration, collective action and political participation, as well as urban citizenship and housing (marginality, exclusion, segregation and camps).

Caterina Mazzilli, Queen Mary University of London

Situated in the field of human geography, Caterina's research focuses on migration, place-narratives, and diversity at the urban level, and, more recently, on labour migration. The present chapter is part of her research on Brighton and Bologna's narratives of receptiveness. She is currently working as a post-doctoral research assistant.

Pierre Monforte, University of Leicester
Broadly situated within the field of political sociology, Pierre's research interests include social movements, migration and citizenship. In particular, he has worked on the protests for the rights of migrants in France, Germany, Britain and Canada, from a comparative perspective.

Timothy Monteath, London School of Economics
Timothy makes extensive use of digital methodologies to investigate questions of inequality, wealth and mobility. His recent research has taken a mixed methods approach to investigating digital data on housing and elites, making use of big data and new digital methods to trace inequality through infrastructure.

Joe Penny, Queen Mary University of London
Sitting between urban economic geography and urban planning, Joe's research explores three main themes: the restructuring of urban governance under conditions of austerity; the financialisation of the local state, public land and housing; and the nature and dynamics of urban politics and democracy.

Ilaria Pulini, Goldsmiths University of London
An urban sociologist, Ilaria's work has focused on place-bound studies of the west London social elite, focusing on change and continuity at street-level. For over 20 years, she was Director of the Civic Museum of Archaeology and Anthropology in Modena, and has published widely on the history of ethnography collections, museums and material culture.

Morag Rose, University of Liverpool
Morag's research interests include public space, gender and access, alongside psychogeography and walking as a political, cultural and creative tool. A lecturer in human geography with a background in performance art, community development, and the voluntary sector, she continues to be committed to equality and spatial justice.

Elisabeth Schimpfössl, Aston University
Elisabeth's current research focuses on philanthropy, both in Russia and the UK. She has also conducted research on media and journalism in Eastern Europe, with a focus on self-censorship. Prior to working in academia, Elisabeth worked in development cooperation under the Austrian Foreign Ministry.

Jonathan Silver, University of Sheffield
As an urban geographer, Jonathan's research agenda concentrates on developing new ideas and vocabularies concerning global urbanisation, with particular interest in infrastructures and housing. He is currently working on two research projects: the ERC funded GlobalCORRIDOR and the ESRC funded Centripetal City.

Amparo Tarazona-Vento, University of Sheffield
With an academic and professional background in planning, urban design and architecture, and a PhD and research interests in line with urban geography and sociology, Amparo has a multidisciplinary perspective on the built environment. Her research investigates the contested politics of urban regeneration and the political economy of urbanisation and city-making, placing special focus on the analysis of the political mobilisation of iconic architecture and the contribution of grassroots politics to place making.

Zoe Williams, *Guardian*
A renowned author, journalist and columnist, Zoe writes regularly for the *Guardian* and the *New Statesman*. Her work provides incisive and passionate political commentary, interviews and reviews, and she has published books engaging with issues in feminism and left-wing politics. She is a patron of Humanists UK.

Preface

Zoe Williams

There was a point in the mid-2010s when the forces of progressive politics looked as though they were starting to win; in retrospect, it was like boiling an ocean, but at the time, victories for insurgent parties like Syriza and Podemos, as well as a surge of energy around the Scottish referendum campaign, were reasons enough for optimism and, moreover, respect. They spored advice – your movement will start to succeed when the reality you describe matches the one that people are living (Podemos); what we need is democracy, democracy and ever deeper democracy (Syriza); and an idea that continued to resonate long after the Scottish referendum was over, from a meeting of one of its campaigning groups, Common Weal – 'we will not succeed until we stop asking qualitative questions about the poor, and start asking qualitative questions about the rich'.

Well, why not? What qualitative questions should one be asking about the rich?

The backdrop was a political mainstream that asked constant qualitative questions about the poor: think tanks asked, are the poor aspirational enough? Are they eating properly? How do they parent, have they a large enough vocabulary? Austerity-era politicians asked, are they striving enough, or are they shirking? Have they got enough skills? Are they cheating the benefits system, should it be reupholstered to preempt that dishonesty? Are they morally corrupt? Why aren't they politically engaged? What has happened to their community spirit? This was all mirrored, culturally, by the poverty safari genre, particularly on television, in which the granular details of life on the breadline were not so much examined as paraded (one programme was literally called Life on the Breadline – these documentaries already look like artefacts). On one memorable occasion, a newspaper columnist attributed an arson attack in which six children had died to a 'benefits culture' that created an underclass breeding for handouts. The systematic study of the poor, the quest to find characteristics that they all shared, had created its own sub-culture of absolute demonisation.

The broader coherent agenda, though, was simply to locate all social problems within the section of society most beset by them. That person is poor because they haven't figured out how to raise themselves from poverty. That one is poor because their parents could not raise them out; three-generations of worklessness became a phrase, without any real mooring in reality. Yet demonising or 'othering' the poor was rarely the stated aim, so rebuttals foundered trying to pin down the intention of any given inquiry: was Benefits Street devised to spur empathy or pour scorn? Were the subjects of a particular study, either as a cohort or as individuals, being judged or merely observed with the aim of improving their lot?

Historically, of course, intention has been important – the careful analysis of a life in poverty has been a great engine of social change. Round about a Pound a Week seeded child benefit and school dinners. The Peckham Experiment launched the idea of preventative public health. Beveridge's Five Giant Evils were the spur of both the NHS and the largest public housing project the UK has ever seen. But if the careful evaluation of poverty was, in the past, a call to arms and to solidarity, how did it latterly become something so different, a trend both judgemental and unjust, one which does more to legitimise the existence of hardship than alleviate the condition of those living in it? It is because no countervailing study has been made of wealth. Inequality is a coin which cannot be understood by studying only one of its faces.

It has become a commonplace to say poverty is systemic, and 'system' here comes to stand for capitalism, at its most specific, or modernity, at its most nebulous. An anarchist might smash the system while a Fabian might reform it, but nobody could adjudicate those options without first understanding the components and circuitry of that system: if capital is no longer boosting wages, where is it going instead? If the majority of wealth is no longer earned, by what rents is it extracted? What is the lived experience of a person whose wealth is unearned? If we accept that the distribution of wealth is not a naturally occurring phenomenon, what decisions determine it, and who's making them? What do great disparities look like in the real world, in its architecture, in its landscape? The necessity of these questions accounts for some of the coyness around studying high net worth individuals, since in examining wealth capture, inevitably one comes to understand poverty not as a condition but as an act of theft and, ultimately, violence. This conclusion is easier to process if the violent side of the equation is impersonal, a number rather than an individual.

We avert our eyes from the people behind the portfolios also out of deference; if there has been a building narrative that poverty stems from personal failure, there is the countervailing and often quite boldly stated idea that wealth accrues from personal greatness, even where we can plainly see this isn't the case, even when the high net worth individual themselves deny it. That innate superiority creates the expectation of privacy, which creates a feedback loop: the less is known about the lives of the rich, the more of a different and better breed they appear to be. What we think of as historical attitudes of class-based respect and reverence are actually functions of inequality, and reassert themselves as inequality grows.

As I write this, the news breaks that the wealth of billionaires over the COVID-19 crisis has risen to $10.2 trillion. The personal wealth of Jeff Bezos today exceeds $200billion, and it will be salutary to see how off that figure is by the time of this book's publication. The problem with the status quo as we have it is that it's not static, it's always worsening. The greater the wealth, the more stratospherically distant it seems, to create this paradox: that the larger it is, the more invisible. This book addresses that invisibility, which shouldn't be the radical and unusual act that it is.

Introduction: how the other half lives

Katie Higgins and Samuel Burgum

Juxtapositions

There is a fascination with how the 'other half' lives. Jacob Riis'
(2016) landmark 1890 photographic study, which bears the same
name as this volume, documented the impoverished conditions of
New York's Lower East Side, challenging the practices of rogue
landlords, sweatshops, and child labour by bringing these issues to
the attention of America's middle and upper classes. In doing so,
he sought to demonstrate that poverty was not an individual choice,
but rather a structural societal failing. In our version of *How the
Other Half Lives*, however, we move beyond a focus on either the
experiences of the poor or the affluent in isolation. We have set out
to consider them both in the same frame.

This is something that has been explored in the arts, but less so
in the social sciences. For instance, stark contrasts of the rich and
the poor is an enduring theme in photography, such as Jim Goldberg's
(1985) *Rich and Poor*, which juxtaposes photographs of residents
on welfare with the suburban upper classes, raising cutting questions
around American myths of social mobility, power, and happiness.
Or more recently, Johnny Miller's (2018) portrayal of urban scenes
of inequality around the globe – from Mexico City to Nairobi and
Los Angeles – which uses drones in order to illustrate the borders
between immense wealth and poverty from the air.

The moral jolt provoked by these direct contrasts is powerful,
offering one response to the problem of 'visualising capitalism'
(Toscano and Kinkle, 2015) in the context of intensifying concentrations of wealth and poverty. In structuring this book we've been

inspired by such creative works that seek to make visible inequalities in new, provocative ways. While the reality is much more complex than such binary portraits of extreme wealth and poverty, it is the contention of this book that greater attention from the social sciences to the differences, similarities, and in-between points where 'the other halves' meet, can provoke new and useful perspectives.

Ultimately, 'inequality' describes a *relationship,* and therefore research (and public perception) needs to move beyond viewing the marginalised or the elite in isolation. As Tawney (1913: 10) wrote over a century ago, 'what thoughtful rich people call the problems of poverty, thoughtful poor people call with equal justice a problem of riches', and this book aims to emphasise these connections: from the accumulation of profound wealth to impoverished communities, from banal decisions by those in the seats of power to increasing levels of violence in austerity-wracked neighbourhoods, and between a world of smooth mobility to oppressive borders. To this end, *How The Other Half Lives* is uniquely structured as a series of oppositions between peaks and troughs, with chapter pairs focusing on a specific subject, including: housing, urban design, place-making, the state, cultures of inequality, and transnational mobility.

We are, all of us, intimately familiar with inequalities. Whether finding somewhere to live, walking in the street, following the news, negotiating international travel, or in our working and personal lives – subtle and crude hierarchies shape our lived experience. Existing texts on inequality have tended to be synthetic, quantitative, and historical. In this book, we contribute detailed, multidisciplinary, and qualitative explorations of the everyday social and spatial realities of inequality, drawing new lines of connection from Manchester to Milan, from Brighton to Bologna. We offer *How the Other Half Lives* as a resource to navigate an unequal world, structured around three overlapping understandings of inequality as: (1) contingent, (2) situated, and (3) interrelated. Each will be explored in greater depth via the editor's introduction that frames each section of the book.

How the other half lives

The contributions to this collection were originally presented at the University of Sheffield, 27–28 June 2018. The event – entitled 'Peaks and Troughs: New Research on Elites, Wealth, Inequality and Exclusion' – was co-organised by the editors of this volume and Rowland Atkinson. 'Peaks and Troughs' brought together emerging scholars in inequalities research (most of whom are now part of this volume), exploring both the connection between the rich/privileged and poor/marginalised, as well as the place and function of critical academic social sciences today. The book is organised into three Parts, each made up of paired chapters illuminating a common theme. One-half of each pair focuses on the 'elite', and the other on the 'marginalised', with the intention of bringing these research agendas together. This collection hopes to raise questions about the role of the social sciences, and to act as a springboard for future research on social and spatial inequalities.

Book outline

Part I Structural inequalities

'The fortunes of the poor', argue de Noronha and Silver, 'are intimately shaped by the fortunes of the rich.' The first two chapters in this section relay a history of housing, capital, and the state in Ancoats, Manchester, reflecting on Engels' landmark work on 'the Housing Question' in the same district 200 years ago. The story of the district is one of peaks and troughs for its inhabitants, moving from its emergence as informal ('slum') accommodation for rural and international migrants meeting the needs of industrialisation, followed by state intervention, post-colonial, and post-industrial decline, and (today) the arrival of intensive capital in the form of financialisation. Ancoats is a space that continues to be shaped by the shifting priorities of state and capital, from the slums and philanthropic interventions, through the double-edged sword of improvement clearances, post-industrial abandonment by the state, followed by regeneration and gentrification by today's state-facilitated investment of global capital. Both chapters highlight the complex relationships between housing, capital and the state, and the impacts of the wealthy upon Ancoats' continually marginalised residents.

As the case of Ancoats demonstrates, one of the most significant recent frames for understanding inequality has been that of neoliberalism: a political economic model which emerged in the post-war period and became ideologically popular throughout the 1970s and 1980s, arguing that principles of competition should be introduced into all areas of both economic, state, and civil activity (Gane 2019), and that the state should actively support this by simultaneously rolling out and rolling back direct responsibility wherever possible (Peck 2010). From the viewpoint of the state, in chapter 4, Penny examines the (in)actions of political elites in local government, who he argues have been conspicuously absent from building resistance to austerity. Compared to Labour-led councils under Thatcher, who actively struggled for an alternative vision of municipal socialism, Penny outlines the way in which those in a similar position today have enabled the smooth administration of cutbacks across ten example boroughs, through structurally inscribed and strategically selective choices. For Ellis, in chapter 5, such regimes are being ideologically supported by claims that there has been a clear decline in violence since the 1990s, when the inevitable rise of inequality under such state withdrawal and policies of austerity has, in fact, produced profoundly violent outcomes. Using statistical evidence, he argues that violence is not only once again on the rise in the UK, but that this is concentrated in poor, politically abandoned communities, and therefore connected to the social breakdown caused by austerity and rising inequality.

Part II Situated inequalities

Chapters 5 and 6 focus on contested public spaces. Tarazona-Vento concentrates on the iconic megastructures that dominate cities as both empirical and symbolic manifestations of wider structures that reproduce situated inequality, and simultaneously obscure such inequalities through the narrative of common wealth and 'growth for all'. She argues that citizens are seduced into such projects through an ethos of entrepreneurialism and competitiveness, in which iconic architecture acts as propaganda through its very design, production, and consumption. Yet there are also tensions, and the same megaprojects can be used to contest neoliberalism by subverting the meanings attached to such iconic structures. On the other side, through her research on material experiences of everyday inequality in the city, Rose explores how intersectional inequality is both embodied and amplified by access to public space (or lack thereof) focusing on issues of gender, everyday sexism, and street-based harassment. Using walking interviews with women, Rose argues that their encounters with poor urban design and strategies of privatisation and commodification illuminate wider social processes of exclusion whilst allowing us to see the importance of the street as a key space for encountering and negotiating difference in the city. A genuinely accessible and safe space, she argues, plays a central role in community cohesion and place-attachment.

Chapters 7 and 8 further explore the role of urban representations and exclusions. Pulini begins with a critical engagement around representations of 'elite' spaces, focusing on a residential street in Kensington (one of the most established wealthy boroughs in London). Using a historical analysis of social patterns on this street, the aim is to better understand such neighbourhoods by tackling the nuances and contradictions of competition for residential space, arguing that the very concept of 'elite neighbourhood' needs to be unpacked in order to reveal the complexities of coexistence between elite and non-elite populations. This chapter is followed by considering representations of 'receptive cities'. Focusing on the cases of Brighton and Bologna, which have both achieved reputations as hospitable and left-leaning cities, Mazzilli argues that, at the institutional level, this public image is rarely scrutinised. Both have constructed such public narratives based on their inclusiveness, which overlook and conceal situated experiences of exclusion, discrimination, and racism.

Part III Interrelated inequalities

As argued above, the frames and narratives which *justify* inequality are key, and notions of 'deservedness' (i.e. who deserves their lot, whether the entitlement of the rich or the fate of the poor) are a central discourse in such legitimation. In chapter 9, Monteath and Schimpfössl outline notions of deservedness for the very wealthy. They analyse the 2018 anniversary edition of the *Sunday Times* Rich List, which suggested that a 'social revolution' had taken place in the UK, as 94 per cent of individuals included on the list were now 'self-made'. They challenge the List's use of 'self-made' through their own analysis of who is included, and argue that this label is not a description of a meritocratic reality but an ideological assertion. In contrast, in chapter 10, Maestri and Monforte demonstrate in their analysis of representations of asylum seekers by both individual actors and charities that 'welcoming cultures' can create limiting and self-fulfilling constructions of 'deserving' refugees as either victims, resilient actors, or entrepreneurial agents. They argue that constructions of migrants through frames of compassion entail a binary division between those who 'deserve' support and those who do not.

Finally, chapter 11 and 12 turn to the different lives of elite migrants and refugees. First, Kunz picks up on contradictions and inequalities of global migrant experiences. Focusing on the everyday lived realities of a German family who have emigrated on multiple occasions since the 1990s, and are now living in Nairobi, the chapter interrogates their trajectory and social mobility, modalities of belonging, and narrations of identity. Finally, Artero's research with refugees in Milan focuses on the lack of adequate reception and assistance they have received, as well as their exclusion from housing and work, which has driven large numbers into irregular seasonal work around Italy and Europe. Instead of being places of arrival, Artero describes Italian cities as places of prolonged passage and unstable residency, focusing in particular on tensions between mobility and presence.

Conclusion

This collection is concluded by Rowland Atkinson who, by drawing together the themes and insights from the various chapters in this collection, outlines their implications for future research on inequality.

References

Gane, N. (2019). Competition: a critical history of a concept. *Theory, Culture and Society*, 37(2), 31–59.

Goldberg, J. (2014). *Jim Goldberg: Rich and Poor*. 2nd edn. Göttingen: Steidl.

Miller, J. (2018). Unequal scenes. www.unequalscenes.com/ (accessed 4 April 2019).

Peck, J. (2010). *Constructions of Neoliberal Reason*. Oxford: Oxford University Press.

Riis, J. A. (2016 [1890]). *How the Other Half Lives: Studies Among the Tenements of New York*. Oxford: Benediction Classics.

Tawney, R. (1913). *Poverty as an Industrial Problem: Memoranda on the Problems of Poverty*. London: William Morris Press.

Toscano, A., and Kinkle, J. (2015). *Cartographies of the Absolute*. London: Zero Books.

Part I

Structural inequalities

Editors' introduction: placing inequalities in context (contingency)

Emphasising the contingency of inequality means demonstrating that inequality is a product of a historical and socio-economic context, and which might, therefore, be otherwise. Yet this also means more, as Doreen Massey (1991: 8) argued, than making 'ritualistic connections to "the wider system" [like] the people in the local meeting who bring up international capitalism every time you try to have a discussion about rubbish-collection … the point is that there are real relations with real content – economic, political, cultural – between any local place and the wider world in which it is set.' A contingent understanding of inequality means recognising these structures and going beyond pervasive and widely accepted notions of natural 'human' traits – such as individualism, entitlement, deservedness, and merit – which are commonly used to explain away historically accumulated and systemically embedded privilege. For people like Boris Johnson, Mayor of London at the time, innate capabilities mean not only that inequalities are unavoidable, but even that they are '*essential* for the spirit of envy and keeping up with the Joneses and so on that is a valuable spur to economic activity'[1] (a point contradicted by evidence that inequality has a dampening effect on economic growth) (Bourguignon, 2015). As he elaborated at the Margaret Thatcher lecture in 2013, some people are just 'too stupid to get on in life' and 'natural differences between human being will always mean that some will succeed and others fail' (Dominiczak and Kirkup, 2013).

Explanations like Johnson's seek to justify inequality as natural, enduring, unavoidable, and even *desirable* for innovation and success, arguing that inequality between human beings has always existed and therefore always will. Yet, once we recognise the role of such normative definitions of 'success', as well as the pivotal part played by inheritance and citizenship in accessing wealth and economic security, we can begin to undermine the idea that people at the top of the economic pile are super-intelligent or have achieved their success through innate ability. His is a clear example of how 'the discourse of inequality is more and more a vehicle for legitimating the upward redistribution of wealth' (Skeggs, 2015: 219), as such a framing of success and failure as 'innate' naturalises and justifies the position of elites who profit from current structural inequalities, as well as those whose lives are made increasingly precarious by global capitalism. These explanations see inequality in the world and assume that it has always been (and therefore always will be) so. This renders inequality a self-fulfilling prophecy.

The chapters below demonstrate the structural nature of inequality through examples of political economy, tracing the impact of successive urban housing regimes as well as of neoliberal governance and austerity. When we think about how each half are housed, we perhaps think of poorer citizens getting by in social housing, substandard accommodation, or living on the streets; while the elite have their country house, a place in the City, and a holiday home abroad. The poor and the rich are often framed in terms of meritocracy and deservedness. Yet chapters 1 and 2 demonstrate that the situation of both are direct consequences of a history of divided access to housing, a retreat of the welfare state and the subsequent rise of equity-based welfare, as well as processes of financialisation, which define the 'value' of a house in economic rather than social terms.

Alongside a programme of austerity, chapters 3 and 4 show that the political economy of neoliberalism has produced a culture of reduced responsibility and individualism, downplaying the interconnectedness of actions. Whether those being punished for their marginalised status, or representatives who have failed to act on behalf of the most vulnerable, the idea persists that while criminals should be held responsible for their own actions; the state cannot be held responsible for the unequal conditions in which suffering takes place.

Note

1 www.theguardian.com/politics/2013/nov/27/boris-johnson-thatcher-greed-good (accessed October 2021).

References

Bourguignon, F. (2015). Revisiting the debate on inequality and economic development. *Revue d'économie politique*, 5, 633–63.

Dominiczak, P., and Kirkup, J. (2013). Boris Johnson: some people are too stupid to get on in life. *The Telegraph*, www.telegraph.co.uk/news/politics/10479466/Boris-Johnson-some-people-are-too-stupid-to-get-on-in-life.html (accessed 4 April 2019).

Massey, D. (1991). A global sense of place. *Marxism Today*, 38, 24–9.

Skeggs, B. (2015). Introduction: stratification or exploitation, domination, dispossession and devaluation? *The Sociological Review*, 63, 205–22.

1

Emergence to clearance: the housing question in the district of Ancoats

Nigel de Noronha and Jonathan Silver

The fortunes of the poor are intimately shaped by the fortunes of the rich. These linked chapters examine the shifting historical-geographical relations that have shaped housing in the district of Ancoats, Manchester. Studies of inequality have long highlighted the ways that elites have structured the often segregated experience of housing for rich and poor alike, through both the location of people's homes and the type, condition and cost of their residence. This scholarship spans from the Victorian reformers (Rowntree, 1899; Booth, 1890; Stedman Jones, 1971), to slum clearance in the 1930s (MUS, 1945), to displacement and race in the 1960s (Coates and Silburn, 1970; Rex and Moore, 1967), and on to gentrification (Smith, 1979) and the contemporary era of neoliberal capitalism (Hodkinson, 2019; Madden and Marcuse, 2016; Minton, 2017). Many of these accounts have drawn inspiration from *The Housing Question* posed by Friedrich Engels in 1872, which outlined a political economy of housing in capitalist society. Here, we return to *The Housing Question* and subsequent scholarship of the Marxist tradition to reflect on how one particular urban space has experienced intense transformation over the last two centuries. In doing so, we highlight the continuing relevance of Engels' ideas for researching the making of urban inequality in the built environment.

Ancoats, a centrally located post-industrial space, is now considered to be a desirable area, regularly featuring in global lists of 'cool' neighbourhoods.[1] Amid old cotton mills, new apartments are being constructed at a rapid pace as the population of the area surges. It has become a neighbourhood in which townhouses are offered for sale at £750,000,[2] and rent for a two-bedroom apartment, in a block interestingly named Engels House, begins at over £950 per month.[3] According to lifestyle website, Manchester Confidential:

> Ancoats is now the epicentre of all that is new and hip in the city's food and drink scene. The coming of shiny new apartment blocks and amenities has initiated a rush to feed all of these young, trendy incomers, with their empty bellies, disposable incomes and penchant for artisanal anything. The last few years have seen a number of the region's most exciting food and drink businesses open new sites in the area.[4]

This transformation of the neighbourhood, from a heavily stigmatised district in which the urban poor were housed from the late eighteenth century onwards to toil in Blake's 'dark, satanic mills' has been dramatic. Who, amongst the new visitors and residents, enjoying £100 per head Michelin starred tasting menus, would know that the streets around them once had the highest cholera and mortality rates in the UK? As Engels (1845: 58) famously wrote on the housing conditions in the district:

> Hence it comes that Ancoats, built chiefly since the sudden growth of manufacture, chiefly within the present century, contains a vast number of ruinous houses, most of them being in fact, in the last stages of inhabitableness ... The working-man is constrained to occupy such ruinous dwellings because he cannot pay for others, and because there are not others in the vicinity of his mill; perhaps too, because they belong to the employer, who employs him only on condition of taking such a cottage.

If Ancoats was paradigmatic of the many newly built districts that accommodated mass urbanisation and the Industrial Revolution, it is also a site in which various interventions into housing, by both state and capital, have proceeded over the last 200 years. As such, it provides a vantage point on the restructuring of the English housing system and the changing relations between state and capital, enabling a broader consideration around the way in which inequalities are produced, embedded and maintained from above. We examine the formation of Ancoats as a site of working-class housing segregated from nearby elite neighbourhoods, such as Ardwick Green or Victoria Park, into the contemporary period in which segregation now divides the district itself. This is a socio-spatial division between new market-rent or owner occupied apartments of middle-class residents and older social housing estates that reflects the role of contemporary state/capital relations in the making of housing geographies. These dynamics also show the continuing relevance of *The Housing Question* in how we interpret these transformations.

Our aim is to better understand the changing geography of housing in England through a focus on Ancoats, a district that has experienced important transformations over the last two centuries. To do so, we historicise relations between state, capital and housing into five distinct eras. In this first chapter, we look at the period between the 1800s and 1890s, when the district was a site of rapid urbanisation, slum landlords, a new urban poor and little state involvement in housing. We then consider the period between the 1890s and 1940s and the onset of municipal intervention into housing, slum clearance, the rise of the council home and a period where marginalised residents were understood as requiring various types of intervention and 'improvement'. In chapter 2 we bring the story into the contemporary era through the post-industrial decline and withdrawal of state and capital, leading to the (re)stigmatisation of the district and population, and the subsequent financialisation of housing that has transformed Ancoats yet again. In developing this historical analysis of what is now a post-industrial urban space, we respond to Engels' ideas to consider the underlying dynamics of class and race in structuring planning logics, and the shifting role of the state and capital in housing provision. We draw from and expand the argument from the editors of this volume that, 'inequalities are historical, geographical and social structures which implicate the past in the present and the actions of the rich in the situation of the poor.' We attempt to broaden the focus on class inequality to consider the relevance of race and migration to this story. We conclude the chapters by reflecting on what lessons the history of this district generates concerning *The Housing Question* in regard to urban inequality.

The housing question

Before we turn to the history of Ancoats, we will set out the ideas Engels contributed to our understanding of housing. Engels is one of the key thinkers in Marxist political economy, and specifically in questions of urban inequality. He moved to work for his father's company based in Manchester in 1842. As a young man he spent the subsequent years researching the emerging slums of industrial capitalism, and in 1845 he published *The Conditions of the English Working Class*. Engels also addressed 'the housing question' in a series of three articles published in 1872, in a radical left critique of the housing crisis in industrial cities across Western Europe. If the polemical nature of the articles and the specific debates are clearly rooted in the socio-economic conditions of nineteenth-century continental Europe, the arguments developed by Engels are of continuing relevance to housing in England. In the first two pieces he addressed the anarchist Pierre-Joseph Proudhon, the bourgeois social reformer Emil Sax, and their respective cases for working-class ownership of homes (Larsen et al., 2016). Engels' third article built on this critique through responding to a supporter of Proudhon with a caustic demolition of the argument for home ownership as reflecting the interests of the petty bourgeoisie. For Engels (1887: 15): 'The housing shortage from which the workers and part of the petty bourgeoisie suffer in our modern cities is one of the numerous, smaller, secondary evils which result from the present-day capitalist mode of production.' Engels (1887: 16) explained how the increasing value of land, caused by mass urbanisation and the Industrial Revolution, contributed to the excessive cost of housing for workers already exploited by capital:

> The growth of the big cities gives the land in certain areas, particularly those which are centrally situated, an artificial and often colossally increasing value; the buildings erected on these areas depress this value, instead of increasing it, because they no longer correspond to the changed circumstances. They are pulled down and replaced by others.

This increasing value of land precipitated demolition of working-class districts and displacement of the residents out of towns and towards the outskirts. Landlords built 'workers' dwellings only by way of exception' (Engels, 1887: 16). Engels criticises the nostalgic approach Proudhon took to the importance of ownership. Whilst Proudhon (1840: 1) is remembered for his claim that 'property is theft', his argument was based on the premise that owning your home was a right that all should enjoy. Engels (1887: 21) believed that the move from the land was part of the historical development of the proletariat:

'In order to create the modern revolutionary class of the proletariat it was absolutely necessary to cut the umbilical cord which still bound the worker of the past to the land … [it is] the very first condition for their intellectual emancipation.' In responding to Sax's support for home ownership, Engels argued this was simply a reflection of the concerns of the petty bourgeoisie. Capital investment in housing for the proletariat was irrational. Capital was bound by its accumulative logic to seek the greatest return. Investment in working-class housing would inevitably lead to a corresponding reduction in workers' wage. Engels argued that the idea the capitalist should invest in adequate housing for the working classes was an irrational moral argument as capital is economically bound by its very accumulative logics to seek the greatest return, even if they were to provide housing for working-class ownership. Furthermore, reduction in living costs would lead to a corresponding reduction of workers' wage. Sax also blamed the behaviour of the working classes for their conditions, in a discourse which is echoed over the timeline of our story (Sax in Engels, 1887: 46; Murray, 1990; CSJ, 2007):

> That if they can only save something on the rent they will move into dark, damp and inadequate dwellings, which in short are a mockery of all the demands of hygiene … in order to spend as little as possible for rent, while on the other hand they squander their income in a really sinful fashion on drink and all sorts of idle pleasures.

It was through this developing political economy of housing that Engels concluded the housing crisis was intimately tied to the logic of capitalism. He argued, 'There are already in existence sufficient buildings for dwellings in the big towns to remedy any real "housing shortage", given rational utilisation of them' (1887: 31). And it is this analysis that remains central to how the political economy of housing has been elaborated over subsequent decades. It exposed the need for state intervention against the rapacious effects of capital. However, Engels was also critical of the state and how it enabled accumulation as rent. He criticised the effectiveness of regulatory measures, describing the state as, 'nothing but the organised collective power of the possessing classes, the landowners and the capitalists' (Engels, 1887: 72–3).

In the second intervention Engels identifies the self-interest of capitalist concerns about the conditions of slum housing and health.

He engaged specifically with the way that liberal reform had been mobilised to protect the class interests of the reformers and address their fears of contamination and pandemic, rather than the working-class slum dwellers. He argued that (1887: 40):

> cholera, typhus, typhoid fever, small-pox and other ravaging diseases spread their germs in the pestilential air and the poisoned water of these working-class quarters ... as soon as circumstances permit it they develop into epidemics and then spread beyond their breeding places into the more airy and healthy parts of the town inhabited by the capitalists.

The third intervention provides a prescient analysis of contemporary gentrification, the 'Haussmann' process that structured the violent remaking of Paris (see also Harvey, 2004). Engels (1887) argued that;

> [by] making breaches in the working class quarters of our big towns, and particularly in those which are centrally situated ...: the scandalous alleys and lanes disappear to the accompaniment of lavish self-praise from the bourgeoisie ... but they appear again immediately somewhere else and often in the immediate neighbourhood.

Engels (1887) described how the development of railways, new streets and prestigious buildings since 1845 had led to displacement as the city expanded (a process that, as we show in the next chapter – is ongoing in the district).

In *The Housing Question*, Engels demonstrated how capitalism produces housing crises, that liberal reform was driven by self-interest and that displacement of working class housing enabled gentrification. Engels articulated a political economic theory that illustrated how capitalism comes to structure and shape housing inequality, which became particularly acute in areas such as Ancoats.

The nineteenth century: an industrialising, working-class district

Ancoats developed in the nineteenth century to accommodate new textile mills, factories and railway yards. Capital required workers to run these industries, and they were housed in appalling conditions in central districts around the mills and factories. The district also met the needs of migrants from rural areas in England, Ireland and Italy seeking work in the mills and factories of the growing industrial city (Rose et al., 2011). A small number of wealthy families, such as the Mosley family in Ancoats, owned large tracts of previously agricultural land, which were leased in small plots to builders to create housing for factory workers. The builders typically paid ground rent for the land for a fixed period of forty years and any investments to buildings or infrastructure on the plots were returned to the owner at the end of the lease. There was little incentive for builders to maintain or improve the housing conditions of these back-to-back dwellings, and the labourers for the mills and factories of the early Industrial Revolution were largely regarded as disposable, with little consideration for the overcrowded and dangerous conditions they lived and worked in. The capital invested in the land provided a guaranteed return to the owner through the leasehold paid to them, while the landlords collected rents as a return on their investment. When a young Engels walked through Ancoats in the 1840s, the government had no role in housing, planning or building regulations, and people were left in the squalor and poverty created by the demands of industrial capitalism.

Engels quoted the Medical Officer for Manchester, Dr Kay, in describing the housing conditions in the working-class districts (Engels, 1845: 62) that remain haunting to this day:

> But when I went through their habitations in Irish Town, and Ancoats, and Little Ireland, my only wonder was that tolerable health could be maintained by the inmates of such houses. ... Not a house in this street escaped cholera. And generally speaking, throughout these suburbs the streets are unpaved, with a dung-hill or a pond in the middle; the houses built back-to-back, without ventilation or drainage; and whole families occupy a corner of a cellar or of a garret.

Fear of cholera through bad housing and sanitation conditions was well founded. The Manchester Board of Health conducted a survey in 1831, which recorded over 55 per cent of homes in Ancoats without plumbing (Niven, 1923). By 1851, with a population of 55,983 in the district (Nevell, 2014), the disposability of the working class for capital was clearly visible in the lives of those living in the cellars and back-to-back housing across Ancoats.

1.1 Back-to-back cottages on Portugal Street, built in 1791 and converted into two-up, two-down dwellings in 1849 (J. Silver)

As Engels had predicted, fear of disease amongst the new middle class, reduced productivity through illness for capital and, for some, concern at these living conditions, inspired political and moral interventions (Platt, 2005). These interventions included the existing housing in Ancoats, some of which was built in the eighteenth century and was barely adequate as basic shelter.

Marx and Engels believed that revolution was the only answer to these conditions. Meanwhile liberal reformers in the city drove the Manchester Corporation to invest in sanitation and other public health measures in districts such as Ancoats, later extended nationally through legislation such as the Local Government Act of 1871 and the Public Health Act of 1872. In Manchester, liberal reformers funded institutions like the Ragged Schools and the Bennett Street Sunday School, which provided religious and moral instruction alongside education (see for example the last will and testament of John Rylands).

The state had little explicit role in housing in the rapidly growing urban spaces of nineteenth-century England but, with political power held by men of property, there *were* state interventions to address major public health concerns through investment in sanitation. This was achieved through new regulatory powers for local government. Towards the end of the century the property-owning elite also became concerned about the housing conditions of their managers and clerks. Thus, as Manchester's industrial quarters developed, mill owners, merchants, other members of the propertied classes and the growing middle classes moved away from the disease and pollution to the suburbs that were developing around the city. The new suburbs were supported by the developing railway infrastructure, while exposure to the risk of infectious diseases was addressed by new sanitation measures, including municipally run sewage and water infrastructure. As the end of the nineteenth century approached, the argument for homeownership expressed by Proudhon was realised for the petit bourgeoisie (as Engels had predicted). The new suburbs were located far away from the streets of Ancoats for the growing middle classes in Manchester, as elsewhere (Cooper, 2002). In the suburb of Chorlton, this development was delivered through the provision of packages of land on a 99-year lease from Lord Egerton. This land was subjected to an annual ground rent and was provided to builders to construct semi-detached houses with access to clean air, improved housing conditions and transport links to their work in the city (for those who could afford it). The suburb became the space of the middle class, many seeking finance from the emerging building society movement (Samy, 2008).

Meanwhile, the city council began to intervene in Ancoats itself using new and growing powers, such as the 1867 Manchester Water Works Improvement Act and public calls for solutions to the housing crisis. The first social housing in Manchester was delivered through tenements in Victoria Square in 1894. This building, designed by Henry Spalding, was constructed on some of the worst slum housing in the district; however the rents were too high for most Ancoats residents. State intervention and investment proceeded in Ancoats for the next few years (Boughton, 2020), including the aptly named Sanitation Street, which contained the first toilets for each individual household in the district, built in 1897. Both the tenements and

1.2 Municipal housing built in 1897 by the Manchester Corporation
(J. Silver)

terraced housing remain to this day as a living reminder of the
capacity of the state to improve housing conditions.

However, while Ancoats briefly became a space of state intervention, the cost of land made these investments prohibitive. As John
Boughton (2020) explains, 'Land in inner Manchester was expensive
– with a consequent impact on rents in schemes intended as self-
supporting. At Oldham Road, the Council had paid over £5 a square
yard; in the city's newly-acquired suburbs, it could be bought for a
little over 3p a square yard.' The next investment created two hundred
houses on the boundaries of the city, most with bathrooms, together
with 50 acres of land for allotments (Boughton, 2020).

Overall, new housing, alongside other small-scale charitable
investments had little impact on the masses housed in the working-
class districts of Manchester. Like Ancoats, nearly all the working-class
housing in Manchester remained owned by private landlords, whose
main concern was generating the largest possible rent at the expense
of the tenants, who often lived in terrible conditions. As Engels had

recognised, capital would always seek return on investment, while the state (which, at the time, was run by the propertied classes) would struggle to compete with rising land values.

In the late nineteenth century, the racialisation of housing also became a political tool for the ruling class in order to divert attention from the profit-driven causes of poor housing conditions in districts such as Ancoats. Engels' analysis foregrounded the salience of race in housing inequality. In the *Conditions of the Working Class in England* (1845), he describes Irish immigrants as essential labour to service the Industrial Revolution, because of their willingness to work for less, resulting in reduction of wages. At a national level, discourses of race and immigration provided an easy scapegoat for politicians and elites failing to address housing shortages, overcrowding and poor conditions. A 1902 parliamentary debate on housing argued about the negative effect of immigration on the conditions of the working class and proposed an amendment to recognise 'the urgent necessity of introducing legislation to regulate and restrict the immigration of destitute aliens into London and other cities in the United Kingdom' (Hansard, 1902: 1284). In moving the amendment, Major Evans-Gordon, MP for Stepney, said:

> Not a day passes but English families are ruthlessly turned out to make room for the foreign invaders. Many of these have been occupying their houses for years. ... Out they have to go to make room for Romanians, Russians, or Poles. Rents are raised 50% to 100% and a house which formerly contained a couple of families ... is made to hold four or five families. (Hansard, 1902: 1973).

In seconding the motion, Mr Forde Ridley, MP for Bethnal Green, argued:

> The British workman is thus squeezed out of his home, and what happens? The house is immediately taken by five, six, eight, or ten of these aliens, who herd together under conditions which are at once degrading and insanitary. I know it has been said by some people that this is a racial question ... This is not a question of Jew or Gentile. We are speaking of foreign paupers and aliens as a whole. (Hansard, 1902: 1983).

This integration of racism into the housing question informed the introduction of the Aliens Act 1905, which restricted immigration from countries outside the empire, while the racialisation of immigrants created the conditions that justified attacks and harassment on those deemed foreign (Holmes, 1988). However, the extent of hostility from the working class in Ancoats towards the new arrivals is less clear. In the nineteenth century, Irish, Italians and eastern European Jews settled in Manchester, and Ancoats was known as 'Little Italy' from the 1870s, with migrants from southern Italy (Holmes, 1988).

Ancoats at the end of the nineteenth century reflected embryonic state intervention to address disease and protect the health of the wealthier inhabitants of the city, while the wealthy were increasingly moving to suburban housing and separate lives from the urban poor. Capital investment by small builders provided the growing middle class with well-built suburban family housing, whilst ensuring a return on the value of the land to its owners. Most working-class housing remained in poor condition, owned by private landlords and insecure. Any financial shocks, whether through ill-health, unemployment or decisions to clear parts of the city, could lead to eviction. Increasingly segregated from the rest of the city, the working class in Ancoats saw little benefit from early state interventions.

1.3 The Round House, L. S. Lowry (Manchester Settlement)

The early twentieth century: municipal-led reform and slum clearance

By the end of the nineteenth century, successive crises of capitalism and the threat of revolution provided the impetus for housing reform in the age of imperialism. The arch-imperialist Cecil Rhodes (1895, in Lenin, 1917: 93–4) wrote about these twin concerns and his own colonial solution;

> I was in the East End of London (a working-class quarter) yesterday and attended a meeting of the unemployed. ... My cherished idea is a solution for the social problem, i.e., in order to save the 40,000,000 inhabitants of the United Kingdom from a bloody civil war, we colonial statesmen must acquire new lands to settle the surplus population

Poor living conditions, insecure employment and punitive conditions for those who fell on hard times contributed to the development of mass movements of trade unions and socialist parties to represent the working class (Stedman Jones, 1971; Booth, 1890). Ancoats had, for many decades, been a hotbed of radical politics, print presses and working-class action against substandard housing conditions. If the contradictions of industrial capitalism were temporarily resolved by imperialist expansion, it still left a growing working-class movement demanding intervention into housing, work and social support. As Engels has suggested, the elite did engage in self-congratulatory social reform, but these interventions were driven by the necessity to maintain the current order in light of working-class mobilisations through tactics such as rent strikes (Hansard, 1903; Gray, 2018). Manchester had already begun to address these conditions with selective demolition to remove back-to-back housing and provision of improved sanitation (Simon and Inman, 1935) that targeted Ancoats' worst housing.

After the First World War, the government promised to deliver 'homes fit for heroes' supported by slum clearance programmes and a combination of state and private investment into housing designed for 'the respectable' working classes (Simon and Inman, 1935; Howard, 1898). The Housing Acts of 1919 and 1924 accelerated state investment through grants to housebuilders, accompanied by restrictions on the rents they could charge – in effect a rent cap. The shifting of responsibility for the implementation of these provisions to local councils, combined with difficulty in securing suitable land, meant progress was slow. The Housing Act of 1930 responded to these conditions. It combined a duty to clear slum housing with the finance needed to do so (Henderson and Maddocks, 1930). The process required a house-by-house inspection to justify declaration of the area to be cleared, a demolition order and finally a notice for households to move. Manchester City Council constructed garden estates away from the city centre, reflecting the earlier development of middle-class suburbs on agricultural land at the edge of the city. In Ancoats, the clearance programme took around four years, but the financial requirements for repaying the loans meant that rents in the new council houses were too high for many working-class residents still living in single rooms in the slums. With the likelihood that slum housing would be cleared, there was little investment in existing provision, and neighbourhoods such as Ancoats deteriorated significantly.

We can get a better idea of the housing conditions through the Manchester University Settlement (MUS), established in Ancoats in 1895 to engage residents through leisure, advice, cultural, and welfare activities, whilst allowing liberal reformers to study the lives of the urban poor. Students involved in the study engaged in the practical development of social work practices and carried out investigations into living conditions. The Settlement developed a plan to survey residents before the clearance and then again once they had moved to the new garden estates. The approach was interdisciplinary, with the first Chair of Geography at Manchester, Professor Fleur, acting as an academic advisor, and with fieldwork and commentary conducted by social workers, and tabulation by statisticians. The resulting portrait of a clearance area provides a comprehensive view of the district. It paints a rich picture of how working-class residents of Ancoats felt threatened by moving out of a cohesive community and the loss of strong kinship and social networks that allowed for mutual aid.

Two objective measures were central to the assessment of the housing conditions of the families living in Ancoats. First, the poverty line was based on a paper from the Royal Statistical Society (George, 1937) and, second, a local standard was used to assess the extent to which a household was overcrowded (MUS, 1945). The survey used household income (after rent) to measure poverty, and captured details of actual expenditure, the use of credit, the effect of having children, being ill or unemployed, social life and attitudes to the clearance.

The report addressed commonly held assumptions that poverty was self-inflicted because of large families, poor eating habits, drinking and poor hygiene. This discourse of seeking to blame poverty on individual – rather than structural – failings, remains a powerful underlying narrative in UK society. The survey results showed that most households were relatively small, household expenditure was appropriate, most families had a balanced diet and they took pride in their homes. The main reasons for poverty were what Engels had identified – the disposability of the working class to capital, leading to inadequate pay, the challenge of supporting young children, and ill-health.[5]

There were different opinions about the clearance of Ancoats, with 60 per cent welcoming the prospect of a better house and amenities, and 20 per cent the prospects of better health for them and their children. Most (94 per cent) were concerned about higher rents and fares to get to work, and some were concerned about their social life or opposed to living in flats. These findings were used by the Settlement in discussions with Manchester's Chief Housing Officer to argue for the residents' interests to be central to the planned clearance. The second survey showed that 70 per cent of the families had been displaced from Ancoats. Whilst households welcomed the extra living space, the majority (93 per cent) were paying more rent and were further away from their workplace. During this era, the state invested significantly in improving working-class housing, at first through direct grants to builders, then through slum clearance and the provision of council housing. The responsibility for implementing the programme was at local state level, which led to significant variation (Boughton, 2018; Harloe, 1995; Simon and Inman, 1935). In Manchester, the new garden estates welcomed council tenants from central districts like Ancoats, Chorlton-On-Medlock and Spinningfields. However, with the start of the Second World War, the programme was halted. Capital investment in suburban parts of the city continued throughout the period, increasingly swallowing the remaining agricultural land.

Conclusion

The actions of the elite – first the 'capital' of factory-owners and land-holders, then the political interventions of the state (even if well-intentioned or driven by the fear of revolution) – shaped the early history and materiality of Ancoats. This was a district frequented by Engels in developing his pivotal ideas on *The Housing Question*. Through historical analysis of the housing geographies, and the shifting state/capital relations across one hundred years of life in the neighbourhood, we have argued that the changing conditions can be grouped into two eras of the governing of housing. Firstly, we explored the rapid growth of Ancoats as representative of the experience of urban housing during the early stages of industrial capitalism, in which workers lived in unsanitary conditions and the state played little role. These conditions were the direct result of a disregard for the urban workforce by both industrial and land-owning elites, who saw workers as disposable through a lens of class, race and nationality.

Secondly, we showed the ways that the state was compelled to act and intervene in these housing conditions through municipal investment and later on slum clearance programmes. Once again, even well-intentioned interventions by the elite had deleterious effects, including displacement, the destruction of communities, and the redirection of resources from improving existing housing (occasionally producing new housing which still remained unaffordable for residents in Ancoats). In reflecting on these transforming housing geographies in Ancoats, shaped by the shifting relations, logics and actions of the state and capital we emphasised the structural character of inequality, including ways in which race and migration might have shaped the lives of the working classes in Ancoats. The next chapter explores how these inequalities and our ways of understanding them have changed over time, the types of people that have been affected, and the changing influence of capital and the state in the housing geographies of Ancoats.

Notes

1 https://ilovemanchester.com/ancoats-is-manchester-coolest-neighbourhood-mana/ (accessed 21 March 2019).

2 www.rightmove.co.uk/property-for-sale/property-72383138.html (accessed 21 March 2019).
3 www.rightmove.co.uk/property-to-rent/property-72856831.html (accessed 21 March 2019).
4 https://confidentials.com/manchester/an-insiders-guide-to-eating-and-drinking-in-ancoats-manchester (accessed 21 March 2019).
5 The original survey papers were found whilst this chapter was being written and offer the potential of exploring the lives of the men and women of Ancoats in the 1930s.

References

Booth, W. (1890). *In Darkest England and the Way Out*. London: McQuordale.

Boughton, J. (2018). *Municipal Dreams: The Rise and Fall of Council Housing*. London: Verso.

Boughton, J. (2020). Municipal housing in Manchester before 1914: tackling 'the unwholesome dwellings and surrounding of the people'. https://municipaldreams.wordpress.com/2014/02/18/municipal-housing-in-manchester-before-1914–improving-the-unwholesome-dwellings-and-surroundings-of-the-people/ (accessed February 2020).

Coates, K., and Silburn, R. (1970). *Poverty: The Forgotten Englishman*. London: Penguin.

Cooper, G. (2002). *The Illustrated History of Manchester's Suburbs*. Derby: Breedon Books.

CSJ (2007). *Breakthrough Britain: Ending the Costs of Social Breakdown*. London: Centre for Social Justice.

Engels, F. (1845). *The Conditions of the Working Class in England*. London: Longmans, Green.

Engels, F. (1887). *The Housing Question*. 2nd edn. Accessed online at Engels The Housing Question.pdf (hlrn.org).

George, F. (1937). A new calculation of the poverty line. *Journal of the Royal Statistical Society*, A, 100(1), 74–95.

Gray, N. (2018). Spatial composition and the urbanisation of capital: the 1915 Glasgow rent strikes and the housing question reconsidered. In Neil Gray, ed., *Rent and its Discontents: A Century of Housing Struggle*. London: Rowman and Littlefield, 49–67.

Hansard (1902). Immigration of Destitute Aliens – Wednesday 29 January 1902 – Hansard – UK Parliament (accessed June 2019).

Hansard (1903). Housing of the Working Classes (18 February 1903) (accessed June 2019).

Harloe, M. (1995). *The People's Home: Social Rented Housing in Europe and America*. Oxford: Blackwell.

Harvey, D. (2004). *Paris, Capital of Modernity*. London: Routledge.

Henderson, A., and Maddocks, L. (1930). *Henderson and Maddock's Housing Acts 1925 and 1930: A Treatise on the Housing Act, 1930, Including the Complete Text of the Act*. London.

Hodkinson, S. (2019). *Safe as Houses: Private Greed, Political Negligence and Housing Policy after Grenfell*. Manchester: Manchester University Press.

Holmes, C. (1988). *John Bull's Island: Immigration and British Society 1871–1971*. London: Palgrave Macmillan.

Howard, E. (1898). *To-Morrow: A Peaceful Path to Real Reform*. London: Swan Sonnenschein.

Larsen, H., Hansen, A., MacLeod, G. and Slater, T. (2016). Introduction: the housing question revisited. *Acme Journal*, 15(3), 580–9.

Lenin, V. (1917). *Imperialism: The Highest Stage of Capitalism*. www.marxists.org/archive/lenin/works/1916/imp-hsc/ (accessed August 2019).

Madden, D., and Marcuse, P. (2016). *In Defence of Housing: The Politics of Crisis*. London: Verso.

Minton, A. (2017). *Big Capital: Who is London For?* London: Penguin.

Murray, C. (1990). *The British Underclass*. Public Interest, 99, 4–28.

MUS (1945). Ancoats: a study of a clearance area: report of a survey made in 1937–38. Manchester: Manchester University Settlement.

Nevell, M. (2014). Legislation and reality: the archaeological evidence for sanitation and housing quality in urban workers' housing in the Ancoats area of Manchester between 1800 and 1950. *Industrial Archaeology Review*, 36(1), 48–7.

Niven, J. (1923). *Observations on the History of Public Health Effort in Manchester*. J. Heywood.

Platt, H. L. (2005). *Shock Cities: The Environmental Transformation and Reform of Manchester and Chicago*. Chicago: University of Chicago Press.

Proudhon, P. J. (1840). *What is property?* www.marxists.org/reference/subject/economics/proudhon/property/ch01.htm (accessed June 2020).

Rex, J., and Moore, R. (1967). *Race, Community and Conflict: A Study of Sparkbrook*. London: Oxford University Press.

Rose, M. with Falconer, K., and Holder, J. (2011). *Ancoats: Cradle of Industrialisation*. Swindon: English Heritage.

Rowntree, S. (1899). *Charles Booth's London: poverty maps and police notebooks*. https://booth.lse.ac.uk/ (accessed 2 August 2019).

Samy, L. (2008). *The Building Society Promise: Building societies and Home Ownership c. 1880–1913*. Oxford: Oxford University discussion papers in

Economic and Social History, 72. www.nuff.ox.ac.uk/Economics/History/ Paper72/72samy.pdf (accessed July 2019).

Simon, E. and Inman, J. (1935). *The Rebuilding of Manchester*. London: Longmans, Green.

Smith, N. (1979). Toward a theory of gentrification: a back to the city movement by capital, not people. *Journal of the American Planning Association*, 45 (4), 538–48.

Stedman Jones, G. (1971). *Outcast London: A Study in the Relationship Between Classes in Victorian Society*. London: Verso.

2

Abandonment to financialisation: Ancoats and the ongoing housing question

Nigel de Noronha and Jonathan Silver

Between 1951 and 2001, the population of Ancoats fell by over 60 per cent (New East Manchester, 2007), leaving a post-industrial landscape in which empty factories and mills, demolished neighbourhoods and widespread abandonment of the built environment were pronounced. The post-war social conditions for residents in Ancoats were characterised by significant unemployment, poverty and social exclusion, reinforced as the area was in many regards forgotten about by capital and the state. The realities of life for the remaining residents were still unequal with other parts of the city, illustrated by a mortality rate that was 50 per cent higher than the UK average (New East Manchester, 2007). The district remained a space in which housing conditions contrasted markedly with the southern, wealthy suburbs of the city. In many regards, the segregated ways in which the working class lived in the city had changed little since the time of the suburban, middle-class expansion of the city. Ancoats was still a stigmatised district, characterised as a place to house the poor, even as state-capital relations were being profoundly restructured.

In chapter 1, we described how Ancoats emerged as a working-class district to house labour required for the expansion of capitalism during the rapid urbanisation of the Industrial Revolution, before concern over slum conditions led to municipal reform and partial clearance. In this chapter we pick up the story after the Second World War when Ancoats entered a period of sustained decline, and eventual redevelopment. In particular, we focus on the use of stigmatisation and a rhetoric of blame towards the working class in the district, which was used to justify segregation, exclusion, and subsequent displacement and regeneration. These dynamics have *structured* the district so that wealth and poverty now live in proximity, even as they remain segregated.

To better understand the transformation of housing in Ancoats, from the Second World War to today, we historicise relations between state, capital and housing into three distinct eras. Firstly, the period between the 1950s and the 1980s, when the area experienced the brunt of post-industrial collapse, population loss, and further displacement with some council housing construction. This era draws to a close with the withdrawal of state and capital, leading to the further stigmatisation of Ancoats as a place of poverty, crime and deteriorating housing conditions. Secondly, we look at the period between the 1980s and 2000s when New Labour's 'Third Way' optimism sought to socially engineer 'mixed sustainable communities' in what had been a segregated, working-class area into a place where rich and poor would live together in an 'urban village'. Thirdly, the period from 2008 onwards has displayed a new phase of relations between state and capital relations in the district. Finance-led restructuring of housing established conditions of gentrification facilitated through globalised circulations of rent-seeking investment into the district.

1950s to 1980s: from welfare state to deindustrialisation

The election of Attlee's Labour government after the Second World War heralded the creation of the welfare state in the UK. To address squalor and wartime destruction, the government implemented a programme to build one million homes, 80 per cent of which were delivered by local councils (Harloe, 1995). Alongside state investment, the Town and Country Planning Act (1947) gave councils the responsibility of planning urban development and creating the green belt to prevent urban sprawl. This period highlighted the potential of state investment to improve the housing conditions of the working class. However, migrants from the new Commonwealth, encouraged to travel to England to support the reconstruction and new investments in social welfare, were often excluded from the benefits through residential qualification periods for council housing, redlining districts that they could not settle in, as well as the direct racism of private landlords (Rex and Moore, 1967; Davis, 2001; Lukes et al., 2018). As a result, new migrants were concentrated in: Longsight, Rusholme,

Hulme, Moss Side and Whalley Range, whilst the Ancoats population continued to move out of the remaining slum housing. The subsequent Conservative government in the 1950s sought to shift back to a marketised governance of housing. They argued that the continuation of the rent freeze from the war was deterring landlords from investing in housing improvement. However, by this stage, Ancoats was dominated by council housing, and by the 1960s the ever-operating slum clearance programmes removed the remaining private housing in Ancoats and other inner-urban neighbourhoods. New estates used technological advances (such as system building) to speed up construction time and reduce costs. The city council built tower blocks and other multi-occupancy structures in areas which had been cleared, including the Cardroom estate in Ancoats. Mr Alfred Morris, Wythenshawe MP and former Ancoats resident, explained the reasons for such transformations:

> In Manchester, in a vast belt immediately outside the central area of the city, there still exist all too many remnants of a planless, knotted chaos of dark, dismal and crumbling homes. Many of these crossed the verge of uninhabited-ableness long before their most elderly inhabitants were born.[1]

Morris went on to highlight the scale of challenge and sheer amount of intervention perceived as required, explaining:

> In 1961, the City Council adopted a target of 4,000 houses to be demolished and 4,000 new houses to be erected each year. Of a total of 201,627 present dwellings in Manchester, some 54,700, or 27.1 per cent, are estimated to be unfit.

Ancoats continued as a space of intense housing intervention by the local state, the (re)making of a part of the district called New Islington being perhaps the most notable intervention by the municipality. It was renamed as the Cardroom estate and incorporated over 350 properties that provided much needed council housing for the city. The estate stood on the site of former terraced housing, industrial buildings and community spaces, such as the beautiful New Islington baths, spanning the land between the Ashton and Rochdale canals. This whole area was cleared in the 1960s and subsequently rebuilt in the 1970s in what would be considered in hindsight as a mistake of town planning. The continuing clearance programmes were systemic and often brutal, displacing whole streets of Ancoats residents, as the street photography of Shirley Baker (1989) evocatively captured. Furthermore, restrictions on access to the new council homes increasingly made them a residual provision for those with significant needs.

As the 1970s progressed, the final decline of the British Empire's global trade networks left Ancoats all but abandoned by capital. The shock of both the 1973 oil and 1976 International Monetary Fund crises left a nation facing what seemed irreversible, post-colonial decline (Dintenfass, 2006; Gamble, 1994). Manchester, like many northern cities, was entering the final stages of deindustrialisation, a seeming death spiral, which neither capital nor state intervention could or would reverse (Tomlinson, 2016). The industrial infrastructures in districts such as Ancoats had become obsolete, with an uncertain future for those still living there, as employment opportunities disappeared.

From 1979, the Thatcher government set out to transform the economy through growth in finance services and deregulation, opening

2.1 Industrial ruins of Ancoats or 'Cottonopolis' (J. Silver)

up industry to global competition, as the ideology of neoliberalism began to take root. These policies accelerated the decline of manufacturing whilst simultaneously blaming the resulting unemployment on the 'underclass' who became victims of structural unemployment (Gamble, 1994; Murray, 1990) in Ancoats, as elsewhere. The commitment to private ownership and a smaller state was also reflected in the sale of council housing at discounted rates, the privatisation of the nationalised infrastructure, and reduced funding to public services. The proceeds of council house sales were returned to central government and as a result the stock of social housing fell from 5.5 million in 1981 to 4 million in 2015 (NAO, 2017). Cuts to public expenditure also meant that the new estates built as part of the earlier slum clearance programmes were not maintained, signalling the beginning of a period of neglect and decline.

In the 1979 election campaign, the Conservatives adopted the racist, anti-migrant rhetoric of the far-right political party the National Front, and in 1981 they introduced the British Nationality Act which removed the right of children born in the UK to automatic citizenship from its enactment in 1984 (Sivanandan, 1992). In 1981, race riots focused government action on structural inequalities facing black communities (Scarman, 1983). In Manchester, this has been seen as the nadir of the decline of the city. It led to significant investment in Moss Side, even as Ancoats and other neighbourhoods continued to be neglected, a political concern for the council, which was reflected in their focus on East Manchester when the opportunities arose in later years. The lack of jobs meant working-class communities in districts like Ancoats were remade into a surplus population, sustained by limited welfare and the informal economy on the margins, awaiting displacement. Once again, as it had with the first generation of migrant workers in the nineteenth century, the racialisation of different groups and neighbourhoods fragmented potential resistance to these attacks by the working class of the city.

1980s municipal entrepreneurialism to New Labour

Primarily since the riots of 1981, the imaginary of the ghetto has repeatedly been adopted in UK policy discourse to describe racialised social problems of the inner city, and has more recently incorporated social housing estates (Hancock and Mooney, 2013; MacDonald et al., 2014). The Housing Act 1988 replaced rent control and security of tenure with the current private rental regime, which allows landlords to set their rents as they choose, reduces security of tenure to six months or a year and, under Section 21, provides a mechanism for eviction within eight weeks even when a tenant fully complies with the conditions of their tenancy. The conditions for the emergence of the private landlord were enabled after years of state ownership of the housing stock.

This stigmatisation of place, together with weakening housing regulation, created the eventual conditions for capital to flow into housing in Ancoats. This making of 'problem places' has fed UK policy discourses and informed Area Based Interventions. Regeneration of Ancoats was premised on an ideological commitment to the market and mixed tenure development. Deas (2013: 2302) argued that a 'post-political consensus' framed regeneration programmes as a technical, managerial challenge, which was 'characterised by the colonisation of decision-making by policy elites.' Through the regeneration of 'problem' places, this restricted the space for democratic dissent. The commitment to social housing was further undermined by the development of the image of the 'scrounger' through media and political reporting, creating an imaginary of the undeserving poor (an echo of Emil Sax's arguments, which were addressed in *The Housing Question* by Engels).

The combination of regeneration based on a pathology of problem places with the allocation of blame for social disintegration on the undeserving poor created a toxic environment. It led to growing 'welfare reform' targeted at residents, the emerging power of property developers, and the conditions for the remaking of urban space in the interests of capital. From the 1980s, Manchester City Council undertook another shift in the state approach to housing. The council moved away from the municipal socialism that had built estates such as the Cardroom, towards municipal entrepreneurialism (Peck and Ward, 2002). This ideology would later find resonance in New Labour's 'Third Way' political programme and a shift towards a logic of marketisation restructured the ways the local state approached housing in the city. Districts such as Hulme became sites of new state/capital interventions, which transformed so called stigmatised estates into mixed tenure neighbourhoods. Hulme's nineteenth-century terraced housing was cleared in the early 1970s and replaced by system-built maisonettes, tower blocks and crescents but, before the end of the decade, such housing was deemed unfit for families with children, and provided shelter instead for single people and squatters.[2] New Labour's solution promised to reduce the proportion of social housing from 85 per cent to 40 per cent by building housing for sale on the open market. Whilst the target to reduce social housing was achieved, most of the properties built for ownership were rented privately. Ancoats, however, remained outside of these new municipal interventions, experiments and market-led approaches as its spiral of decline intensified.

The shift in focus by the Town Hall to East Manchester started with the use of Education and Action Zones in 1998 and was consolidated after the New Labour government had developed a comprehensive, nation-wide urban regeneration programme. The New East Manchester Urban Regeneration Company was set up in 1999 to work across a series of districts including Ancoats. It was boosted by the Commonwealth Games in 2002 and became the governance structure through which a plethora of other housing interventions across this deprived part of the city were implemented. This intense state-led, market driven restructuring of the area led to Ward (2003: 123) describing East Manchester as the most 'policy thick' urban space in the UK. Evaluation of the New Deal for Communities programme suggests that the investment had secured more place-based rather than individual benefits (DCLG, 2010), while a reduction of crime, improvement in housing, and environmental quality increased the attractiveness of one of the 'most deprived' areas in England for private housing investment.

In Ancoats the Cardroom estate's design meant various social problems emerged. Furthermore, the proximity of the Cardroom to the city-centre positioned it as a potential future space for private sector housing investment. This can be partly explained by the idea of a 'rent gap' outlined by Marxist geographer Neil Smith (1987) where, over time, a gap emerges between the potential and actual return on investment in capital held in housing, incentivising redevelopment at higher density or for a more profitable market. The Cardroom had become known as a 'sink estate' in which the council was dumping its 'problem tenants'. This territorial stigmatisation established the conditions through which the eviction and demolition of social tenants would proceed as a New Labour regeneration initiative (Wacquant, 2008). In 2001, the council were successful in securing national-state funding to develop the Cardroom estate in New Islington as a Millennium Community that would be used to represent the best of the new mixed community approach guiding housing policy in the UK. The public land was given to private developer Urban Splash, a company that had established a reputation for converting historic buildings in the city, but had no experience of undertaking neighbourhood regeneration. Luke and Kaika (2019: 584) described what this market-driven Urban Splash vision would entail:

> Total demolition was deemed necessary to rebrand the area, erase the stigma associated with the Cardroom, and open space for new apartments without attention to the spatialised patterns, paths, and practices residents constructed or tended on the neglected Estate.

The plans, concocted by 'starchitect' Will Alsop, were designed to attract the middle class back into Manchester, and had little concern with improving the housing conditions for Ancoats' existing residents. Instead, pushed on by Urban Splash, the focus was on

2.2 Housing waiting for demolition on the Cardroom Estate (J. Silver)

2.3 Urban Splash developments begin from a cleared Cardroom estate
(J. Silver)

how New Islington might create new typologies of marketised housing across the inner-city, with the aim of bringing wealthy people into the district for the first time in its history. No longer would Ancoats be a heavily stigmatised area of the city. Achieving this aim meant expulsion for the urban poor in order to create spaces for these new developments. Luke and Kaika (2019) highlighted that, even a decade after demolition of the Cardroom, only 55 units of new, low income housing had been built, compared to the 106 families that had been displaced (a net loss of 250 council homes). The example established through the Cardroom estate highlighted the way that the state was now focused on enabling capital to invest in housing in the district. Estates such as the Cardroom, which had lasted barely 30 years, were now being demolished as part of an explicit gentrification strategy (Lees, 2008) in Ancoats undertaken by the local state in collaboration with the market. We can again turn back to Engels and his work on the 'Haussmann' remaking of Paris to see how urban renewal is predicated on displacement. Capital was now switching from the primary (i.e. production) to secondary circuit (i.e. not used in the production process but 'sunk' into fixed assets) in Ancoats. This meant that formerly industrial buildings as sites of production or manufacturing were now being transformed into housing, and accumulation was enabled through the rent generated from them.

Owen Hatherley (2010: 146), writing about the area during its economic crisis-induced stasis, offered a withering appraisal:

> The farcical attempt on the part of Urban Splash and their state sponsors to build a 'Millennium Community' on the ruins of the Cardroom estate is a pop-public private partnership farrago which has levelled an area of social housing in one of those gentrification frontiers on the edge of Manchester's ring-road.

Blakeley and Evans (2015: 196), reflecting on the impact of the regeneration in Ancoats and its surrounding neighbourhoods, argued that 'East Manchester was successful in addressing some of the symptoms of poverty, if not the fundamental underlying inequalities which lacerate a multiply deprived area.' Such a view does little to convey the ways in which the regeneration reinforced inequality across the district, nor the ways in which state-capital relations to housing were transforming the lives of the poor in significant ways.

The New Labour market-led approach to housing came to an end with the shock of the 2008 economic crisis and the subsequent brutal waves of the austerity programme of the Conservative-Liberal government. These years saw the further withdrawal of the national state from regeneration programmes, housing intervention and anti-poverty initiatives, leaving municipalities such as Manchester with less powers, finance and capacity to intervene. Attempts to transform the relations between state and capital in the area would now move towards a new wave of market-based housing, which would leave Ancoats a segregated and fragmented district, with stark divisions between incoming gentrifiers and preexisting stigmatised communities.

2008 onwards: financialised municipal entrepreneurialism

The economic crisis of 2008 brought the market-led regeneration of Ancoats, as well as other parts of Manchester and the UK's provincial cities, to a shuddering halt. Investors withdrew from the secondary circuit of capital (Harvey, 1978) as prices dropped; potential buyers struggled to secure mortgage loans from banks facing collapse; and financial returns on new developments evaporated (Van der Heijden et al., 2011). It left the neighbourhood in stasis, with the first wave of apartment blocks visible amongst the few industrial buildings left standing, and large areas of cleared land, particularly the Cardroom estate, facing an uncertain future. The initial influx of new residents had made a home in the district and Ancoats would no longer be a space for the economically excluded. In the years of the Conservative-Liberal coalition government, many low-income households faced an unprecedented assault on social welfare programmes. Waves of austerity and measures such as the Bedroom Tax, which left those with a 'spare room' facing lower housing benefit from the government, meant further impoverishment for people already living on the margins (Gray and Barford, 2018). Ancoats was beginning to develop a housing geography in which wealth and poverty lived proximate but segregated.

Since the post-crisis recovery, beginning around 2014, Manchester has become a city in which large amounts of capital investment from the UK, and increasingly internationally, has been encouraged by a finance-led regeneration model (see for instance Imrie and Thomas, 1993). The pace and scale of the urban development boom has been dramatic. The consultancy firm Deloitte reported a 133 per cent increase in the number of residential units under construction between 2016 and 2017 in the city-centre.[3] And in 2018, 79 development sites were identified with over 25,000 new apartment units on site or with planning permission for the city-regional centre that now included parts of Ancoats and was estimated to be worth billions of pounds (Silver, 2018). Much of this growth has emerged from the local and national government focus on remaking the private rented market, with a shift in emphasis from the 'Buy to Let' sector to the larger scale, institutionally friendly, 'Private Rented Sector' (PRS). These changes in the way in which housing is constructed, operated and owned have been understood through the term *financialisation*, which conveys how financial actors such as pension funds, sovereign wealth funds, billionaires, private equity and other institutions have been able to take ownership of new housing developments as an asset to be speculated on, traded and profited from.

Financialisation has become increasingly important in thinking about housing since the 2008 economic crisis (Aalbers, 2016; Fields and Uffer, 2016). David Harvey (1978), picking up on foundational work by Marx and Engels, explained how housing should be understood as a financial asset that could be held for rent or traded as a commodity. The United Nations defines financialisation as: 'structural changes in housing and financial markets and global investment whereby housing is treated as a commodity, a means of accumulating wealth and often as security for financial instruments that are traded and sold on [the] global market.' The financialisation of housing has been more noticeable in larger economically powerful cities such as London, San Francisco and Sydney. However, in recent years these dynamics are now becoming visible in post-industrial regions of the UK such as Manchester (Silver, 2018). This trend can be explained through the surge of surplus capital into the secondary circuit (global real estate investment was estimated at $1.39 trillion in 2017),[4] and the new opportunities being generated through the restructuring of rental markets (Fields and Uffer, 2016). In the case of the UK, housing developments are increasingly built for rental purposes by or for institutional investors. This process can include developers holding onto the housing units or selling them on to various financial institutions and actors, aimed at the rental sector. This new financial 'product' is the key means through which housing financialisation has taken place and allows institutional investors to purchase property, often at scale (for instance, a whole building or urban development site), creating both ongoing rental income and a capital asset. Encouraged by new national guidance and favourable fiscal conditions, thousands of PRS apartments are in development across Ancoats, and in Manchester more widely. These new housing spaces are intended to capitalise on rising rents but had the effect of reinforcing the housing crisis that has become increasingly acute during the years of austerity. The opportunities to profit from housing have therefore differed considerably from the past because it is now straight-forward for large financial actors to invest in the PRS in the city.

In Ancoats, this financialisation of housing took on a particularly accelerated form through the establishment of the 'Manchester Life' development vehicle. Over the course of a few years, this scheme has built more than 1,000 new housing units, with no social or affordable housing provision included. Manchester Life has also been the partnership through which Manchester City Council have taken the city into a purported £1 billion housing partnership with Abu Dhabi United Group (ADUG). The Group is a United Arab Emirates-based private equity company, owned by Sheikh Mansour bin Zayed Al Nahyan, a member of the Abu Dhabi Royal Family and owner of Manchester City Football Club. The construction of hundreds of new apartments, through a rumoured initial £100 million investment from ADUG and over £50 million of state loans from national government, represents a new phase in the relations between state and capital across the housing of the district. Most visible is the way in which the financial arrangements underpinning housing development in Ancoats have become increasingly complex, internationalised and financialised, as the local municipality and ADUG established a series of companies based in the secretive tax jurisdiction of Jersey, through which 999-year leases of the land have been transferred and all rental income is sent.

If Ancoats' built environment was once broadly connected to the financial life of the primary circuit of capital through production and connection to the global networks of 'cotton capitalism' (Beckert, 2015), during which the purpose of housing was to sustain the social reproductive needs of workers for capital, it has now been transformed. Ancoats has become a space in which the secondary circuit of capital has arguably become the dominant economic activity through investment into housing, supplanting the primary circuit of cotton manufacturing in the nineteenth century. The housing partnership between an English local authority and Abu Dhabi royalty is perhaps the most extreme example of what Beswick and Penny (2018) term 'financialized municipal entrepreneurialism.' They argue: 'The local state is no longer merely the enabler – limited to providing strategic oversight of the private sector – but financializes its practice in a reimagined commercialized interventionism, as property speculator' (2018: 612).

Even since the 1990s, the role of the state in people's lives has fundamentally shifted. It has moved from an enabling function to facilitate private investment into housing in Ancoats during the New Labour era toward an active role as a speculative capitalist actor in the housing market. And it has done this through connecting new flows of petro-wealth into the city and transforming previously public land for marketised housing. In Ancoats, the New Labour focus on creating 'mixed, sustainable communities' has disappeared (Lees, 2008), as the current phase of urban development in the neighbourhood shows little concern with such inclusive, if problematic, discourses. Manchester Life has built housing on the empty land of the old Cardroom estate with the underlying aim of transforming the demographic composition of the district and creating a dramatic shift in the type and cost of housing in the district. It has arguably created a new segregation dynamic in which rich and poor live not in separate districts, but within the district itself: visibly divided by types of housing. Ancoats has become a space in which council housing and former council housing for the working class sit adjacent to new high-density developments for new middle-class residents as an extension of the city-centre. This shift provides a powerful illustration of how we can visualise the operations of capitalism through housing, reminiscent of the photographic work of Johnny Miller (2018) and his portrayal of urban inequality across the globe.

Furthermore, despite the clear demographic change in the socio-economic status of residents that has been instigated in the twenty-first century, the experience of new tenants in Ancoats might not have changed so much after all. In August 2019, Section 21 (6A) Eviction Notices were sent to Manchester Life tenants in 'Smith's Yard' (named as a twisted homage to a pub built in 1775 and demolished for the development). The Notice gave tenants two months to leave before the landlord would apply for a court order to retake possession of the property unless they agreed to rent increases of 5 per cent. Again, we see how Engels' (1887) understanding of increasing land values pushing up the price of housing for workers operates as critical in the operating of capitalist accumulation across urban land. That this mechanism was being used by a company part-owned by the council highlights the contradictions that lie at the heart of the model of 'financialized municipal entrepreneurialism'. As Engels understood back in 1872, capital is bound to seek the greatest return in the built environment, whatever the consequences for the tenant.

Conclusion

Across these chapters, we have sought to understand the role of housing in shaping how the other half lives. To do so we have drawn inspiration from the work of Friedrich Engels, and subsequent thinkers within the Marxist political economy tradition. In particular, we focused on his emphasis on thinking through the way housing is shaped by shifting relations between state and capital. We used a case study of the district of Ancoats in Manchester, the world's first industrial suburb and frequented by Engels in developing many of his pivotal ideas. Through historical analysis of the housing geographies of the district and the shifting state/capital relations across two hundred years of life in the neighbourhood we explored the experiences of residents, and the ways in which they are intimately tied to the interventions and decisions of the elite.

In chapter 1, we outlined the rapid growth of Ancoats during the early stages of industrial capitalism, providing substandard housing for new migrants joining the workforce who were considered disposable by the industrialists. We then showed the ways that the state was compelled to act – through fear of disease and pandemic, revolution, and sometimes by good intention – to address poor housing conditions. This was achieved through municipal investment and slum clearance, which were sometimes successful but nearly always had consequences of displacement, neglect and community destruction. In this chapter, we developed our historical analysis by considering the post-war period clearances and abandonment of Ancoats, as well as the impact of stigma and exclusion for those left living on 'sink estates'. We then highlighted the growth of municipal entrepreneurialism and the role of the state in enabling private sector investment in housing, with the intention of creating so-called 'mixed communities'. Finally, we showed how housing in Ancoats has now been financialised, particularly through a new partnership between the council and ADUG, which has accelerated the changing demographic composition of the district.

Structural inequality and segregation are central to understanding Ancoats, and our analysis also touched upon the impact of race and migration in thinking through the intersectionality of the political economy of housing. Engels understood the social attitudes toward the Irish in relation to housing in a way that can provide analysis beyond class. There was little evidence to differentiate the way that other roles, such as gender, shifted over the period, though the recent emergence of the original survey documents from the slum clearance of Ancoats in the 1930s does provide the potential to develop this analysis further in the future. We acknowledge that these aspects of the district are significant and under-explained parts of the story of housing in Ancoats.

Today, capital and the state continue to remake cities and create new forms of socio-spatial segregation, as well as accumulation opportunities through rent for the elite. Our exploration highlighted some of the ways that these actions have contributed to changing housing geographies in Ancoats. In thinking about the potential future of housing in the district, and more widely in England, the actions of the local state have enabled finance capital to be unleashed in ways that have yet to be fully understood. Through stigmatisation of the neighbourhood and the people who lived there, these new opportunities for capital accumulation have been created. The next stage of relations between the state and capital in the shaping of housing in Ancoats remains to be written. Whatever happens we are certain that the work of Engels will continue to guide interpretations, providing a Marxist political economic foundation to critically explore ways inequality is continually and differentially reproduced across the built environment.

Notes

1 https://api.parliament.uk/historic-hansard/commons/1965/nov/22/slum-clearance-manchester (accessed 24 March 2019).

2 www.manchestereveningnews.co.uk/news/greater-manchester-news/manchesters-lost-council-estates-history-14585553 (accessed 24 March 2019).

3 Deloitte (2017) Transforming the skyline Manchester Crane Survey – www2.deloitte.com/content/dam/Deloitte/uk/Documents/real-estate/deloitte-uk-manchester-crane-survey-17.pdf (accessed 8 April 2019).

4 Cushman Wakefield (2017) Atlas Report www.cushmanwakefield.com/en/research-and-insight/2017/investment-atlas-2017/ (accessed 8 April 2019).

References

Aalbers, M. (2016). *The Financialization of Housing: A political Economy Approach*. New York: Routledge.

Baker, S. (1989). *Street Photographs: Manchester and Salford*. Newcastle: Bloodaxe Books.

Beckert, S. (2015). *Empire of Cotton: A Global History*. London: Vintage.

Beswick, J., and Penny, J. (2018). Demolishing the present to sell off the future? The emergence of 'financialized municipal entrepreneurialism' in London. *International Journal of Urban and Regional Research*, 42(4), 612–32.

Blakeley, G., and Evans, B. (2015). *The Regeneration of East Manchester*. Manchester: Manchester University Press.

Davis, J. (2001). Rents and race in 1960s London: new light on Rachmanism. *Twentieth Century British History*, 12(1), 69–92.

DCLG (2010). *The New Deal for Communities Experience: A Final Assessment. The New Deal for Communities Evaluation: Final report – Volume 7*. London: Department of Communities and Local Government. *Authors*: Elaine Batty, Christina Beatty, Mike Foden, Paul Lawless, Sarah Pearson and Ian Wilson, Centre for Regional Economic and Social Research, Sheffield Hallam University.

Deas, I. (2013). The search for territorial fixes in subnational governance: city-regions and the disputed emergence of post-political consensus in Manchester, England. *Urban Studies*, 51(11), 2285–314.

Dintenfass, M. (2006). *The Decline of Industrial Britain: 1870–1980*. London: Routledge.

Engels, F. (1887). *The Housing Question*. 2nd edn. Accessed online at Engels The Housing Question.pdf (hlrn.org).

Fields, D., and Uffer, S. (2016). The financialisation of rental housing: a comparative analysis of New York City and Berlin. *Urban Studies*, 53(7), 1486–502.

Gamble, A. (1994). *Britain in Decline: Economic Policy, Political Strategy and the British State*. London: Macmillan International Higher Education.

Gray, M., and Barford, A. (2018). The depths of the cuts: the uneven geography of local government austerity. *Cambridge Journal of Regions, Economy and Society*, 11(3), 541–63.

Hancock, L., and Mooney, G. (2013). 'Welfare ghettos' and the 'broken society': territorial stigmatization in the contemporary UK. *Housing, Theory and Society*, 30(1), 46–64.

Harloe, M (1995). *The People's Home: Social Rented Housing in Europe and America*. Oxford: Blackwell.

Harvey, D. (1978). The urban process under capitalism: a framework for analysis. *International Journal of Urban and Regional Research*, 2(1–4), 101–31.

Hatherley, O. (2010). *A Guide to the New Ruins of Great Britain*. London: Verso.

Imrie, R., and Thomas, H. (1993). The limits of property-led regeneration. *Environment and Planning C: Government and Policy*, 11(1), 87–102.

Lees, L. (2008). Gentrification and social mixing: towards an inclusive urban renaissance? *Urban Studies*, 45(12), 2449–70.

Luke, N., and Kaika, M. (2019). Ripping the heart out of Ancoats: collective action to defend infrastructures of social reproduction against gentrification. *Antipode*, 51(2), 579–600.

Lukes, S., de Noronha, N., and Finney, N. (2018). Slippery discrimination: an analysis of the drivers of migrant and minority housing disadvantage. *Ethnic and Migration Studies*, 45(17), 3188–206.

MacDonald, R., Shildrick, T., and Furlong, A. (2014). 'Benefits Street' and the myth of workless communities. *Sociological Research Online*, 19(3), 1, 263–8.

Miller, J. (2018). Unequal scenes. www.unequalscenes.com/ (accessed 4 April 2019).

Murray, C. (1990). The British underclass. *Public Interest*, 99(1), 4–28.

NAO (2017). *Housing in England: Overview*. London: National Audit Office.

New East Manchester (2007). East Manchester: Strategic Regeneration Framework, 2008–2018. www.east-manchester.com/downloads/1/strategic-regeneration-framework-2008–2018/index.html (accessed July 2021).

Peck, J., and Ward, K. (2002). *City of Revolution: Restructuring Manchester*. Manchester: Manchester University Press.

Rex, J. and Moore, R. (1967). *Race, Community and Conflict: A Study of Sparkbrook*. London: Oxford University Press.

Scarman, L. (1983). *The Scarman Report: The Brixton Disorders, 10–12 April 1981*. London: Penguin.

Silver, J. (2018). From Homes to Assets: Housing financialisation in Manchester. Working paper. University of Sheffield

Sivanandan, A. (1992). *A Different Hunger: Writings on Black Resistance*. London: Verso.

Smith, N. (1987). Gentrification and the rent gap. *Annals of the Association of American Geographers*, 77(3), 462–5.

Tomlinson, J. (2016). De-industrialisation not decline: a new meta-narrative for post-war British history. *Twentieth Century British History*, 27(1), 76–99 (doi:10.1093/tcbh/hwv030).

Van der Heijden, H., Dol, K., and Oxley, M. (2011). Western European housing systems and the impact of the international financial crisis. *Journal of Housing and the Built Environment*, 26(3), 295–313.

Wacquant, L (2008). *Urban Outcasts: A Comparative Sociology of Advanced Marginality*. Cambridge: Polity.

Ward, K. (2003). Entrepreneurial urbanism, state restructuring and civilizing 'New' East Manchester. *Area*, 35(2), 116–27.

3

Austerity and the local state: governing and politicising 'actually existing austerity' in a post-democratic city

Joe Penny

This chapter outlines the 'actually existing' contours of austerity urbanism in London, as it is being assembled by local government, and draws out the depoliticising processes and practices through which local actors absorb cutbacks. Given the pace and scale of budget cuts passed down onto local government since 2010, organised institutional resistance from urban political elites has been conspicuous by its absence. During the 1980s, when Thatcher imposed a policy of rate-capping alongside fiscal retrenchment, the response across a small but persistent number of Labour-held councils was to actively struggle against central government on behalf of the residents they represented. Far from simply refusing to set legal budgets, itself a radical act in excess of anything seen today, left councillors back then articulated and sought (albeit unsuccessfully) to create a coalition around a vision of municipal socialism beyond the Keynesian Welfare State and against the emergent New Right. In contrast, since 2010, London Councils have sought to smoothly manage budget cuts and procure consent for a new normal of austerity urbanism in which unprofitable services/assets are pared back and given to resident groups to run, whilst others are commercialised and financialised. To be clear, local state actors were not responsible for the global financial implosion of 2008. But they are playing a role in transforming that event into a slow-burn crisis of social reproduction and its infrastructures.

This chapter moves across and amongst ten London boroughs[1] and draws out the *structurally inscribed* and strategically selective ways in which councillors and officers are remaking local governance at a time of imposed scarcity. The analysis is grounded in empirical research conducted between 2015 and 2017 encompassing: policy analysis; interviews with councillors, officers and activists; and non-participant observation at council meetings and local campaign events. However, following Peck (2017), the chapter leans towards abstraction and conjunctural analysis over thick-description and empiricism. It draws out the shared and symptomatic logics and features that constitute a broad field of (constrained) action in London to suggest that a 'common sense' over how austerity should be managed is being pushed by local urban elites, based on three inter-locking logics: compassionate competence; responsibilisation; and speculative urban entrepreneurialism.

Both myself and Ellis (chapter 4) explore the structural connections between austerity, inequality and violence. But where Ellis explores interpersonal expressions of violence, this chapter engages with a structural violence which has unfolded on the terrain of the local state. Or, to put it more concretely, a slow violence, but enacted by those who make decisions about if and how austerity budget cuts are to be pursued. As such, in addition to drawing out the local state's governing logics, the chapter references on-going struggles to emphasise how this austerity common-sense is contested, even if councillors and officers all too often dismiss the content and visions of grassroots resistance and alternatives.

Compassionate competence and the 'austerian axiomatic'

> This is the point at which Labour councils should be saying no, in a loud and clear voice, with support from their national leadership. We won't make your cuts. We will not pass on the burden of the calamitous economic and financial crisis of capitalism that we did not create. (Former leader of Lambeth Council, Ted Knight 2012).

In 1986, 32 Lambeth councillors were disqualified from political office and ordered to pay nearly a quarter of a million pounds for refusing to set a legal budget in protest against Thatcher's rate-capping policy. This marked the end of a high-stakes political struggle between the Conservative government in Westminster and a handful of 'new urban left' Labour councils in town halls across England, backed for a time by the soon to be abolished Greater London Council (Gyford, 1985). One of the 32 Lambeth councillors was the then council leader, Ted Knight, who has lamented the lack of local political leadership against austerity today.

In contrast to the months between 1984 and 1986, since 2010 there has been no sustained organised resistance to local government austerity led by, or even involving, the political or administrative leadership of a local authority in England and Wales. As Fuller and West (2017: 2095) note: 'At the urban level, what has been striking about the post-2008 landscape is the way in which the macro-economic justifications of austerity have largely been uncontested by urban leaders'. In many respects, far from inspiring local leaders in London today to resist austerity, the 'rate-capping rebellion' has taken on what Kristin Ross (2002) calls a 'cautionary afterlife'. This is nowhere more apparent than in Lambeth, where the spectre of Knight looms large in many councillors' insistence that resistance to central government is not only futile, but recklessly irresponsible:

> We spend the majority of our time focused on tackling inequality, improving people's life chances and supporting the most vulnerable. But we also make sure the bins are collected, that cycling is improved and our parks and green spaces remain beautiful and well-kept … we represent and deliver for everyone and we are practical and pragmatic … No one wants a return to Lambeth Council of the 1980s. (Taken from a letter by Labour councillors in Vauxhall to their residents in 2016)

Beyond signalling the (contested) local legacy of Ted Knight's leadership in Lambeth, these councillors articulate a sensible, managerial and de-politicising stand-point with regards to austerity, which was broadly shared by all of the senior councillors and officers interviewed and which permeates the preambles to all of the ten boroughs' financial strategies. This position can be summarised as follows: resistance to austerity cannot take the form of refusing to set a legal (austerity) budget; doing so would be an abrogation of responsibility and an invitation for un-elected officials from Whitehall to impose cuts in a more ideological and punitive manner, with little knowledge of or regard for local needs; the role of responsible and pragmatic councillors and officers is to competently and compassionately administer the pain of austerity, ensuring that vulnerable groups and front-line services are protected as far as possible.

Far from being struggled over and won in the assemblies, meeting rooms, and corridors of the town hall, let alone in community spaces with residents, the institutionalisation of austerity urbanism – echoing the 'Dented Shield' logic of Neil Kinnock – seems to have been already structurally inscribed in England's central-local relations (Davies et al., 2020). Indeed, following two decades in which outsourcing, privatisation and the sound efficient management of budgets have been held up as signature virtues of local governance, it is unsurprising that the above narrative has become a governing common sense that 'marginalises the counter austerity social logic of social justice, pitting ideologues against pragmatists, utopia versus reality, the grown up custodians … versus the children of populist impulse' (Fuller and West, 2017: 2094).

On the face of it, the acceptance and circulation of austerity as common sense suggests a passive resignation on behalf of Labour-led local authorities, who are resigned to 'administering the local consequences of global historical necessity' (Rancière, 2006: 80). Yet this interpretation falls short in its capacity to appreciate and problematise the ways in which local actors articulate against and with austerity, often *actively* embedding macro-economic logics in local discourse and practice. One common modulation, especially in public and on social media, is that of disaffected consent secured through dull compulsion. Whilst implicitly conceding to the reality of austerity and diligently administering budget cuts locally, many councillors publicly decry the unfairness of budget cuts and pursue institutional channels through which to voice their concerns:

> None of us went into politics to make these cuts, but … if we decide not to set a legal budget and to be all martyr-like the Tories will just parachute in their own administrators who will make worse cuts in a less progressive way. But at the same time I don't want to be seen to be rolling over … on the one hand you have to balance the books locally, and on the other you have to make hell for a government who are balancing their books on the backs of the poor. (Islington Cabinet Member)

Demonstrating that austerity is more than just a centrally imposed condition, other councillors and officers actively 'pull down' austerian discourses (Newman, 2013) to further their own policy agendas.

One Lambeth Officer, for example, stressed that the council at times mobilises 'austerity' as a pretext to push through changes and 'modernise' public services in a way that might not have been politically possible before: 'The austerity thing gives us an amazing platform on which to say, we have got to do this because we cannot afford to do the things that we have been doing previously, and we have got to think of a smart way of thinking about what we continue to do and what we don't continue to do.' (Lambeth Senior Policy Officer).

The above points to the various ways in which some councils have actively sought to re-situate their role at a time of massive budget cuts and potential existential crisis. Whether begrudgingly or willingly, austerity has become a presupposed axiomatic across London's boroughs, pre-empting and infusing all manner of local discussions, deliberations and decisions. Local urban leaders' appeal to govern austerity compassionately and competently works as a powerful form of consensual realism. It separates out, pre-empts and forecloses possibly polemical voices and demands, including from those who would ask fundamental questions about the necessity and legitimacy of austerity. It seeks to channel people's attention and energy into pragmatic, problem-solving efforts to adapt, and even thrive through, the new normal of ascetic municipal statecraft.

By 2016, warnings that the limits of incremental cutbacks and selective 'salami-slicing' of budgets had been reached were consistently being sounded by London boroughs as well as advocacy groups, such as London Councils. With statutory need for social care and waste management rising as budgets continued to fall, a number of councils warned of an inevitable 'tipping point' after which the funding of discretionary services would all but cease. Yet, far from resigning themselves to simply managing organisational, institutional and local decline, all of the local actors interviewed stressed a capacity for resilience and adaptation, albeit within narrow parameters. Broadly speaking, there are two main strategies in this regard. The first centres on discourses of public service modernisation and transformation through new 'creative' public service models that 'responsibilise' residents to achieve 'more for less'. The second is a renewed emphasis on the importance of entrepreneurialism, encompassing ambitious pro-growth forms of privatism and financialisation.

London's libraries and the limits of responsibilisation

The early years of austerity have been characterised by authorities taking action to reduce costs through a range of traditional 'supply side' cost reduction measures ... However, given the severity and duration of austerity, alongside increasing demand for services, local government needs to raise its sights and shift beyond traditional cost reduction approaches. (PwC, 2013: 1)

In the document *Redefining Local Government*, the global management consultancy firm PricewaterhouseCoopers (PwC) reflects and reproduces the axiomatic of austerity described above. Starting with the unquestioned need to administer major budget cuts, PwC offer a framework of the 'new strategic choices' (PwC, 2013: 6) that local authorities must now make. These 'choices', which are in fact presented as incontrovertible exigencies with no realistic alternatives, reflect both what is happening empirically and what 'objectively' must happen normatively. They can be summarised by two concepts: responsibilisation and entrepreneurialism.

Faced with the prospect of making significant cuts to front-line service provision, all of the councils considered here emphasised the importance of reducing the demand for council services in budget documents and in interviews. In a context of dwindling capacity, demand management is being pursued chiefly by enrolling non-state partners in the provision, management and financing of services wherever this is politically possible and technically feasible. In practice, this has meant deepening and extending practices of public service pluralisation along two lines: the responsibilisation of residents, through exhortations that they must do more for themselves or risk losing valued local services; and the outsourcing of service responsibilities, chiefly through outsourcing to local community and voluntary sector organisations, large third-sector providers, and national and multinational companies and corporations.

Rhetorically these two processes – responsibilisation and outsourcing to 'entrepreneurs' – have been presented as alternative, even competing, visions of local government modernisation: the former collaborative and participatory; the latter competitive and privatising. In a 2010 article for *the Guardian*, for example, Allegra Stratton compared and contrasted the approaches of Lambeth and Barnet Council. Dubbing Lambeth the 'John Lewis' council for its cooperative approach and Barnet the 'Easy Council' for its radically outsourced agenda, Stratton suggested that the two councils were going 'head-to-head' in charting opposing flagship models for Labour and Conservative councils respectively in an age of austerity. Yet, as politically elegant as this binary narrative may be, in practice, evidence from the London boroughs suggests that the responsibilisation and outsourcing agendas are less competing visions and more two sides of the same coin of municipal statecraft at a time of imposed scarcity.

That these two agendas should be progressed in tandem is unsurprising given that neither are new to local government. Discourses and practices of responsibilisation have circulated, albeit in varying forms and for different political ends, since at least the 1960s (Cockburn, 1977), and were especially prominent under New Labour through theories and practices of networked governance, partnerships and participation (Newman, 2013). Similarly, outsourcing is far from novel in local government. Since the introduction of Compulsory Competitive Tendering in 1991, all councils have gained competencies in commissioning and contracting private-sector partners across an increasingly diverse range of services (Newman, 2014).

Drawing on their experiences under New Labour, councils across London are seeking to enrol residents in practices of participatory, co-produced, and do-it-yourself governance. In some boroughs, such as Lambeth, Camden and Newham, emphasis has been placed explicitly on reconstituting the relationship between citizen and local state. Mobilising post-welfare discourses of voluntarism, responsibility, resilience and self/community-transformation, as well as austerian inflections of concepts such as creativity, innovation, and sustainability (Forkert, 2016), these boroughs articulate closely with long-held concerns to reduce dependency on the state and encourage collective social action in the co-design, co-production, and community management of local services.

For other boroughs this agenda is promoted with less zeal as the inevitable future for most discretionary services, with residents and community groups exhorted to take part in co-designing and co-producing services, and presented with a series of 'false choices' – either step up and voluntarily take over the running of this library, community centre or adventure playground, or it will close. A common practice in this regard is to offer community groups 'transitional funding' on the condition that they produce business plans showing how they will become financially self-sustainable – a tacit acknowledgement, if not convincing mitigation, of the fragility of some DIY service models.

The fate of London's public libraries – once 'an icon of the public sphere' (Newman, 2007: 887) – is illustrative in this regard. Since 2010, 773 libraries have closed their doors across the UK (Flood, 2019). Beyond these closures, a subtler and slower reconfiguration, or 'slow spoiling' (Penny, 2020), of services within remaining libraries has also been taking place, as professional paid staff are replaced by unpaid volunteers, and a growing number of libraries are transferred to resident-led/private organisations. In Lewisham, for example, data from the BBC (2016) suggests that there have been no library closures since 2010. Yet, between 2010 and 2011, Lewisham council transferred the management of 5 libraries to social enterprises and charities. Furthermore, there are plans for a further three libraries to be run by volunteers, with another becoming a self-service library. This will leave three council-run libraries across the borough. These changes have been controversial locally and were met with considerable local contestation (Forkert, 2016).

In Lambeth, as part of its Cooperative Council agenda, the council sought to absorb budget cuts to its library services by enrolling residents in the provision of DIY-libraries, emphasising to residents that there was no realistic alternative to austerity and that failure to participate constructively in official plans might mean the closure of libraries altogether. When this ultimatum was met with widespread resistance and failed to achieve anything close to consensus during a consultation in 2015, an alternative plan was imposed from above with no consultation: a social enterprise was invited to run three of the borough's libraries as 'healthy living centres'. These centres entail new fee-paying gyms on-site and a loss of library space and of professional librarian time. In response, residents mobilised a campaign against the council's proposal, culminating in the nine-day occupation of the Carnegie library in Herne Hill, and put forward their own alternative solution – a worker-community mutual model – which was summarily dismissed by councillors and officers as unworkable (Robinson and Sheldon, 2019; Penny, 2020).

Since the late Victorian era, libraries have embedded shifting notions of 'publicness' (Newman, 2007). In the more recent history of libraries, from the 1970s, trends towards governing with and through the social and communities have become more pronounced. Certainly, the idea of encouraging greater participation in libraries is by no means new to the post-2010 austerity moment. The pace and scale of local government cuts, however, means that libraries are 'undergoing the most difficult period in their peacetime history' (Anstice, 2015: n.p.) and the trends towards communal self-provision, private management and self-sufficient funding are greater and more generalised than before. The fate of libraries since the onset of austerity, especially visible in Lewisham and Lambeth, points to the limits of responsibilisation as an effective long-term strategy. Indeed, on-going struggles across London to save social infrastructure demonstrate growing tensions and widening divisions between the top-down requirements of those who govern – to make significant savings in discretionary budgets and to mediate decline through a turn to 'community' – and the fears and desires of the governed – who refuse to participate in the slow decline of their services and are now pushing for more democratic and autonomous alternatives. Far from engaging with these fears and desires, however, councils have all too often dismissed residents as at best unrealistic, and at worst irresponsibly 'doing the work of the Tories', by aiming their ire at local Labour councils.

Development vehicles and the struggle against speculative urban entrepreneurialism

Whilst urban entrepreneurialism is by no means new to local government in England, there are a set of novel features which distinguish the current phase of 'austerian entrepreneurialism' from previous phases associated with the emergence of the 'New Right', competitive-funding, and then 'New Labour'. These features include: the dramatic reduction of central government resources (revenue and capital) granted to councils; the decoupling of local government financing from local need; and the primacy of local revenue generation. These conditions of existence mean that increasingly boroughs in London are seeking to fund services, and so secure legitimacy, by facilitating and actively engaging in speculative property development and land value capture urbanism. As an officer for London Councils remarked:

> We have moved from a situation of resource equalisation and funding of need, where each authority had an assessment of need taking account of relative resources [and] what they can bring in from tax, to a system of 'incentivisation' ... This is rewarding councils for a very different purpose, building houses and delivering economic growth. (London Councils Finance Officer)

In a context where 'cities can no longer rely on economic growth in the nation as a source of finance' (Leitner, 1990: 154), the realisation of locally derived revenue is no longer simply one part of the overall funding mix. Rather, it is becoming *the* primary source of income. In other words, economic development has ceased to be an important supplementary function to the delivery of services and is in fact fast becoming the principle means through which services are to be resourced:

> With government grants soon to be a fond memory, councils will depend on growth in council tax and now also business rates for their future financial stability. Without growth in homes and jobs, council services like social care, libraries and street cleaning face inevitable decline. Growth is the only option for a council ... determined to control its own destiny. (Former Leader of Haringey Council, Claire Kober)

In the midst of an intensifying fiscal crisis, Kober here reflects fundamental tensions in London concerning what and who the city is for. With available land in high demand, such tensions play out on the contested terrain of market, and social logics as high exchange-value land uses, for luxury residential and office towers, dominate at the expense of more diverse land uses, including for genuinely affordable housing, light industry and social infrastructure (Edwards, 2016; Ferm and Jones, 2017; Penny, 2020). Given shifts in national planning policy, which mandate the prioritisation of economic viability over broader public priorities (Raco and Moreira de Souza, 2018), London's boroughs are limited in the extent to which they can effectively intervene in these tensions in favour of lower- and middle-income Londoners, although many fail to make the most of the discretionary powers they do have. Moreover, with the loss of centrally provided grants, the financial incentives for councils have been aligned closely with the global accumulation strategies of monopolistic property developers, financial investors and a transnational plutocratic elite (Glucksberg, 2016). Councils have a financial interest in taking an even more permissive orientation towards high-value real-estate speculation and in prompting new rounds of 'accumulation by dispossession' in the hope of capturing a portion of soaring land values.

In this context, 'the idea that city 'success' can be measured in terms of equal access to essential resources has withered as a guiding ideal within political life' (Atkinson et al., 2017: 186). Instead, a sink-or-swim form of what Barnekov et al. (1989: 11) termed privatism – 'a strategy of urban regeneration … [that] ties the fortunes of cities to the vitality of their private sectors and concentrates community attention and resources on economic development and private investment' – has been embraced. Recognising the tendency for this model of growth to push lower-income residents and small businesses out of the borough, one Haringey Cabinet Member referred to it as 'Faustian-esque growth'. When asked how the council could prevent the displacement of those on lower-incomes, he responded by saying that this is the 'million-dollar question to which we do not really have an answer'.

To ensure their financial capacity and legitimacy, London Councils are also looking increasingly to models of 'public entrepreneurialism'. Notwithstanding its commercial and entrepreneurial past, the current configuration of austerity localism is encouraging a step-change in local government thinking about such practices; they are no longer seen as something that councils *can* do, but as something that councils *must* do:

> Entrepreneurialism is a different mind-set. It is not always the mentality people come into public services with. But we need to get them thinking that it is not just a distraction from their day job, now it is their day job, and if they want a job in the future we need their ideas and creativity, to come up with ways to go out and make money. (Islington Cabinet Member)

One way in which councillors and officers in London are seeking to generate long-term returns is by adopting a more commercial and speculative approach to council land and property assets, including council housing and industrial estates. Encouraged by the

2011 Localism Act, which empowered councils to act commercially and generate profit in areas beyond their core service competencies, the number of council vehicles set up to speculatively develop land assets has risen sharply (Beswick and Penny, 2018).

Arguably the most well-known of these was the ill-fated Haringey Development Vehicle (HDV), a 50/50 joint venture between the Labour-led London borough of Haringey and the Australian real-estate giant Lendlease (whose prominent role in the social cleansing of the Elephant and Castle area of Southwark is well documented (Lees, 2014), which would have privatised and redeveloped an estimated £2bn worth of public land. Fearing that existing council housing, schools, libraries and affordable commercial space were set to be replaced by luxury housing, along with some so-called 'affordable' housing, chain stores, and increased land values and rents, a counter-public emerged to scrutinise and challenge the development vehicles business plan. While national media stories of the HDV at the time largely focused on the involvement of the left-wing campaign group Momentum, framing the struggle as a local condensation of a broader fight for the future of the Labour Party, on the ground the resistance was formed of a broad and diverse coalition of residents, tenants and back-bench councillors with varied political affiliations and uneven experiences of activism. Far from all being concerned about the fate of the Labour Party, they were animated by a desire for democratic control over the remaking of urban space and for guaranteeing their continued right to live, work and play in their borough. Senior councillors and officers responsible for the HDV, however, elided these concerns and accused campaigners of factionalism and of irresponsibly ignoring the realities of austerity and the housing crisis.

The HDV was scrapped in 2018 after local elections in which key Labour councillors either resigned or were deselected. However, the underlying forces and tensions animating the HDV and its discontents remain. Indeed, the new Labour-led council in Haringey, dubbed the first Corbyn-council following its realignment after the 2018 local elections, is now itself embroiled in a struggle with market traders and activists over the future of the Wards Corner Latin American Market near Seven Sisters. Elsewhere in London, Labour-led Lambeth, Southwark and Newham councils have also been fighting *against* resident-led campaigns to stop redevelopment vehicles and projects that threaten to gentrify, or socially cleanse, council housing and affordable commercial space. Whilst the details of these struggles differ, they share the same underlying animus: on the one side, governing councillors insist on the need to build new housing and 'regenerate' commercial space to generate income, whilst accusing campaigners of ignoring austerity and accepting decline; on the other, campaigners refuse to consent to proposals that benefit the local state, developers, and investors at the expense of London's diverse working class, calling instead for their right to decide on the pace and quality of change.

Conclusion

This chapter has explored how actually existing austerity urbanism in London is being rolled out, and has drawn attention to tensions between those who seek to 'responsibly' govern and build consensus for fiscal retrenchment locally and those who 'dissensually' refuse to be governed in such a way, who refuse to participate in the spoiling of social infrastructure or the social cleansing of their neighbourhoods.

Instead of resisting their role in the imposition of austerity, local state councillors and officers in London have sought to 'competently' and 'compassionately' manage the slow structural violence of budget cuts by responsibilising residents and speculatively redeveloping urban space. As noted, local state actors are not the chief architects of austerity; they did not choose to transform a financial crisis of capitalism into a fiscal crisis of the state. Yet they do choose to manage the local consequences of that decision. Without gainsaying the difficult position councillors and officers find themselves in, for all of the talk of tough decisions and unprecedented times the managerial response to austerity urbanism has not entailed a rupture in local governance common sense. Rather, the strategic response to massive grant reductions in London represents a deepening of already existing trends. For most of those working in councils, embracing residualisation, responsibilisation and financialisation meant taking a much smaller and well-known step than organising opposition or imagining alternatives to austerity and neoliberal urban growth agendas. Moreover, in seeking consent for and participation in their plans, and by dismissing their discontents, too many councillors are obscuring the violence they are trying to smoothly administer.

In contrast, the emergence of a growing number of local campaigns against austerity and neoliberal urbanisation throws into sharp relief 'the tensions between a 'smooth' framing of consensus-based participation, and a context of urban crisis which … makes processes of governing, and failures to empower citizens or deliver equitable development, increasingly visible' (Watkins, 2017: 2140). A key component of contemporary anti-austerity urban social movements in London is a growing radicalism driven in part by a perceived lack of leadership and solidarity shown by local councils. The activism that responds to immediate ideological and material attacks on hard won social infrastructure refuses to look away as councils seek to manage the contradictions of a situation that, while not of their making, is not beyond their wit or ability to contest. In refusing to consent to new rounds of urban responsibilisation, entrepreneurialism and financialisation, urban social movements in London are decried as petulant and divisive, yet they are revealing the deep divisions present in council proposals to cut social infrastructure and forcibly redevelop people's homes and communities.

An important current in London's emergent urban social movements is that they are pushing beyond calls for a simple end of austerity and a return to the pre-crisis compromise. They are articulating anti-austerity with a bottom-up critique of the local state, especially in its paternalistic 'compassionate competent' mode, and a deeper desire to democratise local authorities. They are, in other words, refusing their position in the local state's governing hierarchy in which they are relegated to cooperative participants in, or supposed beneficiaries of, plans designed by others.

Note

1 Research was conducted in Camden, Greenwich, Islington, Lambeth, Lewisham, Southwark, Westminster, Barnet, Newham and Haringey.

References

Anstice, I. (2015). You don't have to close public libraries to kill the principle upon which they were built. *LSE British Politics and Policy Blog*, 22

December 2015. https://blogs.lse.ac.uk/politicsandpolicy/public-libraries-in-an-age-of-austerity/ (accessed 14 October 2021).

Atkinson, R., Parker, S., and Burrows, R. (2017). Elite formation, power and space in contemporary London. *Theory, Culture and Society*, 34(5–6), 179–200.

Barnekov, K., Boyle, R., and Rich, D. (1989). *Privatism and Urban Policy in Britain and the United States*. Oxford: Oxford University Press.

BBC (2016). Libraries lose a quarter of staff as hundreds close. BBC, 29 March 2016.

Beswick, J., and Penny, J. (2018). Demolishing the present to sell off the future? The emergence of 'Financialized Municipal Entrepreneurialism' in London. *International Journal of Urban and Regional Research*, 42(4), 612–32.

Cockburn, C. (1977). *The Local State: Management of Cities and People*. London: Pluto Press.

Davies, J., Bua, A., Cortina-Oriol, M., and Thompson, E. (2020). Why is austerity governable? A Gramscian urban regime analysis of Leicester, UK. *Journal of Urban Affairs*, 42(1), 56–74.

Edwards, M. (2016). The housing crisis and London. *City*, 20(2), 222–37.

Ferm, J., and Jones, E. (2017). Beyond the post-industrial city: valuing and planning for industry in London. *Urban Studies*, 54(14), 3380–98.

Flood, A. (2019). Britain has closed almost 800 libraries since 2010, figures show. *Guardian*, 6 December 2019.

Forkert, K. (2016). Austere creativity and volunteer-run public services: the case of Lewisham's libraries, *New Formations*, 87, 11–28.

Fuller, C., and West, K. (2017). The possibilities and limits of political contestation in times of 'urban austerity', *Urban Studies*, 54(9), 2087–106.

Glucksberg, L. (2016). A view from the top: unpacking capital flows and foreign investment in prime London, *City* 20(2), 238–55.

Gyford, J. (1985). *The Politics of Local Socialism*. London: George Allen and Unwin.

Knight, T. (2012). We need a coalition of resistance against local council cuts, *Guardian* (30 December 2012).

Kober, C. (2017). Article from Council Leader Cllr Claire Kober on the Haringey Development Vehicle, www.haringey.gov.uk/news/article-council-leader-cllr-claire-kober-haringey-development-vehicle (accessed 8 October 2021).

Lees, L. (2014). The urban injustices of New Labour's 'new urban renewal': the case of the Aylesbury Estate in London. *Antipode*, 46(4), 921–47.

Leitner, H. (1990). Cities in pursuit of economic growth: the local state as entrepreneur. *Political Geography Quarterly*, 9(2), 146–70.

Newman, J. (2007). Re-mapping the public, *Cultural Studies*, 21(6), 887–909.

Newman, J. (2013). Performing new worlds? Policy, politics and creative labour in hard times, *Policy and Politics*, 41(4), 515–32.

Newman, I. (2014). *Reclaiming Local Democracy*. Bristol: Policy Press.

Peck, J. (2017). Transatlantic city, part 1: conjunctural urbanism, *Urban Studies*, 54(1), 4–30.

Penny, J. (2020). 'Defend the ten': everyday dissensus against the slow spoiling of Lambeth's libraries, *Environment and Planning D: Society and Space*, 38(5), 923–40.

PwC (2013). Redefining local government, www.pwc.co.uk/industries/government-public-sector/insights/redefining-local-government.html (accessed July 2021).

Raco, M., and Moreira de Souza, T. (2018). Urban development, small business communities, and the entrepreneurialisation of English local government. *Town Planning Review*, 89(2), 145–65.

Rancière, J. (2006). *Hatred of Democracy* (London: Verso).

Ross, K. (2002). *May '68 and its Afterlives* (Chicago: University of Chicago Press).

Robinson, K., and Sheldon, R. (2019). Witnessing loss in the everyday: community buildings in austerity Britain. *The Sociological Review*, 67(1), 111–25.

Watkins, H. (2017). Beyond sweat equity: community organising beyond the Third Way. Introduction: governmentality and crisis in the 21st century city. *Urban Studies*, 54(9), 2139–54.

4

'They don't know how angry I am': the slow violence of austerity Britain

Anthony Ellis

Tommy's story

The first time Tommy[1] used violence against his father he was 15 years old. On that day Tommy, dressed in his school uniform, found himself pinned against the kitchen wall, his father's forearm pressed across his neck. Not an entirely unusual situation for Tommy, whose father's occasional, and sometimes inexplicable, violence and cruelty had been recurring features of family life throughout his childhood and early youth. As his dad shouted and issued his oft-made threats, Tommy launched his clenched fist into his father's face. Unaccustomed to retaliation, reeling from the impact of knuckles against the soft flesh of his cheek, his father let go and stepped back, stultified by his son's sudden brazen resistance. Tommy, emboldened and sensing weakness for the first time in a man who had seemed impenetrable, advanced towards him: 'Let's have it then you cunt' he shouted, fists clenched, chest puffed out, years of repressed shame now manifesting in a sudden surge of rage. But his father did not 'have it' with Tommy that day. Instead, he did something he had never done in front of his son: he backed down.

In the wake of this event, Tommy increasingly ceased to resemble the boy who had existed for so many years in the shadow of his father's occasional violence. The boy who would sometimes lose continence when his father went to the cupboard to retrieve his belt – the belt used throughout Tommy and his brother's childhood to discipline them – began to change. Outside the front door of their family home the foundations of communal life were changing also. Several years earlier, the mining town, with vociferous political representation, that Tommy's family called home, had been turned into a 'war zone' when police officers from across the country had swept in to root out Margaret Thatcher's 'enemies within'. Daily life in this community had begun to change since the National Union of Miners were defeated in the lengthy and bitter industrial dispute that unfolded during the mid-1980s. Long-term employment at the nearby colliery was no longer a certainty; deep divisions had emerged within the community amongst striking and non-striking families; and the geographical region more broadly was at the beginning of a prolonged period of economic decline as its major industries began to close and government expenditure was reduced.

Many years later, on a warm August evening in 2018, just several months before the Chancellor Philip Hammond would declare the end of austerity in a budget speech, I met with Tommy after he agreed to assist me with my research. We met in the place where he had grown up and still resides. The area's ongoing economic stagnation since many of its mines and steel works closed, and now during the contemporary era of austerity, was made starkly clear in the local council's strategic needs assessment. This indicated that already above average levels of deprivation locally had increased since budget cuts were enacted. The area's persistent economic issues are visibly evident in the numerous unoccupied retail units that dominate its beleaguered and sparsely populated high street. On that balmy August evening, the bare glass frontages of numerous abandoned retail and business units merely reflected the images of the groups of men who walked past; criss-crossing between the run-down pubs that represent one of the area's few remaining viable industries. I met Tommy in one of them: The Bear,[2] a busy, bustling hive of activity and noise behind the muscular frame of two large shaven-headed doormen. In here, cheap beers are drunk, stories are shared, cocaine snorted and distributed, stolen goods sold, and violent reputations occasionally flexed and forged. I found Tommy standing near a large table, dressed in an expensive Hugo Boss shirt, surrounded by an entourage of football hooligans, drug dealers, and Far Right sympathisers. Amid the noise Tommy shouted in my ear, animated by the cocktail of alcohol and cocaine that flowed through his veins:

> The other lads here see me as good old Tommy, a good lad to be around you know? A good lad to back you up in a scrap. They don't

know about the shit I went through as a kid, they don't know how
angry I am ... Ten lads could come in here now and have a go at us
lot and I'll have it with them, I ain't bothered about anyone

An obsessive preoccupation with violence and how to respond
appropriately to perceived bullying and sleights from others has
defined much of Tommy's adult life:

> I have to have it with people that take the piss, I just can't leave it,
> know what I mean? Like when I was a kid the local bully kicked my
> football onto the roof of these garages and fucking laughed at me
> cos I couldn't get it back. I saw him years later and fronted him and
> he's like 'Alright Tommy, leave it pal, we were just kids back then'
> and I'm like 'I don't give a fuck, fuck you, think you can take the
> piss? You're fucking having it.'

Tommy readily acknowledges the lasting effects of his father's violence
during his formative years:

> You grow up with a dad like we had it's going to mess with you isn't
> it? I mean it messed with my brother's head ... he got hold of this
> shooter.[3] ... it's horrible like, but he used it on a kid he'd had an
> argument with.

Tommy emerged from his violent father's shadow determined to
not let anyone take advantage of him; determined to unleash the
humiliation that burned inside him upon those that, as he puts it,
'take the piss'; determined to be 'somebody'. For Tommy, and other
men that reside in some of contemporary Britain's most disadvantaged
areas, crime is now a viable career path, and violence a potentially
significant personal resource. Carrying weapons, hitting first and
hitting hard, become rational pragmatic strategies for physical and
psychological survival, and a means by which a select few can earn
a living in twenty-first-century Britain. The threat and possibility
of violence is often real in these places – an inescapable fact of life
for some groups of both younger and older men, which will eventually
find them no matter how hard they may try to evade it. The prospect
of violence is an accepted part of life for Tommy and the men he
associates with. For many of them, violence has been a persistent
threat at home, in school, on the streets, and something that they
believe has to be faced stoically. A fact reinforced several weeks
prior to that August evening when only metres from where I met

with Tommy, the younger brother of one of the men present with him had been attacked with a sharp object and had to be taken to hospital for surgery.

A detailed examination of the inter-relationship between the various reasons behind such violence lies beyond the scope of this chapter. Rather, in line with the overall aims of this collection, this chapter will consider those who are largely experiencing the recent recorded rise in forms of serious violence. Beginning with Tommy's story and the place where he was born and raised is important, because this story begins to illuminate the reasons for, as well as the socio-historical backdrop to, male violence in contemporary Britain. The reasons are varied, often 'deeply intertwined and tend to reinforce one another' (Currie, 2016: 46), and it is their complex interaction that generates the conditions conducive to more frequent interpersonal violence. Many of the men I have encountered during the course of researching violent crime tell very similar stories to Tommy: they talk about violent domineering father figures, getting into trouble at school, getting into fights with other young men, the buzz of using violence and of having a reputation for using it, and the ignominy of being the victim of violence. While violence has been a fairly persistent presence in their lives, some believe that violence locally and nationally is getting worse. They speak of the increased necessity to defend yourself and those you care about. They speak of a growing minority of disillusioned and dangerous young men desperate for reputation and distinction; young men who are unrestrained, out for themselves, and who feel it is acceptable to carry and use weapons. Some men I have interviewed over the years have spoken at times, albeit vaguely, about notions of 'fighting fair', of informal 'rules' that were often mutually recognised and respected during a fight between men, and of a shared morality around who is 'fair game' for violence and who is not. These various forms of restraint, they argue, seem to be lost on a number of increasingly desperate and volatile men popping up throughout the social networks in which they are embedded. While their belief in this shift from a romanticised past to a dystopian present should be interpreted with some caution, it is arguably grounded, to some extent, in what appears to be a genuine change in recent years towards an escalating pattern of serious violence, which tends to involve largely groups of younger men from deprived neighbourhoods as both offenders and victims.

This chapter seeks to briefly contextualise such lived experiences within the entrenched, structural inequalities that exist in post-recession austerity Britain. Whilst Penny's contribution (chapter 3) outlines a violence that is almost imperceptible, yet devastating and far-reaching in its consequences, what is considered in this chapter is spectacular, instantaneous violence inflicted by human bodies upon other bodies. The chapter seeks to draw connections between violence committed by bodies and the kind of structurally embedded violence discussed in chapter 3 that is obscure, 'slow', and that unfolds gradually over long periods of time (Nixon, 2011). This slow violence, I suggest here, is the harm that results from economic restructuring and the political decisions that accompany it, which is, as Rob Nixon (2011) suggests, 'exponential', as it is capable of escalating subsequent violence that occurs between human bodies.

Violence and inequality in austerity Britain

To consider contemporary changes in the prevalence of serious violence in Britain is important for several reasons. Recorded murder rates have actually been declining over a roughly 12-year period prior to a recent spike. That period of decline in murder rates, which began in the early noughties, was preceded by gradual recorded increases throughout the politically and economically tumultuous period of the 1970s to 1990s (Office for National Statistics, 2019). Following this period of decline in the early twenty-first century, national measures of murder and incidents of serious violence involving sharp implements have begun to increase and have done so consecutively since 2015 (Office for National Statistics, 2019). In the year ending March 2018, 285 people were killed by use of a knife or sharp instrument, the highest number ever recorded in a year since 1946, while the latest figures indicate that between March 2018 and 2019 the police recorded an 8 per cent increase in offences involving a knife or sharp instrument (Office for National Statistics, 2019). The chair of the all-party parliamentary group on knife crime, Sarah Jones MP, recently described the worsening rate of knife attacks in Britain as an 'epidemic'.

However, as has been alluded to briefly already, this is not an 'epidemic' to which the British population as a whole is equally exposed; the risks of being violently victimised contemporarily are closely related to various forms of spatial and structural inequality. Based on data collected between 2017 and 2018 for the Home Office's Homicide Index, the rate at which men are currently being killed by violent behaviour is around double that for women (Office for National Statistics, 2019). This overall pattern of lethal violence changes, though, when we focus exclusively upon the domestic context, where women are much more likely to be harmed or killed by a current or former partner. Currently in the UK, around two women a week are murdered by a man with whom they are, or were previously, engaged in a relationship, and in the latest measurement period, 49 more women were murdered than in the previous year (Office for National Statistics, 2019). The pattern of these recent increases becomes more pronounced when age is included. Young people aged 16–24 experienced the largest volume of increases from March 2017 to March 2018, closely followed by those aged 25–34 (Office for National Statistics, 2019). In London, where considerable media attention has been directed since the rises were first recorded, young people aged 11–20 and identified as Black or Black British, comprised more than two thirds of murder victims during the period 2008–2018 (Irwin-Rogers et al., 2020). A recent analysis of admissions to a trauma centre in the same city found that deprivation increased the risks of being wounded from violence involving a bladed weapon (Vulliamy et al., 2018). When we examine the characteristics of the perpetrators of recent lethal violence, a similar demographic pattern in terms of age and gender emerges, with more than half of all those convicted of homicide during this latest measurement period being male and aged between 16 and 34 (Office for National Statistics, 2019).

In spite of these more recent increases, and the media frenzy that has surrounded them, the UK fortunately has lower, and generally more stable, rates of serious violent crime when compared internationally with many other countries (Currie, 2016; United Nations Office for Drugs and Crime, 2019). It has been argued by some scholars, such as Steven Pinker (2011) for example, that many societies across the world, but predominantly Western affluent states, have experienced considerable declines in violent behaviour amongst their populations over long periods of time. Contrary to considerable popular opinion and the frequent sensationalist media coverage of violent crimes,

Pinker states that we are living in the most peaceful period of human history and that we are becoming kinder and more empathetic. Historian Richard Bessel (2015) is slightly more circumspect, however, suggesting that the use of a term as inclusive as 'we' when referring to humanity's proclivity for violence is potentially problematic given the uneven distribution of violence within countries and across the world.

Indeed, many occupants of Western liberal democracies, in the comfort of relative affluence, consumerism, and security, may now only ever encounter real physical violence on their TV screens. It is slightly more difficult, for example, to include occupants of rural Kenya, where the effects of climate change are being more keenly felt and are disrupting traditional pastoralist livelihoods amongst indigenous tribes, sparking off violent conflicts over cattle and dwindling sources of water (Parenti, 2011). Young men in some Central American states, who are today being murdered at rates similar, or in excess of, some historians' estimations of rates of death by violence in Medieval Europe (United Nations Office for Drugs and Crime, 2019; Spierenburg, 2008), will likely find the kindness and gentility to which Pinker refers more difficult to come by. Even in twenty-first-century Britain, in spite of its wealth, prosperity, and comparatively low national rates of interpersonal violence, there are communities – like Tommy's – where young people and adults are at considerably greater risk of being assaulted or murdered than the population at large (Dorling, 2004).

While Pinker has helpfully drawn our attention towards evidence for an important set of trends in the prevalence of violence across time, the conclusions he reaches appear rather too hastily and enthusiastically drawn. The kind of circumspection displayed by the likes of Bessel is much needed in today's context of growing economic polarisation between social groups, political change, economic turbulence, and environmental degradation that are related to contemporary patterns of violence. However, it would seem that evidence of comparatively low rates of interpersonal violence in countries like the UK are being used to reinforce ideological support for minimally regulated capitalism and neoliberal regimes of government. This economic and political system is often lauded as the best of all possible alternatives for its supposed ability to maximise individual 'freedoms' and generate superior economic growth that benefits everyone, while fostering greater empathy, tolerance, and reduced hostilities amongst citizens.

These claims must also be considered, though, in light of the fact that such regimes have, since the 2008 financial crisis, overseen a continued growth in economic inequality, which began in the 1970s (Dorling, 2015). The business and investment activities of some of those whose wealth has grown during this period have serious consequences for the geography and social life of cities and communities (Burrows et al., 2017), especially as local authorities experience increasing pressures to align with such agendas at the expense of ensuring full provision of services that are accessible to all (see chapter 3 in this volume). In response to the recent economic crisis, the British government initially rushed to aid faltering financial markets; following this up with a prolonged period of fiscal discipline, which has resulted in severe cuts to local authority budgets and associated services upon which largely low-income and vulnerable groups rely (Cooper and Whyte, 2017). Socially and economically marginalised young people, the group that has experienced much of this recent rise in violence, have been adversely affected by reforms to education and youth services under this policy programme (Irwin-Rogers et al., 2020). This recent period of history, rather than experiencing a diminution of tensions, has actually experienced an increasing climate of hostility and anger centred, in particular, around issues of identity and nationhood. Nationalist Far Right formal and street-based movements have received increased support across Europe, to which many who are socially marginalised and feel aggrieved and ignored have gravitated (Winlow et al., 2017). Evans and Giroux (2015) were surely correct when they insisted that a sole reliance upon crude, and likely inaccurate, per capita human death rates from violence globally to present a case for optimism and human progress is not only naïve, but obscures our collective perception of violence contemporarily.

In a country that is experiencing comparatively low rates of serious interpersonal violence between its citizens, despite the recent recorded increases, around 120,000 premature deaths, described as 'economic murder', have been attributed to austerity cuts to health and social services (Matthews-King, 2017). Addressing the timing of, and the reasons behind, this recent increase in mortality rates in Britain, one of the largest documented since records began, Dorling (2017:

48) has suggested that it is the slow violence of 'cuts, austerity and not all being in it together that matter most'. Following a visit to the UK, the UN Rapporteur, Professor Philip Alston, also denounced this recent programme of welfare reforms and cuts given its impact upon the most vulnerable in British society (Office of the High Commissioner for Human Rights, 2018).

Pinker's appeal to historic reductions in levels of interpersonal violence, while likely to have taken place in some geographical regions, does not provide a sufficient account of the complexity of violence in its various guises today, nor how violence correlates in complex ways with structural inequalities and disadvantages. As a result, violence presents inconsistently across nations and within urban spaces. While members of some social groups today are experiencing escalating risks to their physical safety, others are experiencing unprecedented levels of protection and insulation from 'real' violence. The slow violence of austerity in Britain has been unequal in its effects: proving to be literally deadly for some, yet barely registering on the lives of others. Britain's comparatively low rates of interpersonal violence, and claims of historic declines in human brutality, do not negate the necessity for a careful analysis of recent and concerning trends in the country's interpersonal violence rates, which possess a particular geographic and demographic character.

Research on violence does provide quite compelling evidence of a potentially contingent relationship between economic conditions, particularly wealth and income inequalities, and serious violence at both national and global levels (Currie, 2016; United Nations Office for Drugs and Crime, 2019; Wilkinson and Pickett, 2012). The evidence is pretty clear in this respect: the more unequal a society is in terms of how income and resources are distributed amongst the populace, the more violent it is likely to be. Even in economically developed countries, if the benefits of economic growth and prosperity are not distributed more equally amongst the population at large, violence rates are likely to be higher (United Nations Office for Drugs and Crime, 2019). Disparities in income and wealth correlate with the risks of encountering violence and it is poorer groups within the population that are more likely to be caught up in violent crime and who are more likely to die or be seriously harmed by it (Dorling, 2004).

The tendency within much media and political discourse is to divorce serious violence and those involved in it from this social and economic context. The most recent proposed solutions put forward by the current Prime Minister of Britain, Boris Johnson, are reflective of this way of understanding and responding to increasing rates of violent behaviour, with additional funding pledged to help successfully prosecute, imprison for longer, and in larger numbers, those committing violent crimes. It is, in effect, then, pathological individuals and other such individualising tropes that come to define the issue and its causes. Preferred and popular solutions to violence are those which punish, contain and 'correct' individuals, rather than addressing and 'correcting' systemic disadvantage and inequality. In making this point I am not asserting that individual-experiential factors are irrelevant in understanding the causative basis of violent behaviour or the increases recently recorded in the UK, and I have provided more focused analysis of such issues elsewhere (see Ellis, 2016). But these individual issues are linked to, and must be contextualised against, broader structures, or those circumstances and social conditions that lie beyond the immediate control of individuals who become involved in violence. Rather than reflecting solely the actions of a minority of individuals, and in an attempt to redirect society's compulsion to completely individualise the problem of serious violence, Dorling (2004: 190–1) argues persuasively that: 'For murder rates to rise in particular places, and for a particular group of people living there, life in general has to be made more difficult to live, people have to be made to feel more worthless.' Dorling was referring to increases in the murder rate in Britain experienced during the turbulent period of the late 1970s to 1990s, but his analysis is relevant for understanding increasing rates of violent crime today. Just as decades of intensifying economic inequality and policy choices that were detrimental to some of the poorest in society were relevant for understanding increased outbursts of violence in the final decades of the twentieth century, the more recent impact of the recession and the consequences of austerity cuts are important features of the current socio-economic landscape in which these current rises must be situated.

As sociologist Larry Ray has argued, the uneven distribution of interpersonal violence we witness today largely coincides 'with the spatial consequences of neoliberal restructuring' (2011: 82) in the late twentieth and early twenty-first centuries. For Ray, specific spaces characterised by multiple forms of deprivation often develop 'complex patterns of social relationships that persist over time, in which violence is more likely than elsewhere' (Ray, 2011: 82). Tommy, and men of similar socio-economic background, were raised in communities that gradually lost their politicised identities and stable labour markets after losing their long battle with the economic forces of neoliberal capitalism and its political allies. Many of these communities never fully recovered and, in the absence of political representation, continue to suffer in the current context of post-crash capitalism and enforced austerity, which has had a more adverse effect upon groups from deprived parts of Britain (Cooper and Whyte, 2017; Irwin-Rogers et al., 2020). Like many of the other men in his company that evening, whose fathers and grandfathers had once toiled in the area's mines and steelworks, Tommy's life course parallels this recent history of neoliberalism in Britain and the impact that its hegemonic ascent in the late twentieth century has had upon sections of the country's working-class communities and the generations born and raised there since. While the recent violence on the streets of Britain's towns and cities that has filled the pages of newspapers has often been individualised onto the shoulders of economically deprived young men, this has occurred against a background of slow violence and its pernicious effects (Nixon, 2011).

Conclusion: one for the road

It is easy for violence to become subsumed within debates that foreground individuals, while its relationship to structures of inequality remains in the background and largely unacknowledged. Indeed, contemporary Britain's wealth arguably makes this situation more likely, for who would feel the need to behave violently amidst such prosperity and opportunity? The social sciences have done much to dismantle such arguments and expose their simplification of a complex issue. They have also uncovered the socially corrosive effects of inequality and argued passionately for positive change. Sadly, however, inequality persists, with some indications that it is worsening and the world is now littered with examples that current trends may no longer be sustained without serious social breakdown. The anger that has erupted recently in the US, and the state's violent repression of it, following the killing of George Floyd by a police officer, being a recent case in point. The sense of urgency to address inequality is growing and the social sciences must now work collectively and creatively to try to ignite the political will necessary to seriously address it.

After several hours in the company of Tommy and his friends, we shake hands and I thank him for his time. Before I depart he invites me to do a 'line'[4] with him. I thank him for the offer, but decline politely. I exit The Bear and head out into the warmth of the summer night in search of a taxi. On the street outside, where several other pubs and fast food outlets are clustered, stand groups of what appear on first impression to be homeless men and women around benches in the middle of the street. As I search for a taxi I walk past the front doors of a nearby pub that possesses a similar reputation to that of The Bear. Gathered outside, amid numerous extinguished cigarette butts that litter the pavement, is a large contingent of men, smoking and shouting loudly at one another to be heard above the music that emanates from inside. I avert my gaze as I walk past, instinctively avoiding eye-contact and the potential confrontation such a gesture might ignite. I find a taxi located further up the street that is waiting for a fare and I get in. As the seatbelt clicks and the car begins to move forward, some relief comes over me and I exhale audibly. As the car heads further up the street, I glance briefly in the wing mirror at the groups of men congregated on the streets outside the various pubs. Feelings of guilt flicker within me for a moment as I head towards home and away from the fading reflection of those less fortunate than me. The guilt burns in my stomach for a moment as I know I can step out of and escape these more dangerous parts of Britain's towns and cities. There is little such reprieve for the likes of Tommy, his friends, and many generations of men that have been raised, and continue to live, in similar circumstances. I repress the guilt, as I have learned to do as a researcher of violence within deprived communities, pushing it temporarily beyond consciousness.

The next morning, I receive a text message from a friend of Tommy's who tells me that later in the evening Tommy narrowly avoided getting 'lifted'[5] after a confrontation on the street. When asked about it, Tommy claims to have little recollection on account of the amount of alcohol he had consumed and dismisses the encounter nonchalantly. Several weeks later, a friend of Tommy's, and of some of the other men present with him that August evening, had walked the same route that I had after visiting several pubs in the area. As he walked he encountered a group of young men and became embroiled in a confrontation. How it began is unclear, but violence ensued and Tommy's friend was knocked to the floor and beaten. He later died from his injuries.

Notes

1 'Tommy' is a pseudonym to protect the individual's identity.
2 Pseudonym.
3 Firearm.
4 Consume cocaine.
5 Arrested.

References

Bessel, R. (2015). *Violence: A Modern Obsession*. London: Simon and Schuster.

Burrows, R., Webber, R., and Atkinson, A. (2017). Welcome to 'Pikettyville'? Mapping London's alpha territories. *The Sociological Review*, 65(2), 184–201.

Cooper, V., and Whyte, D. (2017). Introduction: the violence of austerity. In V. Cooper and D. Whyte, eds, *The Violence of Austerity*. London: Pluto Press, 1–34.

Currie, E. (2016). *The Roots of Danger: Violent Crime in Global Perspective*. Oxford: Oxford University Press.

Dorling, D. (2004). Prime suspect: murder in Britain. In P. Hillyard, C. Pantazis, S. Tombs, and D. Gordon, eds, *Beyond Criminology: Taking Harm Seriously*. London: Pluto Press, 178–91.

Dorling, D. (2015). *Inequality and the 1%*. London: Verso.

Dorling, D. (2017). Austerity and mortality. In V. Cooper and D. Whyte, eds, *The Violence of Austerity*. London: Pluto Press, 44–50.

Ellis, A. (2016). *Men, Masculinities and Violence: An Ethnographic Study*. Abingdon: Routledge.

Evans, B., and Giroux, H. (2015). *Disposable Futures: The Seduction of Violence in the Age of Spectacle*. (Monroe: City Lights).

Irwin-Rogers, K., de-Lappe, J., and Phoenix, J. (2020). Antisocial shifts in social policy and serious youth violence: evidence from the cross-party Youth Violence Commission, *British Journal of Community Justice*, 16(2), 4–27.

Matthews-King, A. (2017). Landmark study links Tory austerity to 120,000 deaths. *Independent*. www.independent.co.uk/news/health/tory-austerity-deaths-study-report-people-die-social-care-government-policy-a8057306.html (accessed 28 October 2021).

Nixon, R. (2011). *Slow Violence and the Environmentalism of the Poor* (Cambridge, MA: Harvard University Press).

Office for National Statistics (2019). Homicide in England and Wales: year ending March 2018. www.ons.gov.uk/peoplepopulationandcommunity/crimeandjustice/articles/homicideinenglandandwales/yearendingmarch2018 (accessed 25 January 2020).

Office of the High Commissioner for Human Rights (2018). Statement on visit to the United Kingdom, by Professor Philip Alston, United Nations Special Rapporteur on extreme poverty and human rights. www.ohchr.org/en/NewsEvents/Pages/DisplayNews.aspx?NewsID=23881 (accessed 28 January 2020).

Parenti, C. (2011). *Tropic of Chaos: Climate Change and the New Geography of Violence* (New York: Nation).

Pinker, S. (2011). *The Better Angels of Our Nature: Why Violence has Declined* (London: Viking).

Ray, L. (2011). *Violence and Society* (London: Sage).

Spierenburg, P. (2008). *A History of Murder: Personal Violence in Europe from the Middle Ages to the Present* (Cambridge: Polity).

United Nations Office for Drugs and Crime (2019). Global Study on Homicide. www.unodc.org/documents/data-and-analysis/gsh/Booklet1.pdf (accessed 28 January, Vienna).

Vulliamy, P., Faulkner, M., Kirkwood, G., West, A., O'Neill, B., Griffiths, M., Moore, F., and Brohi, K. (2018). Temporal and geographic patterns of stab injuries in young people: a retrospective cohort study from a UK major trauma centre. *BMJ Open* 8(10), n.p.

Wilkinson, R., and Pickett, K. (2012). *The Spirit Level: Why Equality is Better for Everyone* (London: Penguin).

Winlow, S., Treadwell, J., and Hall, S. (2017). *The Rise of the Right: English Nationalism and the Transformation of Working Class Politics* (Bristol: Policy Press).

Part II

Situated inequalities

Editors' introduction: beyond the economic (complex inequalities)

To date, the debate on inequality has largely been driven and shaped by economic approaches, which have played a central role in drawing attention to enduring and intensifying global inequalities and concentrations of immense wealth. To pick out just two, Piketty's (2013) *Capital in the Twenty-first Century* has exposed how the cumulative effect of inherited wealth tends to outpace economic growth and therefore income which can be earned over a lifetime. This pattern creates a world in which already having money begets more money, rather than the meritocratic myths of effort, ideas, or innate talent. Milanović (2016) has also charted the unequal global distribution of economic gain, stagnation, and loss since the early 2000s, as well as the stratospheric growth in fortunes of the richest 1 per cent. In doing so, he mounts a convincing argument about the *economic* drivers behind the rise of political populism, nativism, xenophobia, and border crises. As both Piketty and Milanović show, wealth and income are vital aspects of inequalities, but the references to patrimonial capitalism and the unequal distribution of wealth and poverty globally in their accounts point toward additional sources. There is evidence, for example, that as much as 80 per cent of a person's income is determined simply by whether they were lucky enough to be born in a rich country, plus the income class of their parents, while the remaining 20 per cent or less is due to factors over which individuals have no control (e.g. gender, age, race, disability) and factors over which they do (e.g. effort or hard work)

(Milanović, 2011). Other 'durable inequalities' of gender, citizenship, dis/ability, and race therefore require us to look beyond differentials of wealth or income, for an expanded understanding of inequalities (Tilly, 1999; Treitler and Boatcă, 2016). Some of the most persistent patterns of inequality, after all, do not derive from economic factors, even if the sorting and stratifying of such differences are often *reproduced* as economic disparities.

Studies of inequality in the social sciences have tended to be organised around an enduring intellectual division of labour, which might be summarised as the 'redistribution or recognition dilemma' (Fraser, 1997). For Boatcă (2016: 6), this division has artificially separated our research. On the one hand, studies of wealth and income engage with structural disparities, but minimise processes of othering beyond class. While on the other, studies of gendering, racialisation and ethnicisation engage with the mutual constitution of social divisions but ignore 'the structural causes behind the unequal distribution of resources along gender, racial, ethnic and class lines' (Boatcă 2016: 6). In contrast, a 'situated intersectional approach' (Yuval-Davis, 2015: 9), aims to allow analyses of social inequality which are sensitive to specific geographies, scales and temporalities, 'forming the particular nuanced and contested meanings of particular social locations in particular historical moments, within particular social, economic and political contexts in which some social divisions have more saliency and effect'. Social divisions are not simply additive or cross-cutting, but are mutually constituted, while remaining irreducible to one another. Recognising this, we can mitigate a risk of both vernacularity in many studies of inequality or claims to universality, which assume, rather than explore, the different meanings of social divisions in different locations. Intersectional research on contemporary inequalities requires a sociological imagination which moves between macro-global structures, meso-social formations, and micro-social encounters, to engage both the particularity of situated inequalities *and* the systematic interrelated domains of governance, economy, different politics of belonging, intergenerational, familial and interpersonal networks (Yuval-Davis, 2015).

The chapters in this section focus on inequalities of recognition as expressed by space. No two ways of looking at the city are the same: whether you approach the city as a 'starchitect' and a blank canvas for urban 'improvement' (chapter 5); whether you find yourself dis-abled by non-inclusive designs of the city's paths, roads, and stairways; or whether you are a woman navigating everyday sexism in public spaces (chapter 6). Walking through the city, we shape and are shaped by the urban, whilst experiencing spaces from our own subject position. These alternative perspectives open up prospects for inequality, as decisions made with one set of priorities in mind (e.g. planners or architects) are likely to interconnect with, and have an impact on, those experiencing the city from different positions.

Chapters 7 and 8 build on the theme of situated inequalities by demonstrating how overarching stereotypes and reputations of some neighbourhoods and cities risk brushing over the inequalities that persist underneath. While elite spaces and tolerant cities may enjoy reputations of being comfortable, desirable spaces, the specificity and precision of a molecular perspective illustrates a more complicated reality on the ground. The representation of a place as 'elite' or 'welcoming', in other words, is rarely the full story.

References

Boatcă, M. (2016). *Global Inequalities Beyond Occidentalism*. Farnham: Ashgate.

Fraser, N. (1997). *Justice Interruptus*. New York: Routledge.

Milanović (2011). *The Haves and the Have Nots: A Brief and Idiosyncratic History of Global Inequality*. New York: Basic Books.

Milanović (2016). *Global Inequality: A New Approach for the Age of Globalisation*. Cambridge, MA: Harvard University Press.

Piketty, T. (2013). *Capital in the Twenty-first Century*. Cambridge, MA: Harvard University Press.

Tilly, C. (1999). *Durable Inequality*. Berkeley, CA: University of California Press.

Treitler, B., and Boatcă, M. (2016). Dynamics of inequalities in a global perspective: an introduction. *Current Sociology*, 64(2), 159–71.

Yuval-Davis (2015). Situated intersectionality and social inequality. *Raisons Politiques*, 58, 91–100.

5

Iconic architecture: seduction and subversion

Amparo Tarazona-Vento

Architectural icons are the new monuments of a globalising era. Sklair has defined them as buildings or spaces that are characterised by a 'unique combination of fame with symbolism and aesthetic quality' (Sklair, 2006: 25), and hold a special meaning 'for a culture and/or a time' (Sklair, 2017: 16). Architectural icons include corporate and commercial buildings, but they also include publicly funded buildings, since they are invariably included in urban regeneration projects that promote growth and competitiveness to address urban economic and social decline. As symbols of immense private and corporate wealth, sites of public commemoration for national and sub-national communities, and flash-points of protest, architectural icons mark an important entry point for the analysis of urban politics. The symbolic meaning attached to iconic architecture is actively created by different local and global actors who seek to consolidate these structures as stalwarts of growth and prosperity. On the other hand, iconic megaprojects are often also seen and contested as symbolic representations of the inequalities produced by neoliberalism. This chapter offers a broad-ranging analysis of the practices linked to the political mobilisation of the symbolism of iconic architecture and its resistance.

As a socially constructed cultural form, architecture has historically been seen to contribute to maintaining, legitimating, consolidating and stabilising a given social order (Glendinning, 2010; Jones, 2011). Contemporary architectural icons are linked to the promotion and legitimisation of capitalism. They can be seen as empirical manifestations of global capitalism – because of the often elitist, technocratic and authoritative decision making that underpins their execution, and the social and economic inequalities they produce (Swyngedouw, Moulaert and Rodriguez, 2002). More importantly, they also constitute the symbols that promote it by contributing to making economic imaginaries persuasive culturally (Jones, 2009; Spencer, 2016; Sklair, 2017). Thus, not only does iconic architecture contribute to strengthening citizens' identification with their imagined urban community, it also consolidates a 'global' identity linked to consumerism (Sklair, 2017).

For academics, iconic megaprojects, and in particular state-led iconic megaprojects, are a valuable entry point for the analysis of urban politics. They are the meeting point of global, national, regional, and local political and economic interests, that is, the transnational class, local hegemonies and 'national' political projects. Therefore, such megaprojects reflect the power struggles among different elite groups that want to influence and shape built environments for their own convenience (Hubbard 1996), but also the grassroots contentious politics that oppose such elitist approaches to the governance of cities. As the literature demonstrates, urban policies based on the use of iconic megaprojects often fail to redress the poor employment, social and fiscal situations of cities and, moreover, exacerbate situated inequalities of wealth and income, socio-spatial polarisation and exclusion processes (Swyngedouw, Moulaert and Rodriguez, 2002; Watt, 2013; Tarazona Vento, 2017). Iconic megaprojects can, therefore, also tell us a great deal about the increasingly contested and divided nature of cities as well as the inequalities that underpin its everyday life. In the language used by this volume's introduction, they are significant 'in-between points where "the other halves" meet'.

Architectural icons can be considered visualisations of global capitalism, and they can also contribute to making inequality visible. Private iconic megaprojects such as corporate skyscrapers can convey in people's minds the idea of inequality. After all, they are meant to be testament of the power of private corporations and symbols of capital accumulation. However, in the case of state-led iconic megaprojects that are part of regeneration projects, this connection is more difficult to make, not least because such megaprojects are allegedly built with the objective of reducing inequality by creating jobs and bringing in investment. Moreover, iconic megaprojects, by means of their iconicity, are highly effective at obscuring for the general public the inequalities that they both embody and produce.

This chapter will explore the specific mechanisms used to create and maintain such iconicity, which is used to seduce citizens and win public opinion over to elites' economic and political projects. I will also discuss the ways in which the meanings attached to iconic architecture can be subverted in order to make inequalities visible and, ultimately, contest the 'cultural-ideological mechanisms' related to such icons through which power is exercised (Sklair and Struna, 2013). The first section will focus on exploring how the visual characteristics of architecture – from the aesthetics of the actual structures to their visual representations and mechanisms – are used to influence the meaning attached to them. Recognising that architecture and urban design are also narrative practices, the second section will focus on the discursive practice involved in such meaning-making practices. Finally, the third section will focus on the mechanisms used to create and maintain architecture's iconicity, which are linked to social practice and the use of space.

Place-making is a contested process. The demands of 'marginalised' groups for the right to access urban space safely are a central aspect of struggles against situated inequality and exclusion. This chapter discusses how discourses of iconicity are produced by those in positions of power and how they can be subverted. In chapter 6, Rose further explores mechanisms that can be used to challenge the built environment's intended meaning. Both this chapter and chapter 6 engage with struggles over the representation, interpretation and use of urban space.

The visual: perception and imagination

The symbolic meaning conveyed by buildings and urban spaces depends, to a great extent, on their visual qualities, such as architectural style, materials used, and scale, and these in turn conditioned by powerful actors who commission architects to create a design. As Jones (2009) has argued, dominant political and economic conditions influence not only what is built, but also *how* it is built. While capitalist globalisation has not produced an architectural canon, commentators agree that contemporary iconic buildings share some stylistic characteristics (Jones, 2009; Sklair, 2017). According to Jones (2009: 253), intercity competition for recognisability has brought about the emergence of a '(relatively) coherent iconic style.' He argues that since the function of such iconic architecture is to market a place by re-imaging it and grabbing the attention of the public, the result is an aestheticised architecture in which the design emphasis lies on the visual effect of surfaces and facades (Jones, 2011). Certainly, contemporary global architects have increasingly focused their attention on the design of distinctive and unique shapes and the use of new and eye-catching materials in the facades. Very often, creating a building with a breath-taking sculptural form becomes more important than the perception of space typically prioritised by modernist architects. Iconic architecture often resorts to a strategy of admiration and impact or, in the words of Haddad and Rifkind (2014), the techniques of 'shock.' Thus, the attributes preferred are monumentality and grandeur, an emphasis on what Flyvbjerg (2014) has called the aesthetic sublime. Thereby, architecture has become a means to produce eye-catching images, symbols that can be reproduced in glossy architectural journals in order to advertise the architect, those who have commissioned the project, and the place where the work of architecture is located.

Although architecture has always produced both space and symbols in an intimately linked manner, in a globalising world the production of symbols has shifted from local to global images. The stretching of relationships of power associated with globalisation processes has implied that the meanings and symbols attached to power have acquired global dimensions as well. The audience to which the message is directed is wider than the local communities in the surrounding area, as it intends to reach a global audience through mass media circulation of images and tourism. Even when it is intended in some way to express a distinct local identity, iconic architecture has to be legible as a symbol for a global audience. The symbolism of iconic architecture is therefore both inward and outward oriented. 'Outward' to show to the world and attract tourism and investment; 'inward' as a mirror where citizens can see themselves reflected. This is often related to the creation or reinforcing of different kinds of collective identities (Jones, 2011; McNeill, 2009).

Consequently, while investors of capital are more profit oriented, the style of architecture that governments generally favour is that which they believe to best represent the national identity of their territory (Sklair and Sruna, 2013). According to Vale (1999), this promotion of a national identity is usually linked to three further objectives, namely: promoting an urban identity; promoting the personal identity of the architect and of the client who commissions the work (very often a political leader); and making claims of modernity with the purpose of promoting the mentioned identities internationally. The iconic architecture associated with urban regeneration megaprojects has generally intended to represent a vision for the future and therefore favours 'forward-looking' new aesthetics that break with the past and shock because of their novelty (Jones, 2011: 68). Since one of the key objectives of architectural icon design is to achieve media attention by creating an image that is striking and memorable, the worth of iconic buildings is measured in terms of their capacity to do so (Brott, 2017; Marques and McIntosh, 2018). In the same way that historical architectural styles were designed to be perceived and admired at walking speed, and modernist architecture from the distance or at automobile speed, today's iconic architecture is designed to be consumed as a photograph, disseminated through the media and social media.

Visual representation is a key element in the creation of iconicity from before the building has been completed, during the design and construction processes. In addition to the real architectural object being built, a virtual model is created. Computer-generated representations of the design assist architects in deciding which design will be able to generate more attractive images. They are also used to seduce clients and juries of architectural competitions, and finally for the promotion of the building through the careful selection of renderings of the buildings to be distributed to the media. The increased quality of renderings and virtual 3D modelling has made the real and the virtual indistinguishable from each other. Brott (2017: 29) goes so far as to argue that 'the building must look like a hologram rather than a real building in order to perform its role, and the digital renderings are far more significant to the project than the final building.' In any case, the relationship between object and representation is complex and both contribute to creating a new subjectivity, news ways of perceiving and feeling (Gage and Rancière, 2019).

The very act of producing a visual representation of a building – be it through photography or virtual reality – entails the decontextualisation of the architectural object, both physically and mentally by removing the meaning that comes from its context and its relationships with its geographical and cultural location (Marques and McIntosh, 2018). Notorious, for instance, are photographs of historic buildings such as the Taj Mahal that show what is cut out from promotional images – the contrast of the monument with its impoverished surroundings. Contemporary iconic buildings are invariably decontextualised and perceived as a series of bidimensional images. In this way, by removing them from their context – understood as the physical surroundings and socio-economic conditions in which they were created – we allow the architectural object to be perceived through an alternative set of relations.

As any form of visual representation, photography as well as virtual reality images, incorporates the perspective and the interpretation of the artist, it likewise incorporates the agenda of those commissioning the photograph or rendering (Marques and McIntosh, 2018). Perspectives that better represent the iconicity we are attributing to the building are carefully selected, and favoured views are chosen to become the image of the building (Sklair, 2017). In addition to the perspective and agenda of the creators and curators of architectural photographs and computer-generated renderings, the interpretation of the consumer of these images is incorporated into the process of attaching meanings to buildings and urban spaces. Thus, imagination plays an important role in the semiotic process of signification, representation and meaning making. Imagination is fed by different media such as film, art and literary texts. It is also a reflection of how individuals and communities perceive or wish to perceive themselves. As Çınar and Bender (2007) have argued, the collective imagination allows urban spaces and buildings to become the representation of the collectivity, whether or not individuals or specific groups of individuals are actually able to enjoy or experience them. Thus, public space can be described as democratic in the sense that individuals can imagine themselves being part of it, irrespective of whether they use it or not (Çınar and Bender, 2007). This argument resonates with Natalie Koch's (2018) concept of synecdoche – taking the part for the whole. In her book (2018) on the geopolitics of space in Asia, Koch argues that authoritarian regimes in Asia use the development of their new spectacular capital cities to craft a benevolent image of themselves. In the same way that capital cities are constructed to represent the whole nation, iconic megaprojects are seen to represent the whole city or the whole citizenship.

The same mechanisms used to make architecture *iconic* – such as contrast and decontextualisation – can be used to subvert its intended meaning, make inequality visible and provoke a reaction against it. Images can be used, modified and reinterpreted – through collage or juxtaposition – to try to change the symbolism of architecture. The use of photography as a form of activism has a long tradition (Bogre, 2011), and documenting social conflicts, problems and inequalities can have a huge impact on public opinion. In this sense, contextualising iconic architecture is used to create critical awareness. Iconic architecture is inseparable from, and needs to be understood in relationship with, what Koch (2018) calls the 'unspectacular others', which is not just the background for iconic architecture but also necessary for its production. In this way, images, for instance of the living conditions of migrant construction workers of iconic megaprojects in Dubai, or of Chinese construction workers building the 2008 Olympics, have been circulated alongside images of the spectacular buildings they produce (Molotch and Ponzini 2019). Decontextualisation through, for instance, collage and photomontage has also been an old favourite of artists. While contemporary architects and artists such as Matthias Jung and Fala Atelier make intensive use of architectural collages to change the perception of space, activists are starting to understand the possibilities that the use of digital photography and photomontages distributed via social media provide. Visual activism has even made it onto the curriculum of art colleges such as The Swansea College of Art, which offers a BA in 'Documentary Photography and Visual Activism'.

The narrative: discourses and interpretations

The visual characteristics of architecture are essential for our understanding of a building or space as iconic; the very definition of iconic architecture implies an aesthetic judgement. No less important is how both the architectural object and its visual representations are interpreted by the viewer. Interpretation depends on the imagination, which (as noted above) is fed by various media such as film and literary texts, and is mediated by discourse. In fact, architecture is a discursive practice which, through explanatory discourse and visual representation, reshapes the meaning we give to place (Tarazona-Vento, 2015). As Lawrence Vale (1999) has argued, the marketing and media campaigns used to control the interpretation of 'mediated monuments' cannot be separated from the actual monuments.

Competing narratives condition how we imagine and interpret the built environment. In the same way as people can have diverse and multiple identities – related to questions of class, gender, ethnicity, and so on – architecture and urban space allow for multiple super-imposed meanings to be attached to them (Çınar and Bender, 2007; Tarazona-Vento, 2015). They can be interpreted in divergent ways by different actors with different interests or visions. However, there are actors – for instance professional experts and economic and political elites, but also city marketers, international travel agencies and tour operators and hoteliers – who have more power than others to influence how we interpret place. Importantly, these actors also include professionals such as planners and architects. Starting from how the names of iconic buildings are used to evoke certain feelings and associations, the narratives of the built environment professionals provide clues for the interpretation of architecture. Think, for instance, of Santiago Calatrava's 'Turning Torso', with its poetic associations that present the building as a piece of art, or the 'Signature Towers' – previously known as 'Dancing Towers'– in Dubai, whose name alludes to their aspirations to become iconic. Architects and developers promote the buildings they produce as iconic (Sklair and Struna, 2013). They advertise themselves and their firms while at the same time trying to influence public perception of their architecture.

The high public profile of star architects, who have become celebrities, has put them in a privileged position to intervene in public discourse and social and political debate (McNeill, 2009; Jones, 2011). In fact, in a globalising world in which public image is a crucial asset, the balance of power between an elected politician and a star architect seems to be often somehow almost reversed. Thus, within the architectural world, it is assumed as a fact that it is star architects who choose their clients rather the other way around. This is considered to be evidence of the artistic independence of high-profile architects. As McNeill (2009) has argued, the myth of the architect as an individual 'creative genius' who is sole intellectual and artistic author of his or her office architectural production is one of the most pervasive ideas and is frequently repeated by popular and professional media, critics and architects alike. This is so in spite of the fact that this myth is difficult to maintain in a profession that tends to increasingly favour globalised practice. It is the assumption that architecture is an autonomous cultural practice with a high degree of independence from the socioeconomic and political conditions that give rise to it that serves to maintain existing power relations (Jones, 2011). By claiming autonomy from the interests of those who commission them to create a design, and by placing the focus on aesthetics and philosophical discourse, architects divert attention from socioeconomic relations of power, contributing in this way to reproducing them (Jones, 2009; Glendinning, 2010). The fact that they are able to claim that they are independent from power is what makes architects and architecture so useful to the powerful. In Jones' (2009: 2524) words, 'Field-specific architectural discourse serves to reinforce the "rules of the game"' (Jones, 2009: 2524). It also serves to obscure 'the "silent complicity" (Dovey, 1999) of many architects with regard to political and economic projects' (Jones, 2009: 2524).

City marketing campaigns are another source of narratives in relationship to iconic buildings. Although there are many ways of promoting places, such as advertising or bidding for and organising special events like the Olympics, the most widespread method – and one that is generally included in any other method – is the use of architecture and urban design, because some physical reality is needed in order to support the image of regeneration that is being marketed (Ward, 1998; Marques and McIntosh, 2018). Indeed, architecture constitutes a powerful device deployed to signify a city's economic regeneration and urban vitality (Crilley, 1993). The mechanism in play is the mobilisation of symbolic capital, defined by Pierre Bourdieu as 'the collection of luxury goods attesting the taste and distinction of the owner' (in Harvey 1990: 264). Iconic architecture is a source of symbolic capital, generated not only by mere aesthetics but also through the association with architects who have cultural credentials.

Since one of the main goals of these campaigns is to achieve economic regeneration by attracting investment and tourist expenditure, they tend to emphasise the positive, spectacular, aesthetic features of the architecture (Jessop, 1998; Sklair, 2017). Their other goal

– although it is not always spelt out – is to achieve public support for urban regeneration policies. They intend to achieve such support by diverting the local population's attention away from the issues of exclusion and inequality and focusing it on questions of image (Hubbard, 1996; Ghirardo, 1990; Ward, 1998). Iconic architecture is, therefore, often linked to a populist politics and discourse, appealing to feelings of local pride, identity and belonging, and presenting megaprojects as critical to economic growth (Tarazona-Vento, 2017).

Iconic megaprojects, however, have often provoked tensions and conflicts around questions of social justice and equitable development. While an attractive urban landscape can produce the effect of diverting attention from more essential issues, it may also evidence high levels of expenditure and lead citizens to question who actually benefits from these strategies. The successful mobilisation of the meanings and imaginaries embodied by iconic megaprojects, or the plausibility of the narratives linked to them, depends, as Jessop has argued (1998), on how well these narratives resonate with personal stories. In times of austerity, the contrast between expenditure in megaprojects and declining budgets for social protection make entrepreneurial narratives – which present iconic megaprojects as symbols of competitiveness, as helping to create jobs and success, and appealing to feelings of local pride, identity and belonging – become less plausible. Here, alternative narratives proposed by diverse groups of citizens, which challenge attempts at narrowly defining the city as a site of value extraction, can gain more traction, and iconic megaprojects can come to be seen more clearly as symbolic representations of significant social inequalities.

After the 2008 global economic downturn, narratives emphasising the downsides of iconic megaprojects, rather than their possible economic benefits, became more prevalent. For instance, more and more cities were seen to be voting against bidding for the Olympic Games – such as Oslo in 2014, Hamburg and Rome in 2016, Innsbruck in 2017 and Calgary in 2018 – alleging that the hefty costs cannot be justified by the expected economic benefits. Similarly, in 2016 Helsinki's councillors rejected plans to build a branch of the Guggenheim museum in the city, despite proponents of the project pointing at the benefits the museum could bring by replicating what in Bilbao was known as the 'Guggenheim effect' (Henley, 2016).

Creating and disseminating alternative narratives and new ways of thinking about social and political issues is a key element within urban social movements' long-established battery of strategies (Routledge, 2017), and indeed the case of the contestation of iconic architecture is not an exception. Although access to traditional media is often an obstacle for activists, communication strategies can take new and creative forms. In the city of Valencia in Spain, for instance, various opposition initiatives tried to provide an alternative narrative to the city's urban policy based on the use of megaprojects to that being proposed by city leaders. One of them, 'The Route of Wastefulness', which was a mix of 'citizen journalism' and alternative tourism, was run successfully between 2012 and 2015. It consisted of a series of coach trips around the city's ruinous megaprojects to show citizens the negative effects of an urban regeneration policy based on the use of iconic megaprojects and the hosting of international events such as the America's Cup sailing competition and Formula One racing. Groups of citizens affected by the policy – for instance, because they had been displaced – participated in the routes, explaining their story first-hand on site and raising public awareness of the hidden costs of iconic megaprojects.

The performative: lived experience and social practice

People's relationship to place – including architecture and urban space – is not only mediated by images and discourses; it is also constructed through social practice. How people experience space shapes the meaning they give to it. In fact, even spaces with terrible histories, for instance prisons, can change their meaning through a change of use. This is why architecture can also be considered a performative discipline, because its meaning is constructed through collective experience and the performance of daily life. Designers of iconic buildings, developers and their public and private clients are well aware of such quality of architecture and make extensive use of ceremonies when certain milestones during the development of the project are reached, such as the laying of the first stone, as a way of marking the iconicity of the project (Rego, Irigay and Chaves, 2017). Hence, not only the aesthetics of architecture, and the narratives that accompany them, define them as symbolic; iconic buildings and urban spaces are also the centre of symbolic rituals from their origin.

Once the architectural icon has been completed, its symbolism needs to be maintained if it is to endure. One way of ensuring that the iconicity of a building or public space is long-lasting is through spatial regulation (McDermott 2019). Who can use iconic buildings and spaces, and how they can use them, also becomes part of the construction of iconicity, not least because iconicity is defined in terms of fame and aesthetic judgement and this includes our sensorial experience of it. In order to control how place is experienced, urban space is commodified and complex inequality is hidden. Only those who conform with the market ethos – such as consumers, investors and tourists – are considered appropriate, with the homeless and disenfranchised not considered as belonging to iconic environments. In Tim Hall's words (1998: 28), 'Because the audiences for place promotion are predominantly white and wealthy, the people who populate the imagined cities of place promotion are similarly white and wealthy.' Using Mexico City's historic Zócalo square as a case study, McDermott (2019) has studied how, in some contexts, the spatial regulation of iconic spaces in order to conceal inequality from the tourists' gaze involves both the policing of space and the use of performance, the animation of public space – for instance through the organisation of parades and festivals.

Under those conditions of commodification and spatial control, even the presence of activists in iconic spaces constitutes an act of resistance, and the performance of alternative, traditional, non-consumerist or ethnic performances and rituals become a strategy of contestation. In fact, performance is an important element of protest. As Routledge has argued, equality needs to be performed, in his words 'political activity is that which transforms bodies and places from that which they have been assigned by the political order' (Routledge 2017: 13). Iconic architecture and urban space are important as the site of protest, not just as a backdrop to awake the interest of the media, but because they are symbolic representations of global capitalism as well as spaces of commodified cultural consumption. Performing alternatives of use and changing the types of images associated with those places can change the narratives and meanings attached to them.

Conclusion

This chapter has looked at the myriad of different mechanisms by which contemporary architecture operates to produce and fix symbolic meanings that promote the neoliberal project. These are related to the visual, the discursive and the performative characteristics of architecture and urban space. While the attribution of iconicity entails a judgement based on aesthetics and recognisability – hence the focus on monumentality and eye-catching and sculptural design of volumes and surfaces – meanings attached to architecture and urban space are constructed through explanatory discourse and visual representation, marketing campaigns, symbolic ceremony and spatial regulation.

In the era of neoliberal globalisation, architecture remains one of the main techniques through which elites win the hearts and minds of citizens for their political and socio-economic projects. Iconic architecture, and in particular iconic megaprojects linked to economic regeneration strategies, can be considered not only empirical manifestations of neoliberalism but, importantly, also their symbolic representations. The symbolic dimension of global capitalism epitomised by iconic megaprojects is important because it serves to promote the advancement of neoliberalism by seducing citizens into the ethos of consumerism and competitiveness. While iconic architecture embodies neoliberal governmentalities that reproduce inequalities, it also serves to obscure them through the use of its capacity of seduction. Therefore by means of its design, production and consumption, iconic architecture operates as an instrument of propaganda and compliance.

However, since symbolic meaning is actively created by different local and global actors – including architects and planners, developers, politicians and city marketeers – it can also be subverted. In particular in times of austerity, the tensions created by the clash between the spatialisation of capitalism and the individual and collective life projects of citizens become starker, and iconic megaprojects can come to be seen more clearly as symbolic representations of the inequalities produced by neoliberal policies. In this way, iconic architecture and urban spaces become the site and the target of contestation. The mechanisms used to subvert the meanings attached to iconic megaprojects mirror those used to create those meanings.

These include the contextualisation of images and practices of production, marketing and consumption of iconic architecture, the creation and communication of different narratives for their interpretation, and the enactment of alternative social practices to the commodified consumption of space (as explored in chapter 6).

Further in-depth empirical research on the practices of contestation of iconic megaprojects and the motives behind them can offer theoretical insights into the role of meaning-making in the production and contestation of neoliberal hegemony. Moreover, it can also bring to the fore the political possibilities of subverting the meanings of iconic architecture as a means to challenge the neoliberal emphasis on growth-oriented competitive policies and governmentalities that are, ultimately, the cause of systemic inequality.

References

Bogre, M. (2011). *Photography as Activism: Images for Social Change*. London: Focal Press.

Brott, S. (2017). Calatrava in Athens: the architect as financier and the iconic city. *The Journal of Public Space*, 2(1), 15–32.

Çınar, A., and T. Bender. (2007). *Urban Imaginaries: Locating the Modern City*. Minneapolis: University of Minnesota Press.

Crilley, D. (1993). Architecture as advertising: constructing the image of redevelopment. In C. Philo and G. Kearns, eds, *Selling Places: The City as Cultural Capital, Past and Present*. Oxford: Pergamon Press, 231–52.

Dovey, K. (1999). *Framing Places: Mediating Power in Built Form*. London: Routledge.

Flyvbjerg, B. (2014). What you should know about megaprojects and why: an overview. *Project Management Journal*, 45(2), 6–19.

Foster Gage, F., and Rancière, J. (2019). Politics equals aesthetics: a conversation between Jacques Rancière and Mark Foster Gage. In M. Foster Gage, ed., *Aesthetics Equals Politics*. Cambridge, MA: MIT Press, 9–25.

Ghirardo, D. (1990). The deceit of postmodern architecture. In G. Shapiro, ed., *After the Future: Postmodern Times and Places*. New York: State University of New York Press, 231–52.

Glendinning, M. (2010). *Architecture's Evil Empire? The Triumph and Tragedy of Global Modernism*. London: Reaktion.

Haddad, E., and Rifkind, D., eds (2014). *A Critical History of Contemporary Architecture: 1960–2010*. Farnham: Ashgate.

98 *Situated inequalities*

Hall, T. (1998). *The Entrepreneurial City: Geographies of Politics, Regime, and Representation.* Chichester: Wiley.

Harvey, D. (1990). Flexible accumulation through urbanization: reflections on 'post-modernism' in the American city. *Perspecta,* 26, 251–72.

Henley, J. (2016). Guggenheim Helsinki museum plans rejected by city councillors, *Guardian,* www.theguardian.com/world/2016/dec/01/guggenheim-helsinki-nixed-by-city-councillors (accessed 29 January 2020).

Hubbard, P. (1996). Urban design and city regeneration: social representations of entrepreneurial landscapes. *Urban Studies,* 33(8), 1441–61.

Jessop, B. (1998). The narrative of enterprise and the enterprise of narrative: place marketing and the entrepreneurial city. In T. Hall and P. Hubbard, eds, *The Entrepreneurial City: Geographies of Politics, Regime and Representation.* London: Wiley, 77–99.

Jones, P. (2009). Putting architecture in its social place: a cultural political economy of architecture. *Urban Studies,* 46(12), 2519–36.

Jones, P. (2011). *The Sociology of Architecture: Constructing Identities.* Liverpool: Liverpool University Press.

Koch, N. (2018). *The Geopolitics of Spectacle: Space, Synecdoche, and the New Capitals of Asia.* New York: Cornell University Press.

Lopez Rego, M., Reis Irigay, H. A., and Lago P. Chaves, R. (2017). Symbolic megaprojects: historical evidence of a forgotten dimension. *Project Management Journal,* 48(6), 17–28.

Marques, B., and McIntosh, J. (2018). The spell of the visual and the experience of the sensory: understanding icons in the built environment. *Charrette* 5(1), 68–77.

McDermott, J. (2019). Towards an icon model of gentrification: global capitalism, policing, and the struggle for iconic spaces in Mexico City. *Urban Studies,* 56(16) 3522–39.

McNeill, D. (2009). *The Global Architect: Firms, Fame and Urban Form.* London: Routledge.

Molotch, H., and Ponzini, D. (2019). *The New Arab Urban: Gulf Cities of Wealth, Ambition, and Distress.* New York: New York University Press.

Routledge, P. (2017). *Space Invaders: Radical Geographies of Protest.* London: Pluto Press.

Sklair, L. (2006). Iconic architecture and capitalist globalisation. *City,* 10(1), 21–47.

Sklair, L. (2017). *The Icon Project: Architecture, Cities, and Capitalist Globalisation.* Oxford: Oxford University Press.

Sklair, L., and Struna, J. (2013). The icon project: the transnational capitalist class in action. *Globalisations,* 10(5), 747–63.

Spencer, D. (2016). *The Architecture of Neoliberalism: How Contemporary Architecture Became an Instrument of Control and Compliance.* London: Bloomsbury.

Swyngedouw, E., Moulaert, F., and Rodriguez, A. (2002). Neoliberal urbanisation in Europe: large-scale urban development projects and the new urban policy. *Antipode*, 34(3), 542–77.

Tarazona-Vento, A. (2015). Santiago Calatrava and the 'power of faith': global imaginaries in Valencia. *International Journal of Urban and Regional Research*, 39(3), 550–67.

Tarazona-Vento, A. (2017). Mega-project meltdown: post-politics, neoliberal urban regeneration and Valencia's fiscal crisis. *Urban Studies*, 54(1), 68–84.

Vale, L. (1999). Mediated monuments and national identity. *The Journal of Architecture*, 4(4), 391–408.

Ward, S. (1998). Selling places: the marketing and promotion of towns and cities 1850–2000. In *Selling Places: The Marketing and Promotion of Towns and Cities 1850–2000*. London: Routledge.

Watt, P. (2013). It's not for us. *City*, 17(1), 99–118.

6

Catcalls and cobblestones: gendered limits on women walking

Morag Rose

This chapter shares research focused on gender and public space in the UK. It discusses how inequality is embedded and amplified by the urban environment, with a particular focus on how women's lived experiences of street-based harassment, poor material infrastructure and bad design entrench exclusion. My primary evidence base is a series of walking interviews I facilitated with women within Manchester city centre. I wanted to learn their thoughts, feelings and experiences of the urban environment. I chose a mobile methodology to facilitate richer, more nuanced conversations about place and to disrupt traditional research hierarchies (Pink, 2015; Holton and Riley, 2016; Bates and Rhys-Taylor, 2017). I have lived in Manchester for twenty years, so I am entangled and implicated in this work. The location, and perspective, is that of a post-industrial city in northern England. I will begin by discussing women's experiences of gendered harassment, then discuss features of the built environment which enhance exclusion, and end by sharing some examples of resistance.

This chapter offers a different, but supportive, perspective to the preceding discussion of iconic starchitecture by Tarazona-Vento. There is a symbiotic relationship between architecture and the situated experience of inequality. The built environment embodies a complex web of spatial, temporal, political, historical, cultural, environmental and economic factors (and more). This impacts an individual's behavioural and affective response to a particular place, but they also have power and agency to animate, subvert or recreate space. De Certeau (1984) provides a classic account on how everyday walking can activate architecture in this way.

Approaching the city

Underpinning my research is an assertion that the street is a key site for community building, encountering and negotiating differences (Hall, 2012). Genuinely accessible public space plays a valuable role within cities (Mean and Tims, 2005) but its existence is threatened by exclusionary neoliberal strategies of privatisation and commodification (Minton, 2009; Garrett, 2015). The women I walked with reported how these trends impacted their sense of belonging, with implications for equality and diversity within civic life. For example, Public Space Protection Orders or similar legislation can make campaigning work difficult by prohibiting gatherings or the distribution of leaflets, while a lack of infrastructure, such as toilet facilities, seating or accessible transport and features such as narrow pavements, potholes and cobblestones also mitigate against equal participation.

Women face specific gender-based threats to participation, but because 'women' is a heterogeneous category, I take an intersectional approach. The women I walked with shared how their experiences are impacted by factors including (though not exclusively) age, ethnicity, sexuality (dis)ability, education, faith, class, caring responsibilities, appearance and gender identity. Regardless of their personal circumstances, interviewees shared many commonalities, which are my primary focus. These included frequent gender-based micro-aggressions and 'everyday sexism' (Bates, 2014). The majority of these incidents were reported in a 'matter of fact' way, as just something that happens and must be endured. Individual incidents appear trivial, but their cumulative impact is damaging because 'like other social practices [sexism] becomes meaningful (and powerful) through rehearsal' (Calder-Dawe, 2015: 9). Participants linked their mundane experiences to wider systems of oppression under patriarchy.

Walking is a multisensory and inherently embodied experience. Wherever and however we walk – whether we use assistive technologies such as wheels, sticks or prosthetics – we walk in, and with, our bodies. However, walking as a woman often incorporates a particular form of reflexivity and self-censorship based on gendered experience. This was articulated by Veronica,[1] a teacher in her forties. After work one day she decided to walk along the river near her suburban workplace:

Just to see how far I could get. There was nobody around and I was kind of thinking if something happened now there would be nobody that I could call, I was constantly looking for escape routes ... I think if you were a man you probably wouldn't be doing that, you would be walking and thinking about whatever it is a person would be thinking about.

Despite Veronica's desire to explore she could not fully enjoy the experience. She was unable to relax and let her mind wander. Her experience contrasts with the archetypal flâneur, a figure often evoked in discussions around walking. Invariably male, white, affluent and privileged in many ways he moves through space fearlessly and freely. The conceptual (im)possibility of a flâneuse has been discussed widely (Wolff, 1985; Pollock, 1988; Scalway, 2002). Veronica spoke for many when she discussed a sense of unease and restriction she linked explicitly to gender.

Other women talked about mental maps of safe routes, even though they may not be the most direct or picturesque journey (see also Valentine, 1989; Warren 2016). These maps often have temporal dimensions, as illustrated by Layla. She is mid-thirties, manages a community building and relishes the buzz and vibrancy of living in the city centre. However, her movements change when it is dark:

> I've got a map in my head of where it's okay to walk on a Sunday morning and where I wouldn't necessarily walk on a Friday night, you know like (if it's) late I wouldn't go down that way, I'd go around the long way.

Layla's unease was specifically located in the Northern Quarter neighbourhood. This dense network of streets has a high concentration of pubs and bars. There are also a number of characteristic 'ginnels' or alley ways. Layla told me she enjoyed the atmosphere, and short-cuts, that these provide during the day but was wary at night because they feel enclosed and isolated. Her walk home on a Friday or Saturday evening, prime time for pubs and clubs, was an assemblage based on avoiding both dark alleyways and specific bars which had a high concentration of inebriated young men outside them. There was a delicate balance between the surveillance and protection offered by these eyes on the street, championed by Jacobs (1961), versus the potential threat posed by drunken predators. It's worth noting that the vast majority of women I walked with were not anti-alcohol or anti-pub per se. They appreciated the conviviality and pleasures social drinking can bring, and personally I would echo the need for a nuanced approach here. What they found explicitly threatening was the behaviour of particular people – not necessarily as a consequence of drinking. They also felt there had been a laissez faire approach to licensing, which meant that some areas were particularly unpleasant to navigate.

However, the women were determined to make space for themselves in the city and so developed a range of coping tactics, especially at night. Most reported a constant hyper vigilance, which prevented enjoyment of the environment and atmosphere. Some women had self-imposed curfews and wore (or avoided wearing) specific items of clothing to minimise risk. I suspect many of these strategies will be familiar to readers. Other comments included:

> I'm really just doing 360s all the time, holding onto my phone in one hand, my keys in another making sure that I feel safe, I normally tell someone that I'm doing it (walking at night). (Patti, forties, admin)

> I hate that when I walk to my friend's house, most of the time I go through a park, and then when it gets dark suddenly my right to walk there is compromised. (Fiona, forties, admin)

> I actually run with a key in my hand, between my knuckles, you'll probably be OK, but I can't risk it … And that's a big regret I have that I feel like I can't be quite as intrepid as I would like to. (Rennie, thirties, musician)

The last quote reveals the tension between a desire to assert the right to be in the city and a fear of the potential consequences. Compromises are made by individual women after conducting internal risk assessments. Many stressed the need to hide fear to avoid looking vulnerable (although this is a problematic and mutable term). Jack, a nurse in her fifties said she 'purposely gives a don't you mess with me kind of attitude' and others talked about performativity, of playing the role of a purposeful, efficient walker. 'Looking confident' equated to a particular stance, focusing on the destination whilst moving swiftly with minimal environmental engagement. There is a dichotomy of feigned indifference and hyper alertness, aiming to repel or dissipate threats. Women sense the truth in Butler and Taylor's warning that 'a walk can be a dangerous thing. If you go for a walk you are vulnerable … you assert your rights of mobility and you take a certain risk in public space' (2009: 205). The women I spoke to seek to minimise the risk but were also very vocal against victim blaming. Cheryl moved to Manchester as a student. She recalls a police talk during induction week which meant she never wore high heels despite being acutely aware the warning 'was all about instilling fear in young women to avoid something as opposed to going, boys, could you just not rape girls ... it's the easiest way of shutting something down, to lay the responsibility with the victim or the potential victim'.

Structural change is needed to stop misogyny; it is not the responsibility of individual women. In the meantime, women develop coping tactics based on their personal experiences and wider societal messages. This takes a toll, with many describing the effort as exhausting, frustrating and alienating. Rage, disgust and resignation were also expressed and underneath many comments was an abiding sense of Manchester as a masculine place. Isobelle, a student in her twenties, feels 'the city is built for them, not us' but she often finds this hard to explain to male friends and family. They simply 'didn't get' the need to be constantly alert. She works in a pub and told of several times when men had shouted at her from cars or propositioned her as she walked to the isolated bus stop after closing time. She now chooses to pay for a pre-booked taxi home, but felt her employers and friends were dismissive of her concerns.

A hostile environment

Encounters such as those shared by Isobelle contribute to a hostile environment for women. This can be demonstrated by an extract from my walking interview with Zoe and Jo. They are both in their mid-twenties: Zoe is a carer and Jo works as a PA. We met in Piccadilly Gardens, a public square bordered by a bus station and central shopping areas. I began the majority of my interviews there because its central location gives it a high degree of access and familiarity; it also provides an excellent ice breaker as its redevelopment has been controversial (Pidd, 2014). It provoked a vivid memory of harassment:

> Zoe: I got sexually harassed right here actually [laughs] ... I saw [a friend] from the other side of the street and I felt very free and

happy and called out to her because she hadn't seen me yet, I think I went 'oooooh looking great!' ... and there was this group of men here and they saw that interaction as I ran over the street to hug her and ... they said something like show us your gash and I was like [pause] it felt [pause]

Jo: God!

Zoe: really awful, I didn't really know [pause] it's one of those things that really jolts you and [pause]

Jo: Yes immediately you're like you are sucked down from the level of just being in the world to being a set of sexual organs which are potentially under attack ... it feels like some form of policing ... people coming up to you and saying you're a woman, don't forget it like, you know?

Zoe: Exactly it's just letting you know that you're in a public space that actually isn't really designed for you to feel completely comfortable in ... reminding you you're being watched.

This exchange exemplifies many of the pernicious aspects of street harassment. It is, of course, impossible to divine the intention of the men who shouted out to Zoe. Perhaps some felt uncomfortable and challenged the perpetrator. Maybe they had not even considered the impact of their actions. Or they could have known very well and been deliberately hurtful. However, it is probable that they were not making a literal demand. If Zoe had stopped to display her genitalia to them as colloquially requested we can assume they would have been shocked. Regardless of intent, the impact of their words was real, and damaging, and stole something intangible from Zoe's meeting with her friend. Yet the intentions of individual cat-callers are not as important as the oppressive structures they recreate for women navigating urban space. An analogy can be drawn with arguments about Theresa May's hostile environment (e.g. Jones et al., 2017). Whether May had racist intentions or not, the policies she promoted had racist outcomes.

The comment Zoe received was blatantly sexual, unwarranted and aggressive. Much harassment is subtler and frequently excused as mere banter, such as the 'give us a smile luv' or the shouted compliment. Women who complain are 'feminist killjoys' (Ahmed, 2010). She becomes the problem by naming an issue that had been conveniently ignored – her demand for respect is perceived as depriving her oppressor. Vera-Gray suggests we should frame such encounters as 'interruptions' rather than harassment, better reflecting reality than the legal term which implies direct and obvious harm. Vera-Gray's framing acknowledges the 'sudden feeling of being pulled outside of yourself, without wanting, without warning.' (2016: xiii). Such interruptions are often experienced as a banal nuisance, micro-aggressions, mundane misogyny and everyday sexism. Bates (2014) demonstrates how women's right to be in the city is continuously threatened, mocked and eroded.

Everyday sexism is part of a complex spectrum of symbolic and physical violence that percolates throughout women's lived experiences (Pain, 2015). This violence is absolutely not inevitable or innate, because 'male violence against women is not biological, it is political. And if it is made, then it can be unmade; if it is learnt, it can be unlearnt' (Mackay, 2015: 11). This continuum of gender-based violence, and fear of violence, limits women's ability to inhabit and enjoy public space. Street harassment is one symptom of a historical desire to keep women in what a patriarchal order offers them as their primary place, the private domestic sphere. Of course, domestic violence means this has its own dangers; home is not necessarily a safe haven. It should also be remembered that 'stranger danger' is a comparatively rare occurrence and the experience of crime and the fear it instils is not unique to women. Stanko (1990) discusses the pressures masculinity and male violence place on men and boys, who are harmed in multiple ways by patriarchy. However, the majority of gender-based violence is directed at women and their fear is both logical, and justified, as Stanko states:

> Women's heightened level of anxiety is born of an accurate reading of their relationship to safety. It is not a misguided paranoia. Women's life experiences – as children, adolescents and adults – are set in a context of ever-present sexual danger. Worry about personal safety is one-way women articulate what it means to be female and live, day-in and day-out, in communities where women are targets of sexual violence. (1990: 86)

Gender has a continued and profound impact on women's embodied experiences of the city and how they navigate through it. Wilson (1991), Valentine (1990), Pain (1997, 2001), Bowlby (1990), Kern (2020) and others provide much evidence that women experience encounters with the city as explicitly gendered. They identify sexism, misogyny and gender-based oppression as a key factor in their everyday lives. The embodied, somatic experience of being a woman makes it extremely difficult to conceptualise a space free from these concerns. Women develop a range of survival strategies and find much to relish in the urban, but, as Isobelle told me, it is impossible to truly relax, to inhabit flânerie because 'the city isn't for women really ... I always have to be vigilant ... the world is so much for [men] ... they don't realise what it's like, not feeling like public space is for you.'

Taking the piss: public spaces down the toilet

These embodied knowledges impact on the construction of places and people, as well as the stories we tell about both. Dominant place-narratives betray a complex web of power relations, and my interviews uncovered some of those that are manifested in the cityscape. Tarazona-Vento (in chapter 5) demonstrates what this can mean in relation to starchitects and iconic building projects. Her arguments can equally be applied to the impact of mundane architecture on everyday mobilities, such as walking. Much literature on walking is either ungendered or dismissive of women (Solnit, 2001). Adopting the flâneur as 'typical' erases difference and smooths over power relationships. It imposes an essentialist vision of space and gender, assuming innate and fixed qualities, which disregard the possibility of change and the importance of an intersectional understanding of identity as formulated by Crenshaw (1989). However, there is a rich and growing body of work by artists and academics such as Elkin (2016), Heddon and Turner (2010), Qualman and Sharrocks (2016) and others who all seek to dismantle the dominance of the flâneur. This issue extends beyond walking of course. Armstrong (2018) explores the consequences of this in medicine, and Criado Perez (2019) collates a horrifying plethora of other areas where women are ignored in data. A parallel conversation has also been happening in urban design (Beebeejaun, 2017; Kern, 2020).

Exclusion is entrenched by policy. In my walks with women in Manchester, class, especially, emerged as a particular concern, with fears around gentrification and social cleansing. There was a strong sense that recent developments in the city were excluding those who could not afford to be good consumers and that working-class histories were being ignored (Rose, 2018). This erasure due to income and class is enabled by political and economic decisions (Lees, 2014). Inequality can also be enhanced by design that fails to consider diverse bodies. Access to public toilets provide a salient example. Contemporary media discourse around toilets frequently focuses on transphobic fears around gender free design. This discourse can, and should, be challenged (Jones and Slater, 2020). None of the women I walked with expressed any concerns around gender free design. Indeed, as several pointed out disabled toilets are generally unsegregated. Transwomen are women who suffer escalated levels of discrimination and violence, but Cis women are also at risk from the over-policing of toilet facilities; for instance, women who are deemed too tall, too butch or too masculine may not feel safe. This debate also masks serious issues around how lack of toilet facilities impacts all women. Flanagan (2014) offers a stark historical example of how design inequalities manifest: in the early twentieth century, there were often violent objections to providing toilets for women because 'decent' women should not be in public at all. Today, especially in the context of public service cuts, toilet provision frequently remains inadequate and becomes a very tangible way of exerting control over space and denying the right to be in the city. For example, the 'Piss Daleks' introduced in Piccadilly Gardens to replace closed facilities in Manchester were urinals designed for male anatomies with no additional facilities for menstruation and hygienic disposal of sanitary items (Dunnico, 2014).

The fear of not being able to find a toilet can inhibit when and where people feel safe. Although toilets may be of particular significance to mothers, older people and people with certain disabilities, they are clearly used by all demographics. Slater and Jones (2018) and the Around The Toilet project has highlighted the problem graphically. In Manchester there is just one free public toilet left, on Lloyd Street near the Town Hall, and this is closed at night. The others were closed despite protests. A 'City Loos' scheme to encourage businesses to make their toilets open to everyone was a failure, with only eight places signing up. They were mostly museums, the art gallery, library and shopping centres, that have long been places many will simply pop in to use the toilets anyway. The failure of City Loos illustrates at a micro level the impact of privatisation on public space. Meanwhile, urinating in public can result in an £80 fine in Manchester and the official police advice given to people struggling to find somewhere to go is to 'tie a knot in it' (Dunnico, 2014). This instruction again highlights how the universal male figure continues to dominate discourse as it assumes a penis to tie a knot in.

Toilets are just one example of infrastructure changes that could help reduce spatial inequality. A more holistic approach to urban design and access issues could also contribute to enabling women to feel safer and more comfortable. A subsection of my interviewees – 23 per cent – held a range of expertise and interest in urban design. They were, or had been, working within professions including planning and architecture or studying relevant subjects. Most were members of Manchester Women's Design Group (MWDG). This was a project of the London-based Women's Design Service, which closed in 2012 due to lack of funding and political support. MWDG developed independently as an unfunded voluntary organisation. Arlene works in housing and summed up why she perceived a need for MWDG by telling me 'there is definitely something going on where the built environment is largely designed by men, largely commissioned by men, largely regulated by men, so there's obviously some inequality there.' She believed a lack of diversity at all levels led to a failure to appreciate a full range of human needs.

Arlene felt that the complex and varied needs of women were easily overlooked because there was an implicit assumption that the male experience was 'normal'. This concern was echoed by Rita who worked in planning before her retirement. She said, 'I've always found it difficult to define the things that are purely women's issues because I think those are very few.' For example, Rita spoke about how the majority of caring for children and elders is undertaken by women, and so it is vital that women are included in discussions that impact carers. However, she also wanted to ensure caring was not viewed solely as women's work. She stressed how important it is to make sure design standards work for a range of bodies to avoid 'the height of seats in bus shelters and railway stations and things like that being based on a typical 6-foot male who designed the whole thing.' Rita is currently involved with several national campaigns related to age friendly design and access for disabled people and she was very clear that her guiding principle is that 'accessible design is good for everyone'.

All the MWDG members I spoke to feel their work is of universal benefit. Several told me of internal discussions about changing the name of the group to reflect this, but they concluded there was value in honouring their feminist history. They wanted to acknowledge and remember that advances such as accessible changing facilities had been hard won (Beebeejaun, 2017). Isobelle is a medical student and not involved with MWDG, but illustrates the wider resonance of their work. She has begun to think critically about how design could improve her experience of the city:

> You need to consider are these public places for everyone and if not, you know half of the population is losing out ... you need to think are women going to feel safe here? It's a question that needs to be asked a bit more ... I think in society, the male is the norm, you design the city and spaces with the male as the norm.

The features Isobelle and others are noticing, and demanding action on, include inadequate or inappropriate lighting, isolated bus stops and enclosed spaces such as subways and bridges. The condition of pavements, and the material qualities of the environment were also highlighted. One particular source of concern and conflict in Manchester is areas with cobblestones. Considered by some a sign of character, heritage and authenticity, they can severely inhibit movement. Potholes, broken paving slabs and clutter such as A-Boards and badly placed street furniture also create obstacles for everyone, but particularly blind and visually impaired people and anyone using a wheelchair, mobility scooter or pushing a buggy. Their needs were not considered during design, commissioning and/or maintenance and a choice has been made to ignore concerns raised. To reiterate, these improvements would benefit everyone but the physical environment adds a further barrier to women's ability to fully exercise their right to the city.

Conclusion

There are many signs of challenges to these restrictions. The work of MWDG is one local example but the challenge is international. Other examples include large-scale, spectacular demonstrations of women asserting their right to take up space. Reclaim The Night

(RTN) marches are 'a direct action, public, highly visible and creative mass demonstration against rape and all forms of male violence' (Mackay, 2015: 52). RTN originated in the USA in 1975 where 'Take Back the Night' protested attacks on women and memorialised victims. The first UK events in 1977 were a response to the Yorkshire Ripper and advice from the police for women to stay at home. These marches are a display of defiance, solidarity, strength and community, noisily asserting a being in space. The vigils Reclaim These Streets and others organised in response to the murder of Sarah Everard in London 2020 underlined the continued struggle to assert women's right to life and freedom from male violence. Other international movements such as Million Women Rise led by Black Women and Slut Walk, which originated in Toronto also use women walking together en masse as a tactic. Each creates a temporary mobile space of resistance, solidarity and confidence building. There is something very powerful about being able to physically dominate space whilst evoking the carnivalesque. The atmosphere can be joyous, empowering and invigorating, although debate remains about the lasting impact of such spectacles.

Women walking artists have also created many interventions and creative works which reveal and challenge restrictions and prefigure a more egalitarian city. Over recent years several initiatives have worked to increase the visibility of women walking artists. Examples include Walking Women (Qualmann and Sharrocks 2016, archived online by the Walking Artists Network) and Jo Norcup's radio programmes (2016 onwards). The artists featured include Afghani performer Kubra Khademi. *Armor* (2015) saw her walking in Kabul wearing a costume she made to emphasise her breasts and buttocks. The harassment she received led to the performance being cancelled after eight minutes and ultimately led to her exile in Paris. Monique Beston has created a number of performance walks across Europe, often highlighting environmental concerns. She says:

> It didn't start as an activist act, a political statement or social or cultural research. To some extent it has turned into that. Not because it is what I wanted or aspired to but because that is what the world wanted. I just walked. I walked for weeks, months, and people on the road asked me questions, told me their stories, gave me their opinions. They saw things in my walking I hadn't seen myself.[2]

Beston reminds us that to walk as a woman can mean many things, and to enter into the public realm is to open one's actions up to scrutiny and interpretation. The work of artists has an important role in both drawing attention to problems and modelling alternatives. Paying attention to both the micro and the macro matters because 'when sexism is routinely presented as harmless, its harms become difficult to see and speak of, even as they accumulate around us' (Calder-Dawe, 2015: 89). Walking itself should not have to be a radical, dangerous or political act. It is deeply troubling that for women the very act of moving through, and inhabiting, space can feel like an act of political resistance. We need to work to transform the everyday environment, so it is available to all. The women I spoke to were determined to keep walking in the city, demonstrating (consciously or not) an everyday practice of resistant tactics (de Certeau, 1984). Women make space for themselves on the streets and it is an important feminist task to enable and extend this. Women can, and must, experience public space not just as a site of abuse but also a place of joy, entertainment, serendipity and conviviality. Truly accessible and equitable public space enriches the environment and benefits us all; while spatial inequality has a negative impact, constructing and reinforcing discrimination and exclusion. Uneven power dynamics are revealed through the erasure of public space in Manchester and the multiple obstacles women must challenge to feel safe and welcome in public. A holistic solution is needed which improves material conditions whilst also challenging misogyny and harassment. A city where all women can walk should not be an impossible dream and we need to work to make desire lines a reality.

Notes

1 A pseudonym; all women quoted have been given assumed names to protect their anonymity.
2 https://walkingart.interartive.org/2018/12/monique-besten (accessed 14 October 2021).

References

Ahmed, S. (2010). Killing joy: feminism and the history of happiness. *Signs: Journal of Women in Culture and Society*, 35(3), 571–94.

Armstrong, E. (2018). The gender pay gap in pharmaceutical research. *Voices in Bioethics*, 4. https://doi.org/10.7916/vib.v4i.6008 (accessed 8 October 2021).

Bates, C., and Rhys-Taylor, A. (2017). *Walking Through Social Research*. Abingdon: Routledge.

Bates, L. (2014). *Everyday Sexism*. London: Simon and Schuster.

Beebeejaun, Y. (2017). Gender, urban space, and the right to everyday life. *Journal of Urban Affairs*, 39(3), 323–34.

Bowlby, S. (1990). Women and the designed environment. *Built Environment (1978–) Women and the Designed Environment*, 16(4), 244–8.

Butler, J., with Taylor, S. (2009). Interdependence. In A. Taylor, ed., *Examined Life: Excursions with Contemporary Thinkers*. New York: The New Press, 185–214.

Calder-Dawe, O. (2015). The choreography of everyday sexism: reworking sexism in interaction. *New Formations*, 86, 89–105.

Crenshaw, K. (1989). Demarginalising the intersection of race and sex: a black feminist critique of antidiscrimination doctrine, feminist theory and antiracist politics. *U. Chi. Legal F.*, 139.

Criado Perez, C. (2019). *Invisible Women: Exposing Data Bias in a World Designed for Men*. London: Chatto and Windus.

de Certeau, M. (1984). *The Practice of Everyday Life*. Berkeley, CA: University of California Press.

Dunnico, D. (2014). Inconvenienced: how the cuts have hit public toilets. www.redpepper.org.uk/inconvenienced-how-the-cuts-have-hit-public-toilets/ (accessed July 2021).

Elkin, L. (2016). *Flaneuse*. London: Chatto and Windus.

Flanagan, M. (2014). Private needs, public space: public toilets provision in the Anglo-Atlantic patriarchal city: London, Dublin, Toronto and Chicago. *Urban History*, 41(2), 265–90.

Garrett, B. L (2015). The privatisation of cities' public space is escalating. It is time to take a stand. *Guardian*, 4 August. www.theguardian.com/cities/2015/aug/04/pops-privately-owned-public-space-cities-direct-action (accessed 8 July 2021).

Hall, S. (2012). *City, street and citizen: the measure of the ordinary*. Abingdon: Routledge.

Heddon, D., and Turner, C. (2010). Walking women: interviews with artists on the move. *Performance Research*, 15(4), 14–22.

Holton, M., and Riley, M. (2016). Place-based interviewing: creating and conducting walking interviews. Sage Research Methods https://methods.sagepub.com/case/place-based-interviewing-creating-and-conducting-walking-interviews (accessed July 2021).

Jacobs, J. (1961). *The Death and Life of Great American Cities*. New York: Random House.

Jones C., and Slater J. (2020). The toilet debate: stalling trans possibilities and defending 'women's protected spaces'. *The Sociological Review*, 68(4):834–51.

Jones, H., Gunaratnam, Y., Bhattacharyya, G., Davies, W., Dhaliwal, S., Forkert, K., Jackson, E., and Saltus, R. (2017). *Go Home? The Politics of Immigration Controversies*. Manchester: Manchester University Press.

Kern, L. (2020). *Feminist City: Claiming Space in a Man-Made World*. London: Verso.

Lees, L. (2014). The urban injustices of New Labour's 'new urban renewal': the case of the Aylesbury estate in London. *Antipode*, 46(4), 921–47.

Mackay, F. (2015). *Radical Feminism: Feminist Activism in Movement*. Basingstoke: Palgrave Macmillan.

Manchester Women's Design Group (MWDG). (2017). About Us. http://womensdesign.blogspot.co.uk/p/hello.html (accessed 1 September 2017).

Mean, M., and Tims, C. (2005). *People Make Places: Growing the Public Life of Cities*. London: Demos.

Minton, A. (2009). *Ground Control: Fear and Happiness in the Twenty-First-Century City*. London: Penguin.

Norcup, J. (2016). 'Er Outdoors. *Resonance FM*. www.mixcloud.com/Resonance/her-outdoors-14-april-2016/ (accessed 23 August 2020).

Pain, R. (1997). Social geographies of women's fear of crime. *Transactions of the Institute of British Geographers*, 22(2), 231–44.

Pain, R. (2001). Gender, race, age and fear in the city. *Urban Studies*, 38(5–6), 899–913.

Pain, R. (2015). Intimate war. *Political Geography*, 44, 64–73.

Pidd, H. (2014). Manchester celebrates news that its 'Berlin Wall' is to disappear. *Guardian*, 11 November. www.theguardian.com/uk-news/2014/nov/11/manchester-piccadilly-gardens-berlin-wall-disappear (accessed 1 January 2021).

Pink, S. (2015). *Doing Sensory Ethnography*. 2nd edn. London: Sage Publications.

Pollock, G. (1988). *Vision and Difference: Femininity, Feminism, and Histories of Art*. Abingdon: Routledge.

Qualmann C., and Sharrocks A. (curators) (2016). *Walking Women*. www.walkingartistsnetwork.org/walking-women/ (accessed 23 August 2019).

Rose, M. (2018). Confessions of an anarcho-flâneuse or psychogeography the Mancunian way. In T. Richardson, ed., *Walking Inside Out: Contemporary British Psychogeography*. London: Rowman and Littlefield International, 147–62.

Scalway, H. (2002). The contemporary flaneuse: exploring strategies for the drifter in a feminine mode. www.helenscalway.com/wp-content/

uploads/2013/01/The-Contemporary-Flaneuse.pdf (accessed 23 August 2020).

Slater, J., and Jones, C (2018). Around the toilet: a research project report about what makes a safe and accessible toilet space. https://aroundthetoilet.files.wordpress.com/2018/05/around-the-toilet-report-final-1.pdf (accessed 23 August 2020).

Solnit, R. (2001). *Wanderlust: A History of Walking.* London: Verso.

Stanko, E. A. (1990). *Everyday Violence: How Women and Men Experience Sexual and Physical Danger.* London: Pandora.

Valentine, G. (1989). The geography of women's fear. *Area,* 21(4), 385–90.

Valentine, G. (1990). Women and the designed environment: women's fear and the design of public space. *Women and the Designed Environment,* 16(4), 288–303.

Vera-Gray, F. (2016). Men's stranger intrusions: rethinking street harassment (Vol. 58, pp. 9–17). Presented at the Women's Studies International Forum.

Warren, S. (2016). Pluralising the walking interview: researching (im)mobilities with Muslim women. *Social and Cultural Geography,* 1–22. https://doi.org/10.1080/14649365.2016.1228113 (accessed 14 October 2021).

Wilson, E. (1991). *The Sphinx in the City: Urban Life, the Control of Disorder, and Women.* London: Virago.

Wolff, J. (1985). The invisible *flâneuse*: women and the literature of modernity. *Theory, Culture and Society,* 2(3), 37–46.

7

Inequality in elite neighbourhoods: a case study from central London

Ilaria Pulini

This chapter provides the genealogy of a street in the elite London neighbourhood of Kensington – in terms of its housing and residents – from the late nineteenth century to today. The study concentrates on the manner in which the original built environment has been used and transformed over more than a century, opening up the temporal scope of the investigation. The different types of period properties existing in the street are examined in detail, and their current use is compared and contrasted with past narratives, highlighting ruptures and continuities. By extending the analysis of residential patterns over time, this study demonstrates that the cultural and social distinctions at work today in the street are grounded in a process of transformation of the built environment, which started at the beginning of the twentieth century with the conversion of Victorian single family homes into houses in multiple occupation (HMOs) and the concurrent construction of modern apartment blocks.[1]

This close-up on a single street represents a new approach to the study of the spatial dynamics of London's elite which allows us to uncover contingent specificities and peculiarities, and at the same time, provides insights for broader generalisations. Ethnography and documentary research provide the tools to investigate the built environment of the street over the *longue durée* and to trace the impact of its transformations on current residential patterns. This approach enables insights into social dynamics that do not necessarily coincide with the assumed demographic make-up of an elite neighbourhood. In particular, it shows that the W8 district in Kensington is not just an enclave of elites and upper-middle-class people but, since its heyday, has included residents of intersecting social, economic and cultural backgrounds.

From this point of view, the chapter finds comparisons with Mazzilli (chapter 8). Both studies look at urban spaces with steady reputations: as inclusive and welcoming spaces (in the case of Bologna and Brighton in chapter 8), and as a quintessential elite neighbourhood in the case of Kensington. In both examples, the reputation of these urban spaces to some extent obscures a recognition of difference, which we explore by digging under the surface of their popular images. Both unravel contingencies and peculiarities that provide a re-balancing of mainstream narratives, ultimately highlighting the situated nature of spatial inequalities.

Peaks and troughs in Kensington

Among world cities, London stands out for its high level of economic inequality, due in particular to the growing influx of foreign capital invested in the property market by a wealthy global elite (Atkinson, Parker and Burrows, 2017; Edwards, 2016; Hay and Muller, 2012; Ho and Atkinson, 2017; Minton, 2017). In this context of rising urban inequalities, a new interest in the geography of London's elite has emerged, and in recent years an increasing number of sociologists have contributed to outlining the bigger picture of elite spatialisation in the capital (Atkinson, Burrows and Rhodes, 2016; Burrows, Webber and Atkinson, 2017; Cunningham, 2017; Cunningham and Savage, 2015, 2017). Meanwhile, a number of studies have added insight to the bigger picture, asserting a need for empirical profiles of elite neighbourhoods in order to tackle specificities and contingencies in the spatialisation of London's elite (Atkinson and Ho, 2019; Atkinson et al., 2017; Burrows and Knowles, 2019; Butler and Lees, 2006; Glucksberg, 2016; Knowles, 2017a, 2017b; Webber and Burrows, 2016). Drawing on the rapidly accumulating literature, this chapter focuses on the Royal Borough of Kensington and Chelsea (hereafter RBKC), one of the wealthiest areas in London.

Since the devastating Grenfell Tower fire in North Kensington in June 2017, which left more than 70 people dead and hundreds homeless, social commentators have repeatedly pointed to the stark juxtaposition between the deprived areas concentrated in the northern sectors of RBKC and the rest of the borough (MacLeod, 2018). In particular, they have laid the blame for the extreme level of inequality on the concentration of the new global super-rich in W8, an area of roughly 2 km² in the central sector of the RBKC, which includes some of the most exclusive addresses in London and worldwide. Polarising inequalities in the geography of the RBKC are widely demonstrated by statistics and demography. According to the Mosaic geo-demographic classification, wealth concentrates in W8, with some 58 per cent of its population being 'Global Power Brokers'. They are one of the most affluent and powerful categories in the so-called 'Alpha Territories', where the wealthiest and most successful people cluster together (Burrows, Webber and Atkinson, 2017: 14). A striking picture of the economic and social divide in RBKC is confirmed by a classification based on the English indices of deprivation 2015, where the northern sectors of the borough are ranked among the most deprived 10 per cent in the whole of England, with social housing representing over 60 per cent of the housing tenure, as opposed to W8, which stands among the least deprived 10 per cent areas in the country (MacLeod, 2018: 465).

Yet, despite the stark contrast between the northern sector of the borough and the affluent areas to the south, the borough's demographics also reveal more localised disparities, evidenced by the presence, on the one hand, of affluent middle-upper-class residents at the very core of North Kensington and, on the other hand, of a lower income population in W8 (NOMIS, 2017). Such localised disparities are clearly displayed in the built environment. For example, in North Kensington the top end homes of Oxford Gardens that sell for around £8 million² are less than ten minutes' walk from Grenfell Tower; in Campden Hill Road, at the very core of W8, a large compound of social housing faces a group of super-prime period mansions. Given this background, we may argue that inequalities work at a *multi-scalar* level in RBKC's residential landscape. In other words, the peaks and troughs of wealth are not simply evident across the north-south divide of the borough, but also *within* these sectors.

Such a conceptualisation of RBKC spatial inequalities brings about an understanding of London W8 that differs from the conventional image conveyed by popular and social narratives describing this area as an exclusively elite neighbourhood. The focus on a single street in the following section uncovers contingent peculiarities within a specific area, which may ultimately provide insights for broader generalisations on the spatialisation of London's elite. The underlying idea of this approach to the study of an elite neighbourhood is an understanding of social distinctions and inequalities as the outcome of relationships that are socially and spatially produced and practised, rather than built according to a-priori established hierarchical categories of wealth.

Taking an intersectional approach that acknowledges the particular nuanced social distinctions of places at specific moments in history, this piece of research focuses on a single street over the *longue durée* (Tilley, 2017), exploring the multiple temporalities inscribed in the materiality of the built environment (Pulini, 2019; Tilley, 2019: 19). According to this approach, 'places' are seen in a continual process of 'being and becoming' (Ingold, 1993; Tilley, 2017); and each place is the uneven combination of layers of events (Adam, 1990, 1998; Lynch, 1972; Massey, 1984). From this point of view, the approach adopted in this chapter finds parallels in the work of Tim Edensor (2010) on the materiality of buildings and in a stream of research on urban neighbourhoods and communities, which centres on a diachronic approach linking the past to the present (Bennett, 2014; Blokland, 2003; Blunt, 2008; Degen, 2018; Massey, 2000; McKenzie, 2015; Webber and Burrows, 2016; White, 2003). Ultimately, the analysis of a street over time allows for the conceptualisation of spatial inequalities as historical, geographical and social structures, stretching between past and present.

Cheniston Gardens[3]

Cheniston Gardens is a Victorian development of 39 high-rise terraced houses aligned along an L-shaped street at the core of W8, a stone's throw from Kensington High Street and the tube station. Alongside the terraced houses, there are three different types of buildings: a group of three small cottages tucked in within two rows of terraced houses (Cheniston Studios), a red-brick cottage with a sophisticated façade in Queen Anne style (Cheniston Lodge) and a mansion block with 12 apartments (Cheniston Apartments). According to 2011 Census records, the total number of people living in Cheniston Gardens was estimated at 332 usual residents distributed over 240 households.[4] Census data reports a younger population than in the rest of the borough, with a strong component having an international background, mostly from the EU (Pulini, 2019: 94–7).

In the geo-demographic segmentation based on postcodes developed by Acorn,[5] Cheniston Gardens residents are classified among the wealthy categories of 'Metropolitan Professionals' and 'Metropolitan Money', both made up of individuals in managerial and other professional occupations. The 'Metropolitan Professionals' are described as slightly younger, comparatively less affluent and living in converted flats in the terraced houses, while the more affluent 'Metropolitan Money' are said to reside in the 12 Cheniston Apartments and the three Cheniston Studios. However, the 2018/2019 market values of Cheniston Gardens properties on Zoopla website[6] provide clues to more pronounced socio-economic distinctions between residents. In 2018/2019, one-bedroom flats in the terraced houses sold at £600,000; two-bedroom flats at over £1 million; while small run-down studios in the same type of building were available for rent at £270/ week. At the other end of the spectrum, Cheniston Apartments and Cheniston Studios sell at £3 million to £4 million, while Cheniston Lodge itself is worth almost £10 million.[7]

My interviews with a cross-section of residents in 2014 highlighted a discrepancy in terms of income and social belonging in Cheniston Gardens, where wealthy residents coexist alongside people of lower income. On the one hand, are a Swiss banker, an architect, and a few individuals holding managerial positions in the financial services sector or in IT, who live in fully refurbished two-bedroom flats. And on the other, nurses, social workers, shop assistants and students, who have chosen a small studio or a bedsit in Cheniston Gardens because it is conveniently located for their place of work or college. As shown in the following section, such a nuanced social pattern is the outcome of changes and continuities in the use of space over time, and reflects the manner in which the current residential patterns are structured upon a built environment inherited from the past.

A Victorian upper-middle-class enclave

Cheniston Gardens was developed in the early 1880s. At the beginning, it comprised just the terraced houses, the Studios and the Lodge (Survey of London 1986). The terraced houses were designed to meet the needs of single families with three to five servants, and each house featured 12 to 14 rooms across four storeys and a basement (a total floor space of approximately 400 m²). The Lodge was a comparatively smaller family home (less than 300 m² on two floors), yet more sophisticated and exclusive than the terraced houses. The three Studios were targeted at members of the Victorian artistic community. They are much smaller than the terraced houses, which the artist, usually alone, occupied with just one or two servants across two floors (about 200 m²).

The 1891 Census provides a detailed picture of the social character of the street. Alongside the artists living in the three studios, the people living in the terraced houses were affluent upper-middle-class families. Cheniston Lodge attracted artistically inclined individuals, but also wealthy families who were eager to show off their social status through the elegance and sophistication of their home. Overall, this Victorian street was, in all respects, an upper-middle-class enclave. Living in the lodge and in the studios, rather than in the terraced houses, reflected the different aspirations, inclinations and lifestyles of its residents, but did not entail class or wealth distinctions. This consistent social milieu is acknowledged in the first edition of Booth's Poverty Map, where Cheniston Gardens is represented in yellow, the colour code for the 'Upper-middle and upper classes', and stands out among nearby areas coded from red to black, the colour of the lower-middle class and the poor (Booth, 1891). From this point of view, Booth's map provides clear evidence of Victorian Kensington as an area where upper-middle-class developments were interspersed within less affluent and even deprived pockets, a pattern that would continue, and eventually emerge in full in the course of the twentieth century, and which is still legible in the grain of the contemporary urban layout of RBKC.

The apartment boom

The fact that, despite its name, Cheniston Gardens lacked any sort of greenery was not a real drawback for the people who lived in the street, as they could benefit from a view over the extensive gardens of the properties nearby, a quality that was highlighted also in the advertisements by letting and sales agents (*The Morning Post*, 25 May 1883). Yet such an airy and peaceful environment was not going to last long. Soon, the surroundings started being impacted by the relentless construction of massive mansion blocks, from five to seven storeys high, which swallowed every single bit of greenery, choking the terraced houses with their height. The mansion block at the end of Cheniston Gardens was the first to be completed, in 1894: a six-storey building, subdivided into 12 spacious apartments (ca. 170 m²), each with two reception rooms, a dining room and three bedrooms.

By the turn of the century, mansion blocks had become increasingly popular in England, as they were bringing about a radical change in lifestyle (Marcus, 1999). Not only were the apartments equipped with central heating, modern electrical appliances and lifts, but also entailed a shared concierge who was in charge of many of the tasks traditionally performed by live-in servants in larger family houses. Bearing the maintenance costs of three to five live-in servants had become unaffordable by then, and from this point of view the large terraced houses in Cheniston Gardens were far less appealing than a smaller and cheaper property in a mansion block. The upper-middle class was looking to downsize, and the apartments in the mansion blocks represented an urban alternative to the new suburban developments that provided smaller affordable family houses and offered the advantage of more greenery and much cleaner air than in central London.

Apartments were created to resist the upper-middle-class escape to the suburbs, a trend that can be read in the grain of the advertisement for the apartments of Iverna Gardens, a mansion block just behind Cheniston Gardens. The new apartments were targeted at 'people in excellent positions' looking for an 'ideal healthy and sanitary place of residence', with 'not the slightest vestige of possibility of their ever becoming tenanted by Artisans or the Working Classes' (Survey of London, 1986: 104). Mansion blocks were, in all respects, marketed as upper-middle-class urban strongholds at a time when the large terraced houses that had laid out the texture of the urban fabric of Victorian London were becoming increasingly occupied by lower income people.

Change and continuity in residential patterns

By the turn of the twentieth century, the rush to upper-middle-class suburbs and the availability of modern apartments in the surroundings was actually accelerating the transformation of many Kensington terraced houses from family homes into HMOs. The extent of change in the social character of Cheniston Gardens is highlighted by the new edition of Charles Booth's social map, where the street is now represented as 'red to yellow', with the red standing for 'a hardworking sober, energetic class' (Booth, 1902: 33–62). The concentration of boarding houses and bedsits, occupied by a low-income population, already very large in the interwar period, peaked during the Second World War and its aftermath. The lists of residents in the electoral register show that by the end of the war and throughout the 1960s, at least 27 of the 39 terraced houses in Cheniston Gardens were HMOs. And they were characterised by a relentless tenant turnover that was destined to endure as a typical feature of the street in the years ahead (Pulini, 2019: 83, fig.1.8).

Unlike the grand terraced houses, the 12 apartments in the mansion block maintained their original features throughout the twentieth century, and continued to be used by upper-middle-class families. The three artist studios continued to be the home of artists and other distinguished individuals. By contrast, the sophisticated Cheniston Lodge, after being occupied by a succession of wealthy upper-middle-class families, was purchased in 1940 by Kensington Council and used as an air raid precaution store and depot during the Second World War (Murphy, 2010). In the aftermath of the war and throughout the 1950s, there was no potential market for a luxury home of this type. As Rubinstein points out in his study on wealth in Britain, 'millionaires' had in fact virtually disappeared from the UK, and even where they actually existed, they were fewer in number and far less affluent than in the past (Rubinstein, 2006). After the war the Lodge was transformed into the borough's Registrars' office; and in 1981 it was listed for its artistic interest and aesthetic value. Soon afterwards, it was sold to a private company that rented it out as offices until 2009 (Murphy, 2010).

The situation changed drastically in the course of the 1970s, when people started buying flats in the terraces using government policies supporting home ownership.[8] From the 1980s onward, international speculators joined the Cheniston Gardens scene: Arabs, Middle Easterns, Americans, expats from Eastern European countries, who were converting run-down properties in the terraced houses into flats and bedsits as rental investments. Census figures indicate that in 1981 Kensington had the highest proportion of converted flat purchases in London (Hamnett, 1989: 210). With the spread of flat conversions, the number of HMOs started falling. From the electoral register, however, we can estimate that in 1984, 19 terraced houses were still in multiple occupation, while in 2008 their number had decreased to 13.

Current residential patterns

The present look of the terraced houses is quite uneven, despite the uniformity of their Victorian architecture. Whereas some facades have recently been renovated and repointed, others still stand out with a thick blackish coat caused by long-lasting negligence, worsened by dozens of aerial cables hanging along the frontages; window frames, front doors and tiled steps have different styles and colour, and a number of doorbells are of a poor quality with carelessly scribbled labels. Site visits to two HMOs carried out in 2014 revealed living conditions below any acceptable standard, and hardly conceivable in the assumed elite area of W8: cramped bedrooms, some lacking proper windows, with shared toilets and showers arranged on the landings along the communal staircase.

These run-down HMOs were rented out to a low-income population, both on a short- and long-term basis. At No. 9 a number of rooms were occupied by an enclave of Spanish migrants who had been living there for over 20 years. They had low paid jobs, mostly in the caring and service sectors, and one of them acted as an unofficial house caretaker during time off from his job as a night watchman in a nearby hotel. The house's proprietors were two brothers of Maltese origin. When they bought the house in 1953, it was one of the few single family homes left in Cheniston Gardens, occupied by the same family since 1899. They converted it into an HMO and part of their family resided there until 1965. Despite the substantial income provided by the rent for over 65 years, the owners let the building fall into total disrepair until their heirs eventually evicted the tenants and in 2019 put the property on the market as cheap short lets accommodation after upgrading the building according to HMO standards.[9] A few months later two terraced houses (No. 5 and No. 23) were on sale as HMOs.[10] The resurgence of interest in terraced HMOs is confirmed by a general increase in their licenses in RBKC from 2015 to 2019,[11] in connection with a rising demand for sustainable shared rents all over London. Significantly, the real estate listing for No. 23 reads as follows: 'HMOs are popular investment opportunities as they enable investors to enhance yield due to multiple units in one building. Demand for smaller units in Prime Central London has risen significantly due to the changing nature of the employment market. Corporate budgets have been reduced, leading employees to seek small units in central locations'.[12]

No. 17, another of the dilapidated terraced houses, was sold by public auction in 2014 for £4.5 million (Allsop, 2014). It was subsequently converted into 17 luxury studios, which are rented on short lets for £4,500 per month, to a wealthy transnational population. A previous application to re-convert this terraced house into a super-prime single-family property[13] had been rejected by the RBKC on the ground that the amalgamation of already separated units would be against the borough's policy and strategy aiming at resisting 'the loss of existing small, self-contained flats of one or two habitable rooms' that are a 'typical Kensington feature'.[14] From these examples it clearly emerges that the action of the council in terms of planning is steered by the pre-existing use and history of the properties. HMO licensing policies (RBKC, 2011, 2014), on the one hand, and prevention of flats being reverted into single-use homes, on the other, are two faces of an approach to urban planning aimed at preserving affordable living spaces from being swallowed up by the super-rich taking over the neighbourhood.

It is precisely due to their parcelled layout and size that the terraced houses at Cheniston Gardens are not bound to become super-prime properties for the global super-rich. From this point of view, these large terraced houses radically differ from smaller period properties that can be found in other sectors of W8. Smaller properties, which are either self-contained or divided into a small number of units are in fact among the favourite targets of overseas buyers, who then expand the space of their super-prime properties by digging luxury basement extensions (Baldwin, Holroyd and Burrows 2020; Burrows and Knowles 2019: 81–2).

The uneven condition of the terraced houses sharply contrasts with the impeccable finishing of the Apartments, the Studios and the Lodge, which have continuously been the homes of quite affluent residents. For their larger size, the 12 apartments attract wealthy families with children, of the type described by Acorn as 'Metropolitan Money'. The three studio cottages are particularly sought after for their bohemian character (Orme, 2002) by artistically inclined wealthy individuals, from rock stars to fashion photographers, some of them using the cottage as one of their many homes.

Plans to reconvert Cheniston Lodge from offices to its pristine status as a luxury family home started in 2008,[15] when super-prime properties in Kensington were particularly sought after as financial assets by global investors (Burrows and Knowles, 2019), but works were completed only by 2014. Since then, the property has been left unoccupied most of the time, reflecting a trend that is typical of super-rich investors who regard their Kensington properties mainly as assets or transitory places where they nest for just a few months a year. In summer 2019, the property was again on the market at £9,950 million.[16]

Conclusion

The example of Cheniston Gardens shows how the contingent nature of the built environment is subtly intertwined with the present social fabric of the street. Through the analysis of different types of period properties, this chapter has highlighted the manner in which contemporary residential patterns have become entangled with a process of transformation of the built environment that had started already by the end of the Victorian era. The analysis has focused, in particular, on two major long-term shifts that concurred in re-shaping the character of the residential space: on the one hand, the construction of apartment blocks, and on the other hand, the conversion of the terraced houses from single family homes into HMOs, flats and bedsits. These changes brought about an understanding of dwelling in terms of size, which is materially objectified in the coexistence in the street of larger family homes of the size of the apartments together with small bedsits and studios suitable for single persons. Differences in the size of the properties allow for socio-economic disparities among residents, with wealthy families living in the mansion block, the artist studios and the larger flats in the terraced houses, and low-income residents in run-down studios and bedsits.

Overall, this research is an example of how situated localities can be used to explore broader questions in connection with the spatial distribution of the elites in London. It suggests, in particular, that the history of places, and the characteristics of a built environment inherited from the past, play a crucial role in steering the action of the local government with regard to the transformation of the urban residential space. I argue that to fully understand the socio-spatial dynamics of the elite neighbourhoods it is necessary to reassess the scope of analysis, coupling the information provided by statistics and demography with empirical qualitative research in the *longue durée*, aiming at unpacking distinctions within the built environment of specific places.

Notes

1 The research presented in this chapter draws upon previous works (Pulini, 2015, 2019) and on the material collected through interviews, oral history, documentary and historical sources, for ongoing research on the residential and social patterns in W8.

2 nethouseprices.com/house-prices/london/london/oxford%20gardens (accessed 28 October 2021).

3 Documentary sources for the study of Cheniston Gardens have been accessed at the Kensington and Chelsea Local Studies Library. They include the Post Office Directory, Kelly's Directory, Boyle's Fashionable Court and Country Guide, and Electoral Rolls. Online resources have been accessed through the following links: lbhf.maps.arcgis.com/apps/webappviewer/index.html?id=931fa3b3294b4147a518648579b12d4a; www.rbkc.gov.uk/planning/searches/cardarchive/cardarchiveform.asp (accessed 28 October 2021).

4 Headcounts and household estimates for postcodes in England and Wales, www.ons.gov.uk/peoplepopulationandcommunity/population andmigration/populationestimates/datasets/2011censusheadcounts andhouseholdestimatesforpostcodesinenglandandwales, release date: 28 June 2013.

5 http://acorn.caci.co.uk. Differently from *Mosaic*, *Acorn* can be accessed for free on the web in a trial mode.

6 www.zoopla.co.uk/for-sale/property/london/cheniston-gardens/ (accessed 28 October 2021).

7 www.zoopla.co.uk/forsale/details/52265443?search_identifier=037178 30335b1f8d9485d8f239689b4a (accessed 17 December 2014).

8 The 1967 Leasehold Reform Act.
9 RBKC, building control application registered on 11 June 2019, IN/19/03646.
10 www.rightmove.co.uk/houseprices/detailMatching.html?prop=12883 272&sale=84165570&country=england; www.zoopla.co.uk/for-sale/ details/53175934?search_identifier=03717830335b1f8d9485d8f2396 89b4a (accessed 17 December 2014).
11 www.rbkc.gov.uk/sites/default/files/atoms/files/List%20of%20 currently%20licensed%20HMOs_1.p (accessed 17 December 2014.).
12 www.zoopla.co.uk/for-sale/details/53175934?search_identifier=03717 830335b1f8d9485d8f239689b4a (accessed 28 October 2021).
13 A private company, significantly called Midas, had applied for the 'Conversion of existing 20 units to a single family dwelling including rear extension to existing basement level, second floor rear extension and terrace to rear at second floor level' (RBKC, building control, planning application PP/10/02446).
14 This principle was in conformity with the London Plan, 2011 and the RBKC Core Strategy for 2010. It was included in the Consolidated Local Plan of the RBKC for 2015 (RBKC, 2015: 212).
15 Planning permission ref. PP/08/01440; listed building consent ref. LB/08/01441, granted on 14/07/2008.
16 Zoopla: sale/details/52265443?search_identifier=03717830335b1f8d 9485d8f239 (accessed 28 October 2021). This price is a substantial decrease compared to 2018, when the property was marketed at £11 million.

References

Adam, B. (1990). *Time and Social Theory*. Cambridge: Polity.
Adam, B. (1998). *Timescapes of Modernity: The Environment and Invisible Hazards*. London: Routledge.
Allsop (2014). Catalogue of residential auction, 17 December 2014. www. auction.co.uk/residential/home.asp?JP=LDE&A=881&ID=881000023 (accessed 17 December 2014)
Atkinson, R., and Ho, H-K. (2019). Segregation and the super-rich: enclaves, networks and mobilities. In S. Musterd, ed., *Research Handbook on Urban Segregation*. London: Edward Elgar, 289–305.
Atkinson, R., Burrows, R., and Rhodes, D. (2016). Capital city? London's housing market and the 'super rich'. In I. Hay and J. V. Beaverstock, eds, *International Handbook of Wealth and the Super-Rich*. London: Edward Elgar, 225–43.

Atkinson, R., Burrows, R., Glucksberg, L., Ho, H. K., Knowles, C., and Rhodes, D. (2017). Minimum city? The deeper impacts of the super-rich on urban life. In R. Forrest, Y. S. Koh, and B. Wissink, eds, *Cities and the Super-Rich: Real Estate, Elite Practices, and Urban Political Economies*. New York: Palgrave Macmillan, 253–71.

Atkinson, R., Parker, S. and Burrows, R. (2017). Elite formation, power and space in contemporary London. *Theory, Culture and Society*, 34(5–6), 179–200.

Baldwin, S., Holroyd, E., and Burrows, R. (2020). Mapping the subterranean geographies of plutocratic London: luxified troglodytism? www.researchgate.net/publication

Bennett, J. (2014). Gifted places: the inalienable nature of belonging in place. *Environment and Planning D: Society and Space*, 32(4), 658–71.

Blokland, T. (2003). *Urban Bonds: Social Relationships in an Inner City Neighbourhood*. Cambridge: Polity.

Blunt, A. (2008). The 'Skyscraper Settlement': home and residence at Christodora House. *Environment and Planning A*, 40(3), 550–71.

Booth, C. (1891 [1889]). *Descriptive Map of London Poverty*. Maps first published as appendix to *Life and Labour of the People in London* by C. Booth. London and Edinburgh: Williams and Norgate.

Booth, C. (1902). *Life and Labour of the People in London*, Vol. 1. London: Macmillan.

Burrows, R., and Knowles, C. (2019). The 'HAVES' and the 'HAVE YACHTS': socio-spatial struggles in London between the 'Merely Wealthy' and the 'Super-Rich'. *Cultural Politics*, 15(1), 72–87.

Burrows, R., Webber, R., and Atkinson, R. (2017). Welcome to 'Pikettyville'? Mapping London's alpha territories. *Sociological Review*, 65(2), 184–201.

Butler, T., and Lees, L. (2006). Super-gentrification in Barnsbury, London: globalisation and gentrifying global elites at the neighbourhood level. *Transactions of the Institute of British Geographers*, NS 31: 467–87.

Cunningham, N. (2017). Making and mapping Britain's 'new ordinary elite. Urban Geography,On-line First. https://doi.org/10.108 0/02723638.2017.1390721 (accessed July 2021).

Cunningham, N., and Savage, M. (2015). The secret garden? Elite metropolitan geographies in the contemporary UK. *Sociological Review*, 63(2), 321–48.

Cunningham, N., and Savage, M. (2017). An intensifying and elite city. *City*, 21(1), 25–46.

Degen, M. M. (2018). Timescapes of urban change: the temporalities of regenerated streets. *Sociological Review*, 66(5). 1074–92. ISSN: 0038-0261.

Edensor, T. (ed.) (2010). *Geographies of Rhythms: Nature, Place, Mobilities and Bodies*, Aldershot: Ashgate.

Edwards, M. (2016). The housing crisis and London. *City*, 20(2), 222–37.

Glucksberg, L. (2016). A view from the top: unpacking capital flows and foreign investment in prime London. *City*, 20(2), 238–55.

Hamnett, C. (1989). The spatial and social segmentation of the London owner-occupied housing market: an analysis of the flat conversion sector. In M. Breheny, and P. Congdon, eds, *Growth and Change in a Core Region: The Case of South East England*. London: Pion Limited, 203–18.

Hay, I., and Muller, S. (2012). 'That tiny, stratospheric apex that owns most of the world': exploring geographies of the super-rich. *Geographical Research*, 50(1), 75–88.

Ho, H. K., and Atkinson, R. (2017). Looking for big 'fry': the motives and methods of middle-class international property investors. *Urban Studies*, 55(9), 2040–56.

Ingold, T. (1993). The temporality of the landscape. *World Archaeology*, 25(2), 152–74.

Lynch, K. (1972). *What Time is This Place?* Cambridge, MA: MIT Press.

Knowles, C. (2017a). Walking plutocratic London: exploring erotic, phantasmagoric Mayfair. *Social Semiotics*, 27(3), 299–309.

Knowles, C. (2017b). Walking W8 in Manalos. In C. Bates, and A. Rhys Taylor, eds, *Walking Through Social Research*. London: Routledge, 197–202.

MacLeod, G. (2018). The Grenfell Tower atrocity. *City*, 22(4), 460–89.

Marcus, S. (1999). *Apartment Stories*, Berkeley, CA: University of California Press.

Massey, D. (1984). Spatial Divisions of Labour. In P. Hubbard, R. Kitchin, and G. Valentine, eds, *Key Texts in Human Geography*. London: Sage, 83–90.

Massey, D. (2000). Living in Wythenshawe. In I. Borden, J. Kerr, J. Rendell, and A. Pivaro, eds, *The Unknown City: Contesting Architecture and Social Space*, Cambridge, MA and London: The MIT press, 458–75.

McKenzie, L. (2015). *Getting By: Estate, Class and Culture in Austerity Britain*. Bristol: Policy Press.

Minton, A. (2017). *Big Capital: Who is London for?* London: Penguin.

Murphy, K. (2010). *Cheniston Lodge, Heritage Appraisal*. Report commissioned by Avida Ltd, London.

NOMIS (2017). Official labour market statistics, Office for National Statistics, local output area E00014063. www.nomisweb.co.uk/reports/localarea?search (accessed April 2017).

Orme, K. (2002). Artists' Studios Supplementary Planning Guidance, The Royal Borough of Kensington and Chelsea, www.rbkc.gov.uk/wamdocs/SPG%20–%20artists%20studios.pdf (accessed July 2021).

Pulini, I. (2015). Change and continuity in a central London street (Masters Dissertation in Material and Visual Culture UCL – University College London).

Pulini, I. (2019). Change and continuity in a central London street. In C. Tilley, ed., *London's Urban Landscape: Another Way of Telling*. London: UCL Press, 67–116.

RBKC (2011). *Houses in Multiple Occupation. Guide to Flats in Multiple Occupation and Shared Houses* Version 1. 01/08/11 www.rbkc.gov.uk/pdf/ final%20HMOstds-FMO%20and%20shared%20houses%20version%20 010811.pdf (accessed July 2021).

RBKC (2014). *HMO Standards*. www.rbkc.gov.uk/housing/living-healthy-homes/houses-multiple-occupation/hmo-standards (accessed 14 March 2014)

RBKC (2015). *Royal Borough of Kensington and Chelsea: Consolidated Local Plan*. July 2015.

Rubinstein, W. D. (2006). *Men of Property: The Very Wealthy in Britain Since the Industrial Revolution*, 2nd edn. London: The Social Affairs Unit.

Survey of London (1986). Kensington High Street, south side: Wright's Lane to Earl's Court Road. Survey of London, Vol. 42: *Kensington Square to Earl's Court*: 99–116.

Tilley, C. (2017). *Landscape in the Long Dureé: A History and Theory of Pebbles in a Pebbled Heathland Landscape*. London: UCL Press.

Tilley, C. (ed.) (2019). *London's Urban Landscape: Another Way of Telling*, London: UCL Press.

Webber, R., and Burrows, R. (2016). Life in an alpha territory: discontinuity and conflict in an elite London 'village'. *Urban Studies*, 53(15), 3139–54.

White, J. (2003). *Rothschild Buildings: Life in an East-End Tenement Block 1887–1920*. London: Pimlico.

8

Discrimination in 'receptive cities'? Voices from Brighton and Bologna

Caterina Mazzilli

Brighton and Bologna are two cities that have traditionally had 'receptive' reputations. This chapter compares these popular narratives with the perceptions that Black and Ethnic Minorities (BMEs) in Brighton, and foreign residents[1] in Bologna, have about the city where they live, its local government, and wider community. Several studies have highlighted that ethnic minorities and/or migrants are often amongst the most vulnerable members of society (McLean et al., 2003; Wrench, 2004; Cohen, 2009; Tyler, 2013). For instance, the outcome of a 2017 UK government report revealed that ethnicity is a determinant factor in predicting people's quality of life (Bulman, 2017).[2] This piece sheds light on BMEs/foreigners' accounts of their city's character.

This analysis stems from a wider study on how cities have constructed and established public narratives of receptiveness and the degree to which their respective narratives include or exclude ethnic diversity. It draws on eight months of qualitative field research to gauge how narratives produced from 'above' and from 'below' interact and/or contrast. This includes 58 in-depth semi-structured interviews with representatives of the local government and members of migrants' grassroots associations, plus participant observations at public events held explicitly to foster diversity in the local community. The final comparison of the two cities intends to separate place-specific from reproducible elements. After an overview of the research setting and a discussion of the theoretical concepts guiding the study, the empirical section reports the interviewees' perspective on the cities' character and their lived experiences. The conclusion argues that Brighton and Bologna's liberal-left leaning narrative ultimately obscures our understanding of marginalised experiences.

As in the case of Kensington (chapter 7), dominant place-narratives can obfuscate the recognition of vulnerable or marginalised groups. Unequal levels of income, education, or health often follow spatial divisions. Looking at the neighbourhood and at the city level, both Pulini (chapter 7) and I concentrate on the situated inequalities of urban space. Whilst centring overarching representations of space in our work, we have made an active effort to avoid the 'claims to universality' characterising many studies of inequality 'which assume rather than explore' (see Part II editorial introduction).

Two 'receptive cities'

Bologna is the capital of the northern Italian Emilia-Romagna region, and is the seventh largest city in the country, with 387,044 inhabitants (Comune di Bologna, 2016) living in the city proper, and around 1 million in its greater area. Of those living within the city, in February 2016[3] foreign-born residents accounted for 15.24 per cent (Comune di Bologna, 2016). The town is home to the oldest university in Europe, established in 1088, around which the city has built a considerable part of its prestige, and which attracts both national and international students. This is not the only reason why it is considered a city of culture: unions and associations have been, more than anywhere else in the country, a key feature of the city's active grassroots environment. The public image of Bologna is thus tightly connected both to the 'high-brow' side of culture, represented by the ancient institution of its Alma Mater, and to the 'counterculture' scene, symbolised by social centres.

Emilia-Romagna has long been an industrial area, which also makes Bologna well known for its manufacturing production. The high number of industrial workers is one of the elements explaining the historically deeply rooted presence of the Communist Party and, more generally, the left-wing allegiance of the city, rooted in the local Resistance against the Nazi-fascist regime in the Second World War. The Bologna Urban Centre study (2013) on local city branding describes the city as 'caring and welcoming', 'young and open-minded', 'a workshop of innovation', and as a place 'of culture and creativity'. This mix of factors has, over time, constituted the local 'sense of place' (Campelo et al., 2014). Whether connected to culture, politics, or tourism, the narrative of Bologna as 'welcoming' and 'open' is indeed well known and pervasive from the institutional to the everyday level.

Brighton is located in East Sussex, on the south coast of England, and is the forty-second most populous district in the country (Office for National Statistics, 2018) with a population of 273,369 (Brighton and Hove City Council, 2011).[4] According to the 2011 Census (Brighton and Hove City Council, 2011), 16 per cent of the local population is estimated to be non-UK born, while BME residents count for 19.5 per cent. Brighton, like Bologna, is a popular student city, both thanks to the two local universities – the University of Sussex and the University of Brighton – and to language students. What is locally well established, however, is Brighton's reputation as a holiday and party town, a reputation which it has held from the mid-eighteenth century. This image lies at the very heart of the connotation of the town as an artists' hotspot but also as home to the LGBTQ+ community. Connections to the British colonial past emerge in snippets, such as the town's iconic landmark, the Royal Pavilion, whose style resembles nineteenth-century Indian palaces. In connection to this, Brighton's economy is heavily based on tourism, retail, and the service sector, with the three often merging. The art-loving, flamboyant, and – not to be forgotten – green 'own character' (Massey, 1991) for which this place is most renowned is clearly visible in the central Laines and North Laine areas, which feature a series of vintage shops and independent vegan cafés. In 2018 Brighton was crowned the 'most hipster city' in the world (Dickinson, 2018).[5]

The two cities are both medium-sized within their respective countries, with crucial similarities in their demographics. Both have a significant presence of students and young people, strongly focus on culture, and identify with a political line opposing conservatism. All in all, the dominant image of both cities conveys an idea of openness, inclusion, and receptiveness.

Urban representation, city narratives, and diversity

The first area many might associate with urban representation is mapping. But even this activity, as objective as it seems, involves the ongoing reconfiguration of competing narratives (Dawes, 2014: 227) establishing what is worth representing and what can be omitted. We have access to a representation of the urban space that is necessarily partial and mediated by several factors, at the core of which lies power (Stokowski, 2002). Jansson (2003) expands on this, identifying an oppositional narrative in every context, regardless of the strength of the dominant one. Wherever there is power there is also resistance, thus alternative or oppositional narratives always have the possibility of challenging that mainstream perspective.

Stokowski (2002: 372) argues that 'much of what a person knows about places is initially mediated by others', through oral or written narratives. However, this process is not mono-directional: people do not only teach others the qualities of a certain place, but also 'actively create meaningful places through conversation and interaction' (Stokowski, 2002: 372). Consequently, conversations and every other rhetorical device that follows under the category of 'narrative' are crucial in giving significance to a place. Stokowski (2002) refers to the increasing legitimacy that narratives achieve in the public discourse when repeated for a consistent period – and especially if fostered by individuals in positions of authority, to the point of no longer being questioned. At this stage, if place-narratives are not contested, it means that the identity or character (Massey, 1991) of the place emerging from them is not contested either, becoming the 'truth' about it. However, place-narratives are so powerful not only because they construct meanings, but also – and even more so – because they can 'manipulate [meanings and feelings connected to a place] towards desired (individual or collective) ends' (Stokowski, 2002: 374).

With respect to this, Johnstone (1990) explains that, as our sense of place and community is rooted in narration, so is the framing of issues and needs that affect a citizenry. Above all, this informs the best-suited policies to address those issues. Analysing the impact of power on narratives can allow us to look at social inclusion/exclusion dynamics – and therefore inequality – from a new perspective. Even though the literature on narratives is rich (Goodin, 1996; Papillon, 2002; Sainsbury, 2012; Wodak, 2008) it actually seems to ignore the role of marginalised groups in place-narrative production. Yet the city is much more than just the image publicised by the local government. It is contested, multiple, and shifting. Amin (2006: 1012) observes that: 'Contemporary cities do not spring to mind as the sites of community and wellbeing. For the vast majority of people, cities are polluted, unhealthy, tiring, overwhelming, confusing, alienating.' BMEs/foreigners' narratives are relevant because, in this case, they oppose many points of the ones fostered by local government. While the former are not publicly known, the latter have become established – and thus, a truth – thanks to the political power of their authors.

The recent right-wing drift of many European and world countries has ignited feelings of nationalism, racism, and xenophobia, which can have dangerous effects at both the individual and the wider societal/political level, together with the introduction of more and more restrictive immigration laws. Yet, many scholars, such as Castañeda (2018), argue that, in a context of increasing nationalism, racism, and xenophobia, cities that hold a reputation for being accepting of diversity can be a model, which others can follow to resist these hostile trends. This model is vital, but equally important is the consideration of otherwise often marginal narratives, with the ultimate aim of making these cities even more receptive.

In order to unpack the effects generated by Brighton and Bologna's narratives on the population, it is essential to start from the notion of *diversity*. In both cities, diversity emerges as the main – although not unique – factor on which local receptiveness is built (Mazzilli, 2020). Nevertheless, this concept has a variety of meanings (Berg and Sigona, 2013): it can be framed as a social fact – referring to demographics, as policies, or as a narrative – when it becomes the symbol of a city (Hadj-Abdou, 2014). Well known for being the home of the largest Pride festival in Britain (Pride Brighton, 2018) and of several groups fighting for LGBTQ+ rights, the lines along which diversity is constructed in Brighton are gender and sexuality, together with an unconventional lifestyle. Bologna, instead, with its historical role as leader of the Italian Left and the oldest university in Europe, has a reputation of political activism, the axes along which diversity is constructed.

Aligned with Hadj-Abdou's (2014) work, my findings demonstrate that diversity as a narrative does not necessarily coincide with an ethnically diverse demographic composition. According to Brighton and Hove City Council (2014) indeed, 'Other White[6] 'is the most dominant category among BME groups, at 7.1 per cent. The other minority ethnic groups recorded in the city are Asian/Asian British

(4.1 per cent), Mixed/Multiple Ethnic Group (3.8 per cent), White Irish (1.7 per cent), Black/African/Caribbean/Black British (1.5 per cent), and Arab (0.8 per cent). In total, BMEs comprise 19.5 per cent of Brighton residents – but this does not mean that the local population *looks* diverse. The same goes for Bologna. According to an elaboration of the Italian Institute for Statistics' data (Tuttitalia. it, 2018), the ten most numerous nationalities represented in the city are: Romanian (9,020 residents), Filipino (5,282), Bangladeshi (5,120), Moldovan (4,220), Moroccan (4,037), Pakistani (3,745), Ukrainian (3,673), Chinese (3,476), Albanian (2,656), and Sri Lankan (1,418). Demographically, then, both cities appear 'very white', as a number of BME respondents[7] pointed out in the interviews: in Brighton, the percentage of 'visibly different' (Amin, 2010) BMEs is indeed quite low (in contrast with other cities in England), while in Bologna many among the most represented nationalities, such as Romanians, Moldovans, and Albanians, can pass as white Italians.

Visibility and invisibility in narratives of 'diversity'

As Johnstone (1990) argues, it is not only our sense of place and community that is rooted in such narration. With their force, narratives can also foster specific ideas about who 'fits in' the local environment, depending on their adherence to the sense of place (see Koopmans and Statham, 1999) – or, in this case, the local understanding of diversity. The interviews with members of BMEs/ foreigners' grassroots associations[8] sought to identify their narratives about the city, the degree to which they converged or diverged from the mainstream, and how they felt they were considered as 'fitting in' to the local context by the dominant majority. Similar to the image fostered by the interviews with local government, BMEs/ foreigner interviewees attributed their city's receptive character to its diversity. However, the meaning of diversity was different from its dominant interpretation. This does not mean that grassroots narratives radically diverged from the institutional ones; rather, they built on the institutional narratives to uncover their contradictions.

In connection to their own identity, both BMEs and foreigners attributed a much higher importance to diversity as demographics (Berg and Sigona, 2013) than the representatives of local government.

For instance, in contrast with the prominence ascribed to gender and sexuality by the dominant branding of the city (Landry, 2012), BMEs' framing of Brighton's diversity focused on ethnicity and religion. Respondent 5 [BH[9]/BMEs], a middle-aged man originally from Pakistan and part of a religious association, argued that diversity in Brighton is different from anywhere else in Britain, because:

> You can have diversity or so-called diversity in another town but what diversity means in another town is that you have, for example, a white large indigenous community and then you have a single foreign community [...] But when it comes to Brighton, yeah, it's not just that; it's quite different. There is obviously the white indigenous community but then you have white people, [people] from Africa and the Caribbean and [the] West Indies, also Muslims from all over the world are here, from the Middle East, as well as Asian and South Asian countries, and then you have Coptic Christians ... So there is a real true diversity in Brighton that you don't really find in many other towns and cities.

The respondents were well acquainted with the institutional narratives on the town as renowned 'for its culture of tolerance' (Brighton and Hove City Council, 2014: 3) and generally referred to it as a matter of fact. However, the more the questions narrowed down to their life experiences in the city, the more they responded critically. On the one side, they limited the scope of Brighton's tolerance to certain sections of the citizenry. A man of Caribbean heritage in his seventies, involved in the support of black peoples' rights, articulated his feelings by saying: '[Brighton] it's welcoming and it's tolerant [...] because certain sections of the community are tolerant to each other; [they're] not necessarily tolerant to other people outside' [Respondent 2 BH/BMEs]. He explained that he referred to the acceptance Brightonians have for people's gender and sexuality and their freedom to express it. Yet he did not experience the same degree of openness towards expressions of someone's religion or ethnicity.

Similarly, in Bologna the interviewees emphasised the multicultural composition of the city, which had been less touched upon by representatives of the local government. Interviewees classified as 'foreigners' stressed the high number of nationalities, counting 140 different groups, but complained that, while local government's attention focuses on asylum seekers, there are many other long-settled groups that are not equally visible. However, the contrast between the institutional and grassroots image in Bologna was less clear-cut than in Brighton. I suggest that this might depend on the different prominence of the notion of ethnicity, part and parcel of the British political language but still not normalised in the Italian one. In addition, asylum has recently become one of the hot topics in the Italian media and political agenda alike. In Bologna, the crucial role politics has in the city's narrative can at least partially explain the attention paid to asylum seekers by local governments. The identities deemed legitimate – and almost quintessential to the place – in Brighton are thus the ones corresponding to a diversity of gender and sexuality, while in Bologna they correspond to a diversity as framed alongside culture and political allegiance. BMEs/foreign residents not complying with this image can then be easily ignored. But overlooking their presence might also mean sidelining the discrimination and racism experienced by them.

Is there discrimination in 'receptive cities'?

Participants' accounts of discrimination at the institutional and street level in both cities were quite ambiguous: most of the time they were accompanied by their denial or by an acknowledgement of the blame on migrants for the current urban *degrado*[10] and lack of safety. Several scholars have examined the effect of stigma on marginalised categories (Goffman, 1990; Lamont and Fleming, 2005; Tyler and Slater, 2018), including migrants (Moroşanu and Fox, 2013), uncovering the possible rationale behind their denial of experienced discrimination (Fox, Moroşanu, and Szilassy, 2015). While a few Brightonians openly denounced both institutional and street-level racism, the majority did not address it. When freely talking about their daily life and their interaction with the local white population and/or authorities, they frequently provided examples of discriminatory behaviours and verbal assaults addressed to them. Yet, when directly asked if they had ever been subjects of hate crime and/or racist behaviour, they tended to say no. On the contrary, that was usually the moment when they stressed how good their local institutions/fellow residents were or when they undermined the legitimacy of complaints about racism in the city. This happened

in both Brighton and Bologna. For example, Respondent 12 [BO/
foreigners], a man from Pakistani origin involved in a union supporting migrants' work rights, clarified that:'If a person doesn't
know you, perhaps on the street, or in a café, or in any place, it's
possible to hear some racism. But not in general. Me, I don't feel
it [...] Yes, there is racism, there is racism, but it's not [...] that
every person tells you "Oh, you are a foreigner, go out of the
country." No, I don't feel it.' The quote strongly resembles the
declaration of Respondent 8 [BH/BMEs], a young man of Bangladeshi
heritage involved in a multicultural group, who argued: 'Is there
racism? Might be, might not. But I myself didn't find any [...] that's
why I don't have any evidence about [it]. I believe sometimes it can
be even [a] misunderstanding.' In addition to this, individuals commonly emphasised personal skills, achievements, and wealth when
discussing their position within the receiving society (Wimmer, 2008;
Lentin and Titley, 2011). For instance, a middle-aged woman,
originally from Iran, talked at length about her family wealth, her
higher education, and her successful business, differentiating her
migration from the so-called 'refugee crisis' of 2015. This account
was very interesting, especially in connection to the stories of other
participants. In particular, a woman from Eastern Europe, part of
a cultural association fostering her country's traditions, argued indeed
that'Bologna is very political. If you are a certain type of foreigner,
of migrant, you are welcome, otherwise you are not' [Respondent
6 BO/foreigners]. She felt that the positive image of Bologna as a
politically progressive city, which is open to and supportive of asylum
seekers, clashes with the perception of many migrant groups that
have settled in the city long enough not to need emergency assistance
but who are still not considered integral part of the citizenry by
white Italians.

Conclusion

In this chapter, I have described how narratives of urban representation influence inequalities, based on the lived experiences of BMEs/
foreigners in two allegedly receptive cities. In conjunction with chapter
7, I have treated inequality as situated: a product of a historical
and social context. In comparison with the emphasis representatives

of the local government put on gender and sexuality in Brighton, and on culture and political allegiance in Bologna (Mazzilli, 2019), BMEs/foreigners stressed the relevance of ethnicity when defining the local sense of place (Campelo et al., 2014). According to BMEs/ foreigners, diversity is not only important because it is a symbol, but also – and primarily – as demographic (Berg and Sigona, 2013). Only the most politically engaged individuals in Brighton were explicit about both the racial harassment received on the streets and institutional racism. The majority of the participants instead shared positive responses about local policies for social inclusion, social services functioning, and/or other residents' behaviour towards them. In Bologna, too, respondents classified as foreigners gave the same answers as most of Brighton's BME interviewees. Their accounts were not as enthusiastic, but generally positive, especially when comparing Bologna to other Italian cities. However, episodes of discrimination and racism were not absent in their stories – rather, they were hidden. Instead of addressing racism directly, many participants hinted at it, always speaking in general terms and denying any personal experience. The emerging narrative is therefore a criticism of both cities' selective tolerance concealed under an a-critical positive image of the place. Drawing from the literature (Fox, Moroşanu, and Szilassy, 2015; Lentin and Titley, 2011), I posit the reasons behind this behaviour can be manifold: first, the desire to fit in, and to look like a 'good migrant' who is not ungrateful, and secondly finding genuine comfort in living in a place that is friendlier than average.

Brighton's and Bologna's liberal-left leaning narrative obfuscates the recognition of certain groups' experiences. As was the case for Kensington in chapter 7 with its reputation as an elite neighbourhood, this can overlook the experience and presence of poorer groups living in the same space. In this way, both places involve exclusion and the negotiation of identity in a space where the experience of marginalised residents 'do not exist'. However, we have to remember that Brighton and Bologna *do* remain positive examples within their respective national panorama. An interesting development of this study could interrogate dominant representations of place in other urban realities that do not hold such an image of receptiveness, to better understand how different forms of urban representations are connected to marginality.

Notes

1 The British Census defines as 'Black and Ethnic Minorities' individuals whose ethnicity is 'other than white British' (Institute of Race Relations, 2017). 'Foreigners' is generically used in both official and colloquial Italian to indicate a person with a migration background. I'm personally wary of both classifications but I use it to report the terminology encountered in documents and interviews.

2 According to research, BMEs are twice as likely to be unemployed than their white British counterparts. Black and Asian people and other ethnic groups are also disproportionately likely to be on a low income (Bulman, 2017).

3 Unless otherwise specified, the demographic data refer to 2016, when I conducted my fieldwork.

4 At the time of writing the 2011 Census was the most recent complete report on Brighton's population. The next one was due to take place in 2021.

5 Interestingly, although perhaps less evidently, Brighton also has the highest rate of homelessness outside London, with 1 in 69 people sleeping rough (*The Argus*, 2016). Three areas within the city, East Brighton (particularly St. James' Street and Eastern Road), plus 'Queen's Park, and Moulsecoomb and Bevendean, have also been ranked in the top 10 per cent of national deprivation' (*Hastings and St. Leonard's Observer*, 2016). These figures not only show some of the many faces of the city, but also problematise its narrative of openness, receptiveness, and harmony.

6 Despite being personally wary of this classification, in this chapter I use the same breakdown of ethnic groups used in the UK Census to make the connection with governmental data more straightforward.

7 In contrast, only two respondents from the local government pointed this out.

8 I selected only members of grassroots associations who had migrated during their life and had been living in the destination country for more than ten years, to make sure they were well acquainted with the local government functioning.

9 BH stands for Brighton and Hove; BO stands for Bologna.

10 *Degrado* is an Italian word that translates as disrepair, neglect and/or degeneration. I decided to use the Italian word instead of a translation because it feels to me more complete and suitable for its inherent meaning: a mix of dirt, abandon, and disrespectful behaviours ranging from loud noise to petty crime and lack of public safety.

References

Amin, A. (2006). The good city. *Urban Studies*, 43(5–6), 1009–23.

Amin, A. (2010). The remainders of race. *Theory, Culture and Society*, 27(1), 1–23.

The Argus (2016). One in 69 people in Brighton and Hove is homeless.

Berg, M. L., and Sigona, N. (2013). Ethnography, diversity and urban space. *Identities*, 20(4), 347–60.

Bologna Urban Centre (2013). *É Bologna. Progetto City Branding. City Branding Project*. Bologna: I Quaderni.

Brighton and Hove City Council (2011). 2011 Census Briefing. www.brightonhove.gov.uk/content/community-and-life-events/census-2011 (accessed 3 May 2021).

Brighton and Hove City Council, Corporate Policy and Research Team (compiled by) (2014). City Snapshot – Report of Statistics. www.bhconnected.org.uk/sites/bhconnected/files/City%20Snapshot%20 Report%20of%20Statistics%202014%202.pdf (accessed 3 May 2021).

Bulman, M. (2017). Racial inequality in the UK: the appalling reality of how a Briton's ethnicity affects their chances of a good life. *Independent*.

Campelo, A., Aitken, R., Thyne, M., and Gnoth, J. (2014). Sense of place: the importance for destination branding. *Journal of Travel Research*, 53(2), 54–166.

Castañeda, E. (2018). *A Place to Call Home. Immigrant Exclusion and Urban Belonging in New York, Paris, and Barcelona*. Redwood City, CA: Stanford University Press.

Cohen, E. F. (2009). *Semi-citizenship in Democratic Politics*. Cambridge: Cambridge University Press.

Comune di Bologna (2016), Cittadini stranieri a Bologna. Le tendenze www.comune.bologna.it/iperbole/piancont/Stranieri/StudiStranieri/ Stranieri_aBo/2017/Stranieri_2016_12.pdf (accessed 3 May 2021).

Dawes, S. (2014). Representing the city: non-representation, digital archives and megacity phenomena. *Theory, Culture and Society*, 3(7–8), 227–38.

Dickinson, G. (2018). Is Brighton really the world's most hipster city? *Telegraph*.

Fox, J. E., Moroşanu, L., and Szilassy, E. (2015). Denying discrimination: status, 'race', and the whitening of Britain's new Europeans. *Journal of Ethnic and Migration Studies*, 41(5), 729–48.

Goffman, E. (1990). *Stigma: Notes on the Management of Spoiled Identity*. London: Penguin.

Goodin, R. E. (1996). Inclusion and exclusion. *European Journal of Sociology/ Archives Européennes de Sociologie*, 37(2), 343–71.

Hadj-Abdou, L. (2014). Immigrant integration and the economic competitiveness agenda: a comparison of Dublin and Vienna. *Journal of Ethnic and Migration Studies*, 40(12), 1875–94.

Hastings and St. Leonard's Observer (2016). Levels of deprivation across Sussex revealed by charity report.

Institute of Race Relations (2003). Definitions. www.irr.org.uk/research/statistics/definitions/ (accessed 4 May 2021).

Jansson, A. (2003). The negotiated city image: symbolic reproduction and change through urban consumption. *Urban Studies*, 40(3), 463–79.

Johnstone, B. (1990). *Stories, Community, and Place: Narratives from Middle America*. Bloomington, IN: Indiana University Press.

Koopmans, R., and Statham, P. (1999). Ethnic and civic conceptions of nationhood and the differential success of the extreme right in Germany and Italy. *How Social Movements Matter*, 10, 225–52.

Lamont, M., and Fleming, C. M. (2005). Everyday antiracism: competence and religion in the cultural repertoire of the African American elite. *Du Bois Review: Social Science Research on Race*, 2(1), 29–43.

Landry, C. (2012). *The Creative City: A Toolkit for Urban Innovator*. London: Earthscan.

Lentin, A., and Titley, G. (2011). *The Crises of Multiculturalism: Racism in a Neoliberal Age*. London: Zed Books.

Massey, D. (1991). A global sense of place. *Marxism Today*, 38(1), 1–5.

Mazzilli, C. (2019). Receptive cities? Institutional narratives of migrants' integration and migrants' own perceptions of receptiveness in Brighton and Bologna (PhD Thesis, University of Sussex).

Mazzilli, C. (2020). 'The happiest city in England': Brighton's narratives of diversity between 'success stories' and sidelined issues. *Ethnic and Racial Studies*, 1–19.

Mclean, C., Campbell, C., and Cornish, F. (2003). African-Caribbean interactions with mental health services in the UK: experiences and expectations of exclusion as (re)productive of health inequalities. *Social Science and Medicine*, 56(3), 657–69.

Moroşanu, L., and Fox, J. E. (2013). 'No smoke without fire': strategies of coping with stigmatised migrant identities. *Ethnicities*, 13(4), 438–56.

Office for National Statistics (2018). Population estimates for the UK, England and Wales, Scotland and Northern Ireland: mid-2017. www.ons.gov.uk/peoplepopulationandcommunity/populationandmigration/populationestimates/bulletins/annualmidyearpopulationestimates/mid2017 (accessed 4 May 2021).

Papillon, M. (2002). *Immigration, Diversity and Social Inclusion in Canada's Cities*. Ottawa: Canadian Policy Research Networks.

Pride Brighton (2018). 'About'. www.brighton-pride.org/pride-festival/ (accessed 4 May 2021).

Sainsbury, D. (2012), *Welfare States and Immigrant Rights: The Politics of Inclusion and Exclusion*. Oxford: Oxford University Press.

Stokowski, P. A. (2002). Languages of place and discourses of power: constructing new senses of place. *Journal of Leisure Research*, 34(4), 368–82.

Tuttitalia.it. (2018). Cittadini stranieri a Bologna – 2016. www.tuttitalia.it/emilia-romagna/provincia-di-bologna/statistiche/cittadini-stranieri-2016/ (accessed 4 May 2021).

Tyler, I. (2013). *Revolting subjects: Social Abjection and Resistance in Neoliberal Britain*. London: Zed Books.

Tyler, I., and Slater, T. (2018). Rethinking the sociology of stigma. *The Sociological Review Monographs 2*, 66(4), 721–43.

Wimmer, A. (2008). Elementary strategies of ethnic boundary making. *Ethnic and Racial Studies*, 31(6), 1025–55.

Wodak, R. (2008). 'Us' and 'them': inclusion and exclusion – discrimination via discourse. In G. Delanty, R. Wodak, and P. Jones, eds, *Identity, Belonging and Migration*. Oxford: Oxford University Press, 54–77.

Wrench, J. (2004). Trade union responses to immigrants and ethnic inequality in Denmark and the UK: the context of consensus and conflict. *European Journal of Industrial Relations*, 10(1), 7–30.

Part III

Interrelated inequalities

Editors' introduction: relations of inequality
(never in isolation)

In a context of intensifying economic and political disparity, this book presupposes that inequalities are historical and geographical *structures*, which implicate the past in the present and the actions of the rich and privileged in the situation of the poor and marginalised. As C. Wright Mills argued over half a century ago, 'the accumulation of advantages at the very top parallels the vicious cycle of poverty at the very bottom' (2000: 111) and we therefore make the case that research on wealth and poverty needs to be brought into conversation. There is a danger that research focusing on describing elites independent of wider political-economic concerns becomes merely a taxonomic exercise that effectively describes the accumulation of privilege, but 'risks repeating the elite fantasy that their rising fortunes are not interdependent with the dire straits of the lower orders; that, to paraphrase Mario Tronti, capitalists have at last emancipated themselves from workers' (referenced in Toscano and Woodcock, 2015: 513). Research focused purely on describing the lives of the impoverished isolated from wealth and its creation, at best, only tells a partial story and, at worst, risks placing the blame for poverty with those experiencing it. When developing independent concepts for advantaged and disadvantaged communities, social scientists risk falling into the trap of 'reserv[ing] structure for poverty, and culture and agency for elites' (Cousin et al., 2018: 277). Rather than a passive role for the poor, or a moralising tale of individual failings for the rich, the task for social scientists is to situate 'the other half', rich or poor, within the production and reproduction of wider structures that generate contemporary inequalities, including global legacies of colonialism, gendered social reproduction, and processes of racial capitalism (Bhambra, 2007).

One clear example of the connection between the accumulation of wealth and the exploitation of the disadvantaged is the financialisation of households, a pattern especially evident in the Global North. The 2007/2008 financial crisis – which itself was intersected by racist, gendered, and classist histories (Moten, 2013) – was 'precipitated by housing debts among the poorest US workers [and was therefore] directly related to the financialisation of personal income, mostly expenditure on housing but also on education, health, pensions and insurance' (Lapavitsas, 2012: 15). Households have themselves become sites of profit-making as a consequence of stagnating workers' wages, expanding credit systems, and the withdrawal of previously public provisions – such as education, health and housing – which are now increasingly only accessible through debt. What Lapavitsas describes as 'financial expropriation' captures a process of 'extracting financial profit directly out of the personal income of workers and others' (Lapavitsas, 2012: 15), clearly linking financialisation to the processes of capital accumulation. Thus we can connect, for instance, 'the astronomic house prices of London to the people forced to live on the streets, and bonuses in the city to individuals borrowing on high interest credit cards to make ends meet' (Toscano and Woodcock, 2015: 518). In sum, rather than being driven by isolated individuals, inequalities are produced, embedded, and maintained in ways that are structural, situated, and *interrelated*.

The case studies in the following four chapters are interrelated because they share common structures of understanding, albeit at different 'ends' of society. For example, the notion that 'you get what you deserve' either through working hard or being work-shy is a prominent norm in contemporary capitalist-individualistic societies, where ideas of meritocracy are widespread. As highlighted by chapters 9 and 10, a common framing of *deservedness* demonstrates how the parallel experiences of rich and poor are interrelated. While the rich are celebrated for their dynamism and innovation (which they are invariably considered to have developed under their own merit), refugees and asylum seekers who overcome enormous obstacles in order to make a better life for themselves and their families must fit particular criteria, as either passive victims or entrepreneurial, depending on context, to be deemed deserving.

Similarly, in chapters 11 and 12, it is shown how the wealthy can more easily cross borders in search of opportunities, while asylum seekers and less wealthy migrants in search of safety and opportunity under international law, are denied these freedoms by securitised, classed, and racialised borders. Kunz and Artero illustrate the way that differential inclusion is a key mechanism that shapes experiences of border crossing, comfort and a 'range of belongings' (chapter 12) for both rich and poor migrants. It is only by placing these examples of migration in parallel that we can understand such double standards that perpetuate inequalities.

References

Bhambra, G. (2007). *Rethinking Modernity: Postcolonialism and the Sociological Imagination*. Basingstoke: Palgrave Macmillan.

Cousin, B., Khan, S., and Mears, A. (2018). Theoretical and methodological pathways for research on elites, *Socio-Economic Review*, 16(2), 225–49.

Lapavitsas, C. (2012). Financialised capitalism: crisis and financial expropriation. In C. Lapavitsas, ed., *Financialisation in Crisis*. Leiden: Brill, 114–48.

Moten, F. (2013). The subprime and the beautiful. *African Identities*, 11(2), 237–45.

Toscano, A., and Woodcock, J. (2015). Spectres of Marxism: a comment on Mike Savage's market model of class difference. *The Sociological Review*, 63, 512–23.

Wright-Mills, C. (2000). *The Sociological Imagination*. Oxford: Oxford University Press.

9

The *Sunday Times* Rich List and the myth of the self-made man

Elisabeth Schimpfössl and Timothy Monteath

Introduction: a 'new wave of self-made billionaires'

'Britain has been transformed into a country where the self-made can succeed [...] today 94% of those in the Rich List are self-made entrepreneurs', wrote Robert Watts, the compiler of the 30th edition of *The Sunday Times* Rich List, an annually compiled catalogue of the 1000 richest people in the UK. Watts (2018) explained this 2018 figure of 94 per cent – compared to 43 per cent in 1989 when the Rich List was first published – as a 'wave of new self-made entre-preneurs' who have built their own fortunes, many of whom stem from 'humble backgrounds'. 'Today the self-made are running the show' because, as Watts claimed (2019: 10), it is them who are prepared to 'take the risk of starting their own business, put in mammoth hours and become wealthy by providing goods and services that people want to buy'.

We challenge *The Sunday Times* Rich List figure that 94 per cent of their 2018 entries were 'self-made' and consider this to be a purely ideological assertion. To back up our claim, we carried out an inquiry into the social backgrounds of the top fifth (203) of the 2018 Rich List.[1] In 2018, the cut needed to make it onto the list stood at a minimum of £110 million and there was a record number of 147 billionaires. Combined, their fortunes added up to £724 billion, a figure which had risen by 10 per cent from 2017, when their collective wealth was £658 billion. Our aim was to find out where those who were included came from, what might have facili-tated their business activities, and what privileges they might have enjoyed. Along the way we ponder how and why being self-made is such an unquestioned and powerful claim.

Despite their apparent distance, it is this overarching understanding of deservedness that demonstrates the interrelation between the Rich List and refugees. In chapter 10, Maestri and Monforte ask what it takes for post-2015 refugees in Europe to be judged as worthy of support in the eyes of volunteers and humanitarian organisations. While refugees demonstrate deservedness through victimhood or entrepreneurialism, when it comes to the 'self-made' super-rich, deservedness is typically associated with the latter, couched in terms of individual merit, agency, achievement and risk taking.

Researching the Rich List

We collected data on the top 203 entries, denoting the ranking of either individual or family wealth. A focus on the richest 20 per cent may well mean losing out on potentially 'truly' self-made people and skew the database towards the more privileged; however, the further down the list, the thinner the publicly available information tends to become.

The Rich List supplement included a section where the compilers present their methodology. These 'rules of engagement' explained how estimations about wealth were gathered and assessed (Watts 2018). However, they stop short of providing definitions of what it actually means to be 'self-made' or of 'humble background', terms they use throughout. Hence, we came up with our own categories to explore this question in more detail. From our perspective, the following parameters are, in descending order, incompatible with the idea of being self-made (see also Freund, 2016; Freund and Oliver, 2016: 8):

First, there is a clash between a claim to being self-made and having been born into the nobility. We therefore cross-referenced people whose names appear on the Burke's Peerage (Burke's Peerage Foundation, 2003), a genealogical encyclopaedia of people with aristocratic titles, among them peerage, baronetage, knightage and landed gentry. We found the names of 18 per cent of our UK sample listed here. Unless their noble standing is widely known, we were not able to confirm noble backgrounds of those born and raised outside the UK, as there are no comparable registers.

Having been born into the British establishment is almost equally incompatible with self-made claims. The boundaries of this exclusive social group of high-status people with vast political and economic resources are diffuse and permanently subject to change. Therefore, beyond anybody with a well-known name, we were not able to ascertain whether they had such a background.

Easier to identify were families with established dynastic wealth, our second parameter. We set the threshold for pre-existing family wealth very high, applying this term only to where a family had been a matter of public reporting for several generations. An example here is Alejandro Santo Domingo who, together with his wife, Lady Charlotte Wellesley, ranked at position 29 on the 2018 Rich List. Domingo's grandmother was from Colombia's political establishment, and his grandfather built a fortune during the Great Depression of the 1930s. If we combine the international entries of dynasty-based Rich Listers with those born in the UK and add noble-born wealth, we arrive at 44 per cent of our sample who were born into either aristocratic families or families of long-established business empires.

Third, there is the divide between comprehensive and independent schools, which remains a key indicator used by social scientists to differentiate between the better off and the less well off (see Social Mobility Commission report, 2019). We broke this down further into state schools, grammar schools and independent schools. Within independent schools, we added the category of Clarendon schools, led by Eton, Harrow, St Paul's, Westminster and Winchester College. We categorised graduates from Clarendon schools as those who are unlikely to be classified as 'self-made' because of the very high fees their parents would have had to pay, the selectivity in admission and the institutions' long association with the British elite (Reeves and Friedman, 2017). As for schooling, we limited our analysis to the British entries, as data for international Rich Listers was patchy. Even within the British sample, we were still unable to verify the schooling of 15 per cent. Among those we found data for, 33 per cent went to state school, 13 per cent to grammar school and 25 per cent to a private school, compared to 6–7 per cent among the general UK population (Ryan and Sibetia, 2010); 16 per cent of them attended a Clarendon school.

Graduating from Oxbridge is another status marker (Reeves and Friedman, 2017). Overall, 72 per cent of those who went to university graduated from a Russell Group university or a renowned university abroad. Higher education is, however, not to be overestimated as an indicator for elite belonging, especially in aristocratic circles (see, for example, Rubinstein, 1986). Compared to 14 per cent of those from international backgrounds who had no higher education, it was 40 per cent of our British entries who did not have university degrees (we could not find information about higher education for a fifth of our overall sample).

In addition, there are those who became familiar with business activities from a young age, which might have facilitated their later entrepreneurial success – very much on a par with the advantages granted by any other intense childhood exposure to exclusive and prestigious practices, knowledge and social environments. Although we did add this category to the overall figure, we cautiously suggest that entrepreneurial activities among the parental generation tend to contradict the idea of being 'self-made'. Such advantage applies to a most heterogeneous mix of people, from the media tycoon Richard Desmond (position 48), whose father briefly managed a film distribution company, to Anil Agarwal (position 60), whose father was a small-time scrap metal trader, a business from which Anil built an industrial empire. In total, we identified 20 per cent as having been born into families where parents or other family members exemplified business activities.

Alongside these parameters, which we regard as either fully exclusionary to 'self-made' status or as highly incompatible with it, we further distinguished between Rich Listers who grew up in Britain and those whose link to the UK appeared and strengthened later in life. We labelled only those as 'British' who had spent the majority of their lives in the UK and, hence, had passed through UK-specific social institutions (most notably, Britain's school system). Following this definition, our sample appears highly international: 110 of the 203 entries were classified as British and the remaining 93 moved to the UK later in life. We opted for the term 'international', rather than immigrant: although individuals have a strong link to the UK to be included on the Rich List in the first place, they might have not made the country their prime and exclusive centre of life, either in terms of where they or their family live or where their businesses are located. An example of this is Mohamed Bin Issa Al Jaber (position 16), who splits his time between the UK, France, Austria and Saudi Arabia.[2]

If we add up the first three categories (aristocratic background, inherited dynastic wealth, and attendance of a well-known public school), we end up with 48 per cent of the 203 top entries on *The Sunday Times* Rich List having enjoyed at least one of these privileges. Difficulties in confirming biographic details for some entries on the list, particularly those from an international background, was a significant hindrance. For 23 per cent of them we could not find solid information for any of these categories. However, if we take only those whom we classify as 'British', we find that 81 per cent of them stem from a privileged background. Only 8 of them do not fall into a single one of the three categories. These figures clearly contradict the claims of social mobility made by *The Sunday Times*.

An inherent supremacy

Our data demystifies *The Sunday Times*' statement that there has been a 'self-made triumph over old money' (Watts, 2018). In fact, there seem to be fewer self-made super-rich in the UK than globally because, for example, many tech industry billionaires and emerging markets entrepreneurs are based elsewhere, primarily in the US (Freund and Oliver 2016: 2). However, even there the vast majority of the country's billionaires were born into wealth (Carney and Nason, 2016). In any case, the claim of 94 per cent being self-made is without any ground – even if measured by the most conservative parameters, of inherited money versus the rest.

Yet such claims remain hugely influential. For many, they serve as proof that potentially anybody can get rich. References to the odd rags-to-riches story, like the one of Jim Ratcliffe, the UK's richest man of 2018, who grew up in a council house near Manchester, obfuscate statistics that show a general picture of a country where inequality has become entrenched 'from birth to work'. According to the government's Social Mobility Commission's *State of the Nation 2018 to 2019* report, people born into a privileged background are nearly 80 per cent more likely to end up in professional jobs, compared to those from a working-class background (2019: 105). Rather than acknowledging the existence of structural advantages, of privilege and luck, the rich and powerful tend to be convinced of their individual supremacy and that their success is down to their personality, talents and merit (Gaztambide-Fernandez, 2009; Khan, 2011; Kraus and Keltner, 2013; Kraus and Callaghan, 2014).

Many journalists and academics actively repeat these ideas of entitlement and deservedness and they prove to be popular, no matter how many times researchers have debunked such assertions for their lack of scientific rigour. A classic example is Harvard's Greg Mankiw whose studies apparently prove that the wealthy have a higher IQ than the rest of society (2013) – claims which have been repeatedly proven wrong – yet his standing has only gone up. More subtle was the contribution to the 2018 supplement by the then chairman of Patisserie Valerie, Luke Johnson. He invoked a study by Rainer Zitelmann, a conservative German historian-turned entrepreneur, who concluded that self-made multimillionaires are optimistic, nonconformists, driven by gut instinct, and good at selling, a skill many of them acquired at a young age (Johnson, 2018: 8).

Studies of this kind share the assumption that great fortunes can be explained by their creators' and holders' personality traits, isolated from and unrelated to wider society. Arguments that justify wealth by reference to individual merit overlook the wider societal structures upon which the accumulation of these fortunes rest, such as the returns to capital over wage labour (as Piketty has demonstrated, 2014); or that the super-rich benefit from the current legal and economic setting (for example, through offshore financial structures, which allow them to shelter their wealth from taxation; see Bullough, 2018). There currently exists an economic environment that is advantageous to wealth accumulation for those who already have wealth to build upon. As the founder of *The Sunday Times* Rich List, Philip Beresford, who compiled the first 28 editions, notes, Margaret Thatcher and her neoliberal reforms were key for rich individuals to rise in numbers and to accumulate the level of wealth we have seen in recent years (McCall, 2018).

The ideology of meritocracy

Narratives of meritocracy symbolically reproduce contemporary capitalist culture (Littler, 2017), and belief in meritocratic values is strengthening at the very same time that inequality is growing (Mijs, 2021). Those at the top are presented as deserving and entitled; they are there because they 'work the hardest' and are 'the most able' (Littler, 2017: 2). Such portraits can benefit from, but do not rely on, a story of self-made wealth. Instead, what is crucial is effective performance. Ethnographers have identified this skill as being part of an elite education, one in which the language of meritocracy is learned as a justification for privilege (Khan, 2011; Khan and Jerolmack, 2013). Such training also perfects social eloquence and the ability to swiftly switch between cultural registers (Laurison and Friedman, 2013).

Meritocratic claims to wealth are further reliant on the argument that merit-based wealth is 'good' (Carney and Nason, 2016). 'Good' wealth is supposed to have been created by honest means. It should preferably be tangible and of use to society, as are many consumer goods and services. In contrast, 'bad' wealth is unearned, corrupt, nepotistic and down to parasitic methods, such as the exploitation of natural resources. 'Bad' rich do not reinvest and develop infrastructure and technology but take their money offshore (for distinctions of this kind, see Freund, 2016). Any moral judgements about 'good' and 'bad' wealth are highly functional for the sustainability of capitalism and the social acceptance and concentrations of great wealth in the hands of a few. The basic ideological premise is that capital accumulation through private ownership and its subsequent socio-economic inequality are natural and desirable. Most of the system's faults and flaws we experience today are down to the 'bad' rich. This implies that if these black sheep changed their behaviour, most of these flaws would be eradicated.

Even if this was the case, there is little chance for the public to identify 'bad' wealth. Wealthy individuals have the power to launder their image and reputation (Cooley et al., 2018; Goodrich, 2019). For example, Len Blavatnik, the billionaire who led the Rich List in 2015, has successfully rewritten the story of how he accumulated his fortune in the 1990s, after the break-up of the Soviet Union (Foy and Seddon, 2019). He has reinvented himself as 'good wealth': a US philanthropist of Jewish-Ukrainian origin, he joined the ranks of the British establishment and has become part of public life, most famously by funding the construction of a new wing of the Tate, which is named after him. Blavatnik was knighted in 2016.

The French economist Thomas Piketty is highly critical of any attempts to establish a moral hierarchy of 'good' and 'bad' wealth. He argues that reducing social inequality to personality is meant to distract from the problems inherent in our socio-economic system, while judgements about which rich individual is 'good' and which is 'bad' are usually based on little more than a few arbitrary assertions about a person's merits and character. For many, Bill Gates – until recently the richest man in the world – epitomises meritocratic entrepreneurship and philanthropy. But Piketty challenges this idea by pointing to the virtual monopoly on operating systems from which Gates has profited, as well as to the work of thousands of engineers and scientists who worked for him. They did not patent their scientific papers, but Gates' success depended on them (Piketty, 2014: 444–5).

Conclusion

An ideology of self-made deservedness and entitlement has been a foundational cornerstone of *The Sunday Times* Rich List from its inception. By the time the supplement was first published in 1989, neoliberal thinking had successfully conquered the mainstream (Harvey, 2011) and ever since, the Rich List has played its part in reassuring its readership that the capitalist system as we see it today is unrivalled, not least because it allows for everybody to make it (if only one tries hard enough). Its proclamation in 2018 of a 'social revolution' by the self-made who allegedly make up 94 per cent of the super-rich might, however, have been the most outlandish (McCall, 2018: 39).

It begs the question what will come next. The fortunes which we have seen rising to an unprecedented scale will keep doing so, simply because of their size (if Piketty's 'r>g' is to be believed); it is completely irrelevant whether these fortunes were inherited or entrepreneurial in origin, or whether their owners work or not (Piketty 2014: 439–40). Next there is the question of how these supposedly self-made fortunes will be assessed in future, once they themselves will have turned into inherited wealth. We will not have to wait for too long to see this. Many people on the 2018 List are advanced in age; at least three of them are no longer alive at the time of writing. The most likely outcome is that inheritance will be paired with a reputation for being morally deserving and, consequently, nourish narratives of meritocracy. Philanthropic activities can greatly facilitate a smooth transition of wealth and status across generations (Schimpfössl 2019; Monteath and Schimpfössl, 2019).

When compared with Maestri and Monforte's research (chapter 10), we suggest that attitudes towards refugees and the rich are interrelated. Both volunteers with refugees and the journalists writing for *The Sunday Times* Rich List support the idea that worthiness and deservedness is, in the end, down to personality, character and conduct. While we, as social scientists, are unlikely to reproduce such crude ideas, we might still fall into another trap: focusing on structural processes when analysing refugees but on culture and agency when examining elites (Cousin at al., 2018: 227). With our research, we were partly guilty of doing this when taking the individual as the basic unit of our analysis; however, we believe we have remained reflexive of this potential pitfall with our attempt to demystify an ideology of meritocratic wealth.

Notes

1　This odd number (203 rather than 200) is down to the fact that the bottom six entries are all estimated the same net wealth of £700 million.

2　Although not relevant in terms of our inquiry into social backgrounds, it would have been interesting to establish the Rich List members' legal migration status, as this defines whether they are obliged to pay tax in the UK or not. In general, of course, with the exception of sensational cases such as Roman Abramovich, whose visa was not renewed by the Home Office in 2019, Rich List members are highly unlikely to be subject to visa and citizenship obstacles (Transparency International 2015). The investor visa scheme remains the main instrument to obtaining British citizenship.

References

Burke's Peerage Foundation (2003). *Burke's Peerage, Baronetage and Knightage. 107th edition.* London.

Bullough, O. (2018). *Moneyland: Why Thieves and Crooks Now Rule the World and How to Take it Back.* London: Profile Books.

Carney, M., and Robert S. Nason (2016). Family business and the 1%. *Business and Society*, 57(1), 1–25.

Cooley, A., Heathershaw, J., and Sharman, J. C. (2018). The rise of kleptocracy: laundering cash, whitewashing reputations. *Journal of Democracy*, 19(1), 39–53.

Cousin, B., Khan, S., and Mears, A. (2018). Theoretical and methodological pathways for research on elites. *Socio-Economic Review*, 16(2), 225–49.

Foy, H., and Seddon, M. (2019). From Russian oil to rock'n'roll: the rise of Len Blavatnik. *Financial Times*, 6 June. www.ft.com/content/c1889f48–871a-11e9–a028-86cea8523dc2 (accessed 15 January 2020).

Freund, C. (2016). *Rich People, Poor Countries: The Rise of Emerging Market Tycoons and Their Mega Firms.* Washington, DC: Peterson Institute for International Economics.

Freund, C., and Oliver, S. (2016). The origins of the superrich: the billionaire characteristics database. Peterson Institute for International Economics. Working Paper Series 16–1 (February). www.piie.com/system/files/documents/wp16-1.pdf (accessed 15 January 2020).

Gaztambide-Fernandez, R. (2009). *The Best of the Best: Becoming Elite at an American Boarding School.* Cambridge, MA: Harvard University Press.

Goodrich, S. (2019). *At Your Service. Investigating how UK Businesses and Institutions Help Corrupt Individuals and Regimes Launder their Money and Reputations.* Transparency International UK. Report 24 October.

Harvey, D. (2011). *The Enigma of Capital: And the Crises of Capitalism.* London: Profile Books.

Johnson, L. (2018). What it takes to be a successful entrepreneur. *The Sunday Times Magazine. Rich List 2018.* May.

Khan, S. R. (2011). *Privilege: The Making of an Adolescent Elite at St. Paul's School.* Princeton, NJ: Princeton University Press.

Khan, S., and Jerolmack, C. (2013). Saying meritocracy and doing privilege. *The Sociological Quarterly* 54(1): 9–19.

Kraus, M. W., and Callaghan, B. (2014). Noblesse oblige? Social status and economic inequality maintenance among politicians. *PLOS One* 9(1).

Kraus, M. W., and Keltner, D. (2013). Social class rank, essentialism, and punitive judgment. *Journal of Personality and Social Psychology*, 105(2), 247–61.

Laurison, D., and Friedman, S. (2013). *The Class Ceiling: Why it Pays to be Privileged*. Bristol: Policy Press.

Littler, J. (2017). *Against Meritocracy: Culture, Power and Myths of Mobility*. London: Routledge.

Mankiw, N. G. (2013). Defending the one per cent. *Journal of Economic Perspectives*, 27(3), 21–34.

McCall, A. (2018). 30 years on: how the Rich List has undergone a social revolution. *The Sunday Times Magazine. Rich List 2018*. May, 38–9.

Mijs, J. J. B. (2021). The paradox of inequality: income inequality and belief in meritocracy go hand in hand. *Socio-Economic Review* 19(1), 7–35.

Monteath, T., and Schimpfössl, E. (2019). The culture of elite philanthropy: Russia and Britain compared. In Peter J. S. Duncan and Elisabeth Schimpfössl eds, *Socialism, Capitalism and Alternatives*. London: UCL Press, 49–65.

Piketty, T. (2014). *Capital in the Twenty-First Century*. Cambridge, MA: Belknap Press.

Reeves, A., and Friedman, S. (2017). The decline and persistence of the old boy: private schools and elite recruitment 1897 to 2016. *American Sociological Review* 82(6), 1139–66.

Rubinstein, W. (1986). Education and the social origins of British elites 1880–1970. *Past and Present* 112(1), 163–207.

Ryan, C. and Sibetia, L. (2010). *Private Schooling in the UK and Austria*. London: Institute of Fiscal Studies. www.ifs.org.uk/bns/bn106.pdf (accessed 15 September 2019).

Schimpfössl, E. (2019). Russian Philanthrocapitalism. *Cultural Politics* 15(1), 105–20.

Social Mobility Commission (2019). *State of the Nation 2019: Social Mobility in Great Britain*. London. www.gov.uk/government/publications/social-mobility-in-great-britain-state-of-the-nation-2018-to-2019 (accessed 15 August 2019).

The Sunday Times (2018). Rules of Engagement. 13 May. www.thetimes.co.uk/article/sunday-times-rich-list-2018-rules-of-engagement-nvw0lwzck (accessed 15 January 2020).

Transparency International (2015). *Gold Rush: Investment Visas and Corrupt Capital Flows in the UK*. London.

Watts, J. (2018). The Rich List: at last, the self-made triumph over old money. *The Sunday Times*, 13 May. www.thetimes.co.uk/article/sunday-times-rich-list-2018–at-last-the-self-made-triumph-over-old-money-0qx8tqvjp (accessed 15 August 2019).

Watts, J. (2019). The age of uncertainty. *The Sunday Times Magazine. Rich List 2019*. May, 7–10.

Zitelmann, R. (2018). *The Wealth Elite: A Groundbreaking Study of the Psychology of the Super Rich*. London and New York: Lid Publishing.

10

Victims and agents: the representation of refugees among British volunteers active in the refugee support sector

Gaja Maestri and Pierre Monforte

This chapter analyses how volunteers make sense of their engagement within the charities and networks composing the European 'Refugees Welcome' movement.[1] More precisely, we ask how they represent the beneficiaries of their collective actions, in order to explore the moral boundaries underpinning different representations of the deserving refugees and migrants. Since the peak of the so-called refugee 'crisis'[2] in 2015, individuals across Europe have mobilised to show compassion and solidarity towards the refugees and migrants trying to reach the European Union territory. Often labelled as the 'Refugees Welcome' movement, this wave of mobilisation has led to the engagement of entire new sectors of society in charities and networks that were already mobilising for the rights of migrants and refugees. This wave of action has led to the construction of new organisations and networks at the local, national and transnational level, as well as the spreading of initiatives such as organised hosting networks, language courses, food and clothes donations, legal support, and rescue missions at the European borders.

This chapter draws on comparative research that explores the engagement of refugee-support volunteers in the UK and France. We focus here on the British case and on 72 interviews with volunteers in different charities and networks in the pro-refugee sector. The interviews took place in London, Birmingham, Sheffield and the Midlands and were conducted in a variety of organisations, from large well-established ones, to smaller, more local ones. We also included informal networks that emerged in the context of the 'refugee crisis' in 2015, such as hosting groups, and volunteers supporting migrants in Calais and Dunkirk. In these groups, our participants were dedicated to different types of activities: legal advice, emotional and therapeutic support, advice for finding a job or accommodation, donations of food and clothes in the Calais 'jungle', hosting of refugees in their home, organisation of social events, support with the English language, and so on. Our sample is composed of volunteers with different profiles in terms of age, gender and socio-economic background. The majority of our participants started volunteering in the context of the 'refugee crisis'.

To begin, we discuss the main academic literature, as well as governmental and media discourses, around the idea of deservedness of refugees. We then move to our empirical findings, showing how volunteers mobilising for the support of refugees define different figures of the individuals who deserve their compassion: the figure of the vulnerable victim, on the one hand, and that of the proactive and resilient actor on the other. We will do so by also pointing out the tensions and ambiguities of these representations. Finally, we will consider how these figures are distributed across different charities and support groups and we will draw conclusions on how different experiences of volunteering shape different representations of the refugees.

By similarly mobilising the concept of 'deservedness', Monteath and Schimpfossl (chapter 9) argue that the image of the self-made entrepreneur has become increasingly salient in distinguishing between deserving and undeserving wealth. Interestingly, though applied to social groups at opposite ends of the social ladder, both highly marginalised groups (such as refugees and asylum seekers) and the very wealthy are morally evaluated on the basis of their (presumed) ability and effort to invest in themselves in order to succeed economically. At the same time, despite this interrelation, international wealth elites are not depicted as 'migrants', since this term is usually used to refer to poor, ethnically marked and lower-skilled mobile people (Sandoz and Fabian, 2019). Furthermore, another difference lies in the contextualisation of agency of these two groups and in the appreciation of systemic processes: while the privilege of the super-wealthy is often presented as detached from broader dynamics (e.g. patent laws or international taxation), the refugees' capacity to act is appreciated as part of a system that penalises them.

Representations of deservedness

The literature on charities, volunteering and humanitarian action shows that acts of support towards particular individuals and groups are based on specific representations of who these individuals and groups are (Boltanski, 1999; Fassin, 2011). Volunteers and humanitarian actors engage in 'acts of compassion' (Wuthnow, 1991) because they assume that those they seek to help have specific needs, and it is expected that the beneficiaries of their actions will display certain moral characteristics. In other words, beneficiaries need to demonstrate that they deserve the support of volunteers and humanitarian actors, especially by showing the extent of their suffering and by giving evidence of their 'good character'. This idea has been explored, for example, in studies drawing on Marcel Mauss' (1990 [1923]) analysis on gift-giving and exchange practices, whereby the gift-giver and the gift-receiver construct a relation of interdependence maintained by reciprocation (Ostenn, 2002). In this relation, each actor responds to mutual representations of who they are and to expectations about how to behave accordingly. In the context of charity or humanitarian action, as the gift-giving (e.g. in the form of help provision, protection and care) is based on unequal power relations (as the receiver depends on the benevolence of the gift-giver), and is generally non-reciprocal (i.e. the beneficiary is not expected to give in return), representations and judgements about the 'deservingness' of recipients are central.

It is on the basis of these representations and judgements that the relation between volunteers and beneficiaries is constructed and that help, protection and care are provided. As developed by Levinas (1961), voluntary, unconditional and non-reciprocal gift-giving in the form of charity action is based on representations of the typical recipient as the stranger, widow or orphan (Silk, 2004). As these representations of the deserving recipient of charity action suggest, the figure of the vulnerable and powerless individual is central (Vitellone, 2011). It is through the demonstration of their vulnerability and powerlessness that individuals prove their needs, and hence deservedness of support. And it is also through the demonstration of their vulnerability that they demonstrate their 'good character': it is a way to show that their suffering is not intentionally caused by their own action. This idea has been, for example, developed by Nussbaum (1996) in her study on compassion and by Ticktin (2017) in her analysis of representations of innocence in humanitarian action. They both show that humanitarian and charity action is underpinned by representations and moral judgements on the part of those who provide help, protection and care. These representations produce worthiness: they are used to establish binary distinctions between the deserving and undeserving, for example the suffering victims in need of protection and the others (Ticktin, 2017; Fassin, 2011).

As we have developed elsewhere (Maestri and Monforte, 2020), representations of 'refugees' are central in the processes of mobilisation of individuals involved in the 'Refugees Welcome' movement. In the course of their compassionate collective actions, volunteers construct and adjust their representations and moral judgements about who the refugees are and why they deserve support. Here, we want to develop this idea further and explore more specifically how different – apparently contradictory – representations about the deservedness of refugees can coexist in the narratives of volunteers engaged in this movement. In particular, we show that the representation of refugees as vulnerable and passive victims coexists with representations underlining their agency, resilience and resourcefulness. In doing so, we aim to underline the heterogeneity of the movement, as well as more generally the lines of inclusion and exclusion on which it is based. Our general argument is that these different figures coexist in the narratives of volunteers because they are used as (sometimes complementary) indicators of the moral worth of refugees.

Our analysis shows that notions of deservedness mobilised to evaluate the morality of the refugees are not isolated, but embedded within broader discourses on citizenship and worthiness. As we illustrate below, while the representation of the refugees as vulnerable victims is rooted in a humanitarian logic, proactivity, resilience and entrepreneurship also reflect the spreading of a neoliberal discourse on citizenship, whereby the access to rights (or, in this case, support from charities and collective actors) is conditional on showing one's activation and responsibility (Monforte et al., 2019; Suvarierol and Kirk, 2015). Nevertheless, we argue that both humanitarian and neoliberal frames are based on the centrality of agency (or lack thereof) as a criterion of judgement of a subject's moral worth: a lack of capacity to act in the former, and a positive demonstration of proactivity in the latter.

Articulations of deservedness in compassionate acts: between victimhood and agency

During the interviews, we observed that participants rely on seemingly divergent – and sometimes even contradictory – representations of refugees. As illustrated below, the individuals and groups they seek to help are sometimes depicted as vulnerable and passive, and sometimes as resilient, proactive and resourceful. These representations are not mutually exclusive though: while we will show how they are mostly spread in certain organisations rather than others, individual volunteers at times endorse both in their personal accounts. In fact, volunteers directly engaged in the refugee support sector do experience tensions and ambiguities around these representations as the expectations they produce around conducts and behaviours often clash with the realities of relationships with the refugees. These images are developed in opposition to negative stereotypes in public debates around recipients of charity support, but at the same time resonate with governmental and media discourses around deservedness (to describe refugees and more generally the recipients of charity action). As we have shown elsewhere (Maestri and Monforte, 2020), these discourses can be observed more specifically in public debates around migration. On the one hand, the representation of refugees as vulnerable and in need of protection resonates with a framing of immigration and asylum issues through 'humanitarian reason' (Fassin, 2011). On the other hand, the figure of the proactive and resilient migrant reflects neoliberal discourses that portray migrants as resilient and productive individuals who are keen to demonstrate their contribution to society. In both cases, however, there is an attempt to situate the agent within a broader unfavourable structure. As the next two sections show, refugees are not innately 'vulnerable' or 'proactive' but are either victims of abuses and difficulties or are entrepreneurial *despite* the challenges they have faced. This is a crucial point in understanding the interrelated construction of deservingness between social groups since, despite sharing the relevance of a neoliberal framing of citizenship, refugees and the super-rich differ in the role given to systemic processes. While the worthiness of refugees is appreciated through a consideration of the broader context, the deservedness of the wealthy is constructed through dismissing the larger dynamics that might facilitate creating and maintaining privilege (see chapter 9).

While these representations might appear to be opposites at a first sight, they both foreground the capacity to action of the refugees. In the first case, the refugees are represented as harmless victims who have been subject to violence and who were not in a position to react (except by fleeing). In the second case, refugees are evaluated through their capacity to behave proactively. These discourses have been central in recent years in debates around austerity and the Big Society and beyond, and they produce a distinction between 'deserving' and 'undeserving' service users (e.g. the urban poor, refugees, people with disabilities) on the basis of their good character (Tyler, 2013; Garthwaite, 2017). In opposition to the 'undeserving' service users being represented as responsible for their own suffering (in particular because of their poor life choices), the 'deserving' subjects are characterised by their individual suffering and perceived lack of agency, but also through the focus on their commitment to invest in themselves and contribute to society. From this perspective, in a context of retreat of the welfare state, the role of charities and volunteers is presented as a way to empower and responsibilise 'deserving' service users, while being directly or indirectly involved in the exclusion and disciplining of 'undeserving' subjects. As Donoghue (2013: 88–9) argues, this leads to viewing the role of volunteers through a logic of conditionality which 'implies an active/ passive binary whereby citizens are simultaneously in need of empowerment while also being actively responsibilised'. From this perspective, the apparently opposite figures of the vulnerable and proactive recipients of charity action in fact complement each other as they are both based on a judgement about the moral worth (i.e. the good character) of the individuals in question.

Deservedness I: refugees as passive victims

The analysis of our interviews shows that, for many participants, refugees need help because they have been victimised, either in their country of origin or in their country of destination. This representation resonates with the humanitarian logic shaping governmental and media discourses during the recent migration crisis (Della Porta, 2018; Karakayali and Steinhilper, 2019). It highlights the suffering and helplessness, as opposed to the threatening images of the 'illegal' migrant invader or potential terrorist (Grohman, 2017; Rettberg and Gajjala, 2016). For instance, vulnerability was explicitly brought up by a volunteer from a London-based hosting network, who argued that refugees deserve more help than British homeless people because they are 'more vulnerable':

> I know many homeless people have very little recourse to anybody else. But these people specifically have less recourse to the other actors in the field, such as homeless charities. I think they are more vulnerable. (Interview 3, Female, 58 years old, London)

According to the participants, vulnerability can be produced by different situations at different moments in the lives of the refugees, such as suffering in their country of origin, during the journey, or in the country of destination. Vulnerability, thus, is perceived as the result of broad contextual factors. War and persecution from authoritarian governments are very often evoked as the most relevant causes of people being pushed out of their countries. Some volunteers stressed the vulnerability of the refugees during their journey to Europe, often contrasted with the negative figure of the smugglers. This idea was underlined by a volunteer who set up an informal group bringing donations to Calais:

> It's a sweeping generalisation, I know but, you know, they get sold by the smugglers that England is this place you can go to, that's this, this, this, and this. The volunteers coincidentally have become part of the package that the smugglers sell. (Interview 35, Female, 31 years old, Midlands)

In this case, refugees are depicted as being in the hands of the smugglers and as not having the resources to know if what they are told is true – which can be read through Ticktin's (2017: 578) notion of 'innocence' as a form of ignorance or lack of knowledge. In addition, the challenges faced within the country of destination are often evoked, especially those linked to the Home Office. Participants also mentioned difficulties in the everyday life of refugees, such as not speaking the language and living in a hostile environment, as argued by a volunteer from an informal group in Sheffield offering legal support to asylum seekers:

> Like they've got all that, just as much as like a British person has got who is from a minority background, but they've got it ten times worse because they don't speak English as well or they've got an accent or God, they've just got so many problems. So many problems. 90% of it is problems [laughs]. [...] And we're just like, as a society we can be really like dehumanising about people as well [...] (Interview 23, Female, 26 years old, Sheffield)

In the words of this participant, refugees are vulnerable because they face processes of 'dehumanisation'. The engagement of the volunteers is thus constructed through a focus on the 'bare life' (Agamben 1998; Fassin 2011) of those they want to help.

While the perception of the refugees as victims plays an important role in the volunteers' motivations for engaging in collective action, some participants also question the gravity of the suffering of the people they support. For example, a participant hosting a refugee in her home told us how she started asking herself whether her guest genuinely needed help:

> The thing I feel is challenging to myself is, is her need great enough? Like, because she has friends, she has family here, and she is gonna go into social services, and again, I don't know, is that a calculated decision that she's made to then get into social [...] (Interview 32, Female, 32 years old, Birmingham)

As this extract shows, volunteers' questions about the vulnerability of refugees can lead to broader questions about their moral worth: here the participant feels challenged because she believes that the person she helps has a deliberate strategy to access social services.

The analysis shows that these types of questions and personal challenges can emerge in different situations and through different experiences of volunteering. For example, a similar tension was experienced by a detention centre visitor who had the feeling that the person she was supporting was lying or 'playing the system' in their favour (Interview 44, Female, 71 years old, London). From a similar perspective, other volunteers question the moral worth of refugees because of their perceived lack of agency. For instance, a volunteer host described one of her guests as 'too troubled' and complaining:

> We had this young doctor who was here for two weeks and every time he came down he had his head in his hands and he was 'oh my goodness, what shall I do, this is a problem, that's a problem'. I really wanted to help him but I knew I didn't have the emotional space to help him [...] I know it's terrible! So far it's been great, apart from that one, which was fine but he was a bit too troubled. (Interview 12, Female, 52 years old, London)

Being traumatised and in need of help was, in this case, not considered as an indicator of good character. As explored in the next section, this shows how – beyond the figure of the vulnerable victim – volunteers can also endorse and reproduce neoliberal representation of deservedness based on resilience and proactivity.

Deservedness II: refugees as proactive contributors

Further analysis shows that during the interviews, participants also referred to the refugees as proactive and resilient agents, which counters the idea of the 'scrounger' or bogus refugees (Banks 2012) as a burden to society. These volunteers acknowledge that the refugees withstood horrible situations. However, in contrast with the previous image of the passive victim, the difficulties are not used to stress victimisation and vulnerability but – on the contrary – to highlight determination and strength. This was clear, for example, in an interview with a volunteer from a local charity in Sheffield, who underlined the 'courage' and 'stoicism' of asylum seekers, despite the challenges they are faced with in the UK:

> It's all psychologically draining. But I've never ever heard one person moan, ever. No moaning, and the stoicism, and the courage, the resilience is phenomenal. It's humbling to witness it. (Interview 15, Female, 62 years old, Sheffield)

In this view, *in spite of* very unfortunate circumstances, refugees do not behave as victims. For example, the host who was mentioned at the end of the previous section criticised one of her guests for being 'too troubled', but at the same time she praised the other because he showed willpower despite his previous traumatic experiences:

> He was great and he was working to get his licence, he had a job with Crisis, he had a job coach, a house coach, he had a plan and still got a place. He was really on. He might have been tortured, but he wasn't traumatised by his country being blown up. [...] Now he works with Domino's pizza and he's working incredibly long shifts so he can buy a motorbike ... he's a man with a plan! (Interview 12, Female, 52 years old, London)

This quote not only shows how volunteers evaluate refugees through their resilience but also through their proactivity and entrepreneurial spirit, something that emerged in many interviews. This was, for example, the case of another London-based volunteer, who stressed how pleased she was when her guest became a 'British tax payer' (Interview 1, Female, 61 years old, London).

Within this understanding of deservedness, refugees are seen as proactive and productive subjects, who should be enabled to develop their full potential to contribute to society. This was often brought up by volunteers who work on employment services for the refugees, like this participant volunteering for a national charity in London:

> Through the training I had I'm able to empower people, to move on and settle. We begin by getting them into the asylum process, and once they get status in this project they can begin to get permission to work, they can utilise all their skills they have. We've got a project that's called [NAME REMOVED]. If I can do a little bit by getting them a National Insurance Number, benefits and let them have an independent life ... that's good. (Interview 9, Female, 70 years old, London)

However, the analysis shows that, as for the image of refugees as victims, a proactive attitude is not always seen in a positive light. For instance, some volunteers mentioned the difficulty in engaging with refugees who are not as isolated or vulnerable as they initially thought. Speaking of her guest, a host remarked how she hoped they would spend more time together while 'he [i.e. the refugee guest] prefers to feed himself' and to spend time with his friends outside the house (Interview 13, Female, 78 years old, London). Appreciation of resilience and proactivity can also be difficult when it is perceived as channelled towards personal gain. For example, a London-based host described his guest through the stereotype of the 'immigrant sponger' (a representation that, however, he dissociated himself from):

> [NAME OF GUEST 2] said he would bring his family here and he thought the council would give him a flat. No, I said, it's not that simple, they might not give you a flat. This is like the Daily Mail idea of immigrants spongers. He worked in a car factory. I said you should get an Arab-English dictionary ... how didn't he buy one? So I phoned up the Arabic shop and gave him the address to go and get it, but he didn't. (Interview 14, Male, 88 years old)

A similar tension was experienced by a volunteer who went to a camp in Dunkirk with a local group from the Midlands, and who underlined her feeling of 'confusion' and disappointment with a woman lying to her:

> There was one woman, an Iranian woman that we absolutely bust a gut for because the traffickers were after her [...]. One of [her] children developed an eye condition, so I arranged a hospital visit so this little boy could be looked after, we arranged hotels where she was safe, where literally we would sleep in the room with her because she was so scared of traffickers. It turned out to be a complete lie, complete lie. She wasn't even Iranian, she was Iraqi. (Interview 36, Female, 57 years old)

These examples epitomise the controversial nature of representations of deservedness. Indeed, the refugees mentioned in these examples are criticised for being both too proactive (i.e. wanting to bring their family over to the UK and demanding a council flat, or lying for their own personal gain) and not industrious enough (i.e. not doing enough to learn the English language). Also showing religious zeal is not necessarily perceived as a positive form of proactivity. For example, the London-based host above explained how she felt uncomfortable during Ramadan:

> I found Ramadan quite challenging. It's very easy to be super liberal when someone is out. There were fantastic things about it, like the meals and a lot of people around the house, praying. I felt as a sort wishy-washy liberal because I was thinking 'you have to get out and find a job!' You can't be hungry and not operating properly and basically put your life on hold for a month, when really you should be out getting jobs, instead of claiming JSA [Jobseeker's Allowance].

I had an extreme dialogue that goes in my head, like when I'm teaching for A level, can you please eat before you have A level?! (Interview 12, Female, 52 years old, London)

As much as proactivity and entrepreneurship are seen as positive characteristics, when the spirit of initiative does not reflect the volunteers' values, ways of life, or expectations, it can also become a representation that discredit the refugees.

Overall, our analysis of participants' representations of refugees shows that volunteers are constantly engaged in processes of evaluation of the moral worth of the individuals they aim to support. The figures of the passive victim and of the proactive contributor can be used against each other and produce different lines of deservedness. However, at a more general level, they are also complementary because they are used to evaluate the person who is in need of support, either in their genuine impossibility to react to violence (vulnerability and victimhood) or in their full exploitation of their capacity to act (proactivity). While different representations can be evoked by the same volunteers, we noticed that some notions of deservedness are more frequent among certain volunteer roles than others. The analysis highlighted that the representation of refugees as vulnerable victims who are voiceless and passive is much more diffused among volunteers who operate in emergency contexts and spaces of 'exception' (Agamben, 1998), such as the camps in Calais or Dunkirk or the detention centres in the UK. In contrast, images of refugees as resilient and productive tend to be more frequently evoked by those who engage in activities promoting social integration in the country of destination, such as casework, job access services, or hosting.

We argue that these differences in representations are linked to contrasting volunteering experiences. On the one hand, volunteers who engage in spaces of exception engage in activities that reduce the refugees to their 'bare life' (i.e. providing food and clothes) and that create a strong relation of dependence between the 'victim' and the 'helper'. On the other hand, volunteers who engage in spaces that are closer to their everyday experience in the country of destination and whose activities aim to address the inclusion of refugees (e.g. access to housing or work) tend to define a different role for themselves and for the refugees. Indeed, their role appears to be aimed at empowering refugees rather than providing immediate humanitarian support. This can lead them to endorse representations based on a neoliberal construction of subjectivities, which increasingly characterises citizenship at large, stressing the resilience and productivity of the refugees. This is especially present among volunteers who host refugees, revealing how intimate and domestic spaces have fully become sites of negotiations of neoliberal values, as the worth of someone who is welcome in the privacy of the home is often measured through notions of proactivity and entrepreneurship.

Conclusion

Volunteering plays a crucial role in the support of marginalised groups who often only rely on charity help. Although we acknowledge the importance of benevolent action, the aim of this chapter is to contribute a critical reflection on this form of engagement. The analysis of how volunteers articulate different representations of refugees allowed us to unpack the image of the deserving refugees, which is not only shaped by governmental and media discourses but is also increasingly influenced by the narratives of charity actors and their experience in the field. Representations of refugees as passive victims and as proactive agents are used to counter various negative views of refugees, such as that of the invader, the bogus refugee or the scrounger. However, the interviews also revealed that these figures equally contribute to drawing lines between desirable refugees (and therefore deserving of compassion) and the undesirable ones (therefore undeserving). Indeed, as argued by Anderson (2013) and Chauvin and Garcés-Mascareñas (2014), representations in terms of desirability and deservedness are about acceptance as much as domestication, which can reproduce and reify violent distinctions between 'Us' and 'Them'.

This chapter has demonstrated how meanings around deservedness are never fully settled but constantly open to collective re-definitions and re-negotiations throughout the practice of supporting refugees. While volunteers might endorse governmental and media representations of the refugees as passive victims or proactive contributors, they are also faced with dilemmas and tensions in their volunteering experience. Furthermore, the ways in which deservedness is articulated change according to the activities and *loci* of the volunteers. On the one hand, those who witness the violence of state borders and the 'bare life' of the refugees are more likely to endorse a narrative around vulnerability and victimhood – although this is often used to blame the government and not to support their policies. On the other hand, volunteers who mostly operate within the field of social integration within the UK appear to engage more with a discourse around proactivity and entrepreneurship. Overall, we have shown that what is at stake is the moral worth of refugees: throughout their experience of volunteering, participants navigate ambivalent processes of judgement-making about the good character of the individuals they aim to support. As opposed to the articulation of moral worth in the *Sunday Times* Rich List, where the super-wealthy are represented through their supposedly individual heroic success, the agency of deserving refugees is never completely free, but always confronted with the ineluctability of broader systemic processes.

Note

1 The research on which this chapter is based was supported by the Economic and Social Research Council. Project title: Exploring the Frames of Altruistic Action, 2017–2020. Grant number: ES/N015274/1.

2 Although we refer to the term refugee 'crisis' as it was widely used in public discourse, we agree with Lendaro et al. (2019) that we should be critical of this notion as it omits the failure of governments to comply with their international obligation to welcome refugees.

References

Agamben, G. (1998). *Homo Sacer: Sovereign Power and Bare Life.* Stanford, CA: Stanford University Press.

Anderson, B. (2013). *Us and Them? The Dangerous Politics of Immigration Control.* Oxford: Oxford University Press.

Banks J. (2012). Unmasking deviance: the visual construction of asylum seekers and refugees in English national newspapers. *Critical Criminology*, 20(1), 293–310.

Boltanski, L. (1999). *Distant Suffering: Morality, Media and Politics.* Cambridge: Cambridge University Press.

Chauvin S., and Garcés-Mascareñas B. (2014). Becoming less illegal: deservingness frames and undocumented migrant incorporation. *Sociology Compass*, 8(4), 422–32.

Della Porta, D., ed. (2018). *Contentious Moves: Solidarity Mobilisations in the 'Refugee Crisis'*. Basingstoke: Palgrave Macmillan.

Donoghue, M. (2013). Welfare and cohesion contested: a critical discourse analysis of New Labour's reform programme. *British Politics*, 8(1), 79–100.

Fassin, D. (2011). *Humanitarian Reason: A Moral History of the Present*. Berkeley, CA: University of California Press.

Garthwaite, K. (2017). 'I feel I'm giving something back to society': constructing the 'active citizen' and responsibilising foodbank use. *Social Policy and Society*, 16, 283–92.

Grohman, Stefania. (2017). Space invaders: the 'migrant-squatter' as the ultimate intruder. In Pierpaolo Mudu and Sutapa Chattopadhay, eds, *Migration, Squatting and Radical Autonomy*. London: Routledge, 121–9.

Karakayali, S., and Steinhilper, E. (2019). L'été de l'accueil en Allemagne: les deux versants du bénévolat en temps de crise des réfugiés. In Annalisa Lendaro, Claire Rodier and Youri Lou Vertongen, eds, *La crise de l'accueil: Frontières, droits, résistances*. Paris: La Découverte, 251–72.

Lendaro, A., Rodier, C., and Vertongen, Y., eds (2019). *La crise de l'accueil: Frontières, droits, résistances*, Paris: La Découverte.

Levinas, E. (1961). *Totality and Infinity*, trans. A. Lingis. Pittsburgh, PA: Dusquesne University Press.

Maestri, G., and Monforte, P. (2020). Who deserves compassion? The moral and emotional dilemmas of volunteering in the 'refugee crisis'. *Sociology*, 54(5), 920–35.

Mauss, M. (1990 [1923]). *The Gift: The Form and Reason for Exchange in Archaic Societies*, trans. W. D. Halls. New York: Norton.

Monforte, P., Bassel, L., and Khan, K. (2019). Deserving citizenship? Exploring migrants' experiences of the 'citizenship test' process in the United Kingdom. *British Journal of Sociology*, 70(1), 24–43.

Nussbaum M. (1996). Compassion: the basic social emotion. *Social Philosophy and Policy* 13(1), 27–58.

Ostenn, M. (ed.) (2002). *The Question of the Gift: Essays Across Disciplines*. London: Routledge.

Rettberg J. W., and Gajjala R. (2016). Terrorists or cowards: negative portrayals of male Syrian refugees in social media. *Feminist Media Studies* 16(1), 178–81.

Sandoz, L., and Fabian, S. (2019). Who receives more help? The role of employer support in migration processes. In I. Steiner and P. Wanner, eds, *Migrants and Expats: The Swiss Migration and Mobility Nexus.* Cham: Springer, 57–81.

Silk, J. (2004). Caring at a distance: gift theory, aid chains and social movements. *Social and Cultural Geography,* 5(2), 229–51.

Suvarierol, S., and Kirk, K. (2015). Dutch civic integration courses as neoliberal citizenship rituals. *Citizenship Studies,* 19(3–4), 248–66.

Ticktin, M. (2017). A world without innocence. *American Ethnologist,* 44(4), 577–90.

Tyler, I. (2013). *Revolting Subjects: Social Abjection and Resistance in Neoliberal Britain.* London: Zed Books.

Vitellone, N. (2011). Contesting compassion. *The Sociological Review,* 59(3), 579–96.

Wuthnow, R. (1991). *Acts of Compassion.* Princeton, NJ: Princeton University Press.

11

Entwined stories: privileged family migration, differential inclusion and shifting geographies of belonging

Sarah Kunz

This chapter discusses the case of a family – a married couple and their two children – who emigrated from Germany in the mid-1990s and have lived in various countries since. It interrogates their migration trajectory and how migration was productive of social mobility in ways more often associated with less privileged migration; it also explores family members' shifting modalities of belonging and accordant narratives of identity, making sense of these dynamics by mobilising the concept of 'differential inclusion' (Mezzadra and Neilson, 2012). This concept theorises incorporation beyond the prevailing inclusion/exclusion binary, and the chapter uses it to focus on contingent inclusion and partial belonging at the more privileged end of the migratory spectrum. The chapter demonstrates how forms of 'differential inclusion' can be the result of privilege and a mechanism of its reproduction, and ow migratory privilege is an intersecting, relational and contextual construct formed at the juncture of place, life-stage, personal biography and ascribed personal characteristics.

A growing body of work examines privileged instances of migration (Fechter and Walsh, 2010; Kunz, 2016; Leonard and Walsh, 2018). Research has explored, for example, how migratory privilege is produced and enacted, the forms of community it engenders, and the self-identification and belonging migrants privileged by citizenship, class and 'race' narrate. Scholars have also begun to address how the terminology of migration itself participates in the production of privilege and have urged a conversation about what the growing understanding of privileged migration means for received migration theory and concepts, generally formulated in response to less privileged migration (Croucher, 2012; Klekowski von Koppenfels, 2014; Fechter and Korpela, 2016).

This chapter arises out of a project on 'expatriate' migration, for which I conducted five months of ethnographic research in Nairobi, Kenya, in 2016. Quite soon upon my arrival, I was invited to an event at the Canadian High Commission in the lush Gigiri neighbourhood, a part of town historically associated with the European colonial community and now host to the United Nations (UN) headquarters and foreign embassies. Here I met Andreas Schmidt,[1] a jovial man in his early fifties who works for the UN. Over the next five months, I met Andreas and Claudia, his wife, at several social events, and interviewed them and their two adult children, Anna and Jonas, who I talked to via skype video call. I spoke to them about their twenty-odd years living abroad, in particular about a decade spent in France and about life in Nairobi, where the family had spent three years before, and where Andreas and Claudia had just returned on their own, while their children attended university in Germany and the United States.

This chapter thus discusses four entwined migration stories, drawing on interviews, informal conversations and on my observations recorded in fieldnotes. It explores a family life structured by migration, marked by shared narratives, memories and joys but also tensions and compromises. While this particular story is hardly generalisable, it produces insights of broader relevance for our understanding of family migration, incorporation and identity, and the role, production and lived experience of privilege in migration. The chapter's focus on life course and position within the family speaks to work that has shown the gendered structuring of privileged migration and calls for attending to the experiences of children (Coles and Fechter, 2008; Fechter and Korpela, 2016). The chapter thus also contributes to an 'overdue shift towards placing children's own perspectives at the center of enquiry' and gives 'due recognition to the relevance of geographical, social and political positionalities, and how these impact on, and shape ideas of children growing up transnationally mobile' (Fechter and Korpela, 2016: 424).

In the following I will, first, sketch the Schmidts' migration trajectory and examine how it is productive of social mobility. I will then discuss geographies of belonging and constructions of identity that evidence shared privileges but also different life stages and positions within the family.

Mezzadra and Neilson (2012: 62) argue for the necessity of 'mov[ing] beyond the binary inclusion/exclusion', and point to 'the proliferation of subject positions that are neither fully included nor fully excluded from the space of citizenship and from labour markets, of subjectivities that are neither fully insiders nor fully outsiders.' As Artero shows (in chapter 12), people seeking refuge in Milan experience differential inclusion, inasmuch as legal residence does not protect them against discrimination when negotiating the city, its welfare system and socio-economic fabric. In this chapter, I argue that analysing the experiences of more privileged migrants through the lens of 'differential inclusion' offers distinct, yet equally useful and complementary insights into how practices of bordering produce inequality in and through mobility.

The pairing of these two chapters is pertinent for another reason. Artero's respondents and the Schmidts have different, yet structurally interrelated, migratory trajectories. Violent conflict or natural catastrophes are generally associated with the movement of those seeking refuge. However, these events also result in the numerically smaller but socio-politically significant movement of military, humanitarian and bureaucratic personnel who, like Andreas, migrate in order to intervene in the conflict, help overcome the catastrophe, or 'manage' the movement of those seeking refuge. Their movement tends to be characterised by a much greater level of choice and privilege and is often linked to career progression and social mobility; it also directly impacts on the movements of those seeking refuge. In this sense, the two chapters look at structurally related yet unalike migrations and highlight the wide and unequal spectrum of interconnected movement set in motion by violent conflict or natural catastrophe (see also Sheller 2013; Fechter and Korpela, 2016).

Privileged migration and social mobility: shared journeys and different positionalities

All four members of the Schmidt family narrate migration as a family decision and project. Nevertheless, there exist multiple stories of migration when one family moves. Andreas (the father) tells their migration story as structured by his career and, to some extent, dictated by work contracts. As such, Andreas' migration – and that of his family – enabled career progression and substantial social mobility. Andreas joined the German police force at age 16 and was in his early thirties when he had the opportunity to join the peace-keeping mission following the war in former Yugoslavia in the early 1990s. Andreas had always wanted to work abroad, to 'do something else and see something else'. Another decisive factor was pay. Going abroad implied a generous per diem on top of Andreas' normal salary, a welcome bonus as they had two young children and had just built a house. Andreas left for six months. He enjoyed working abroad, meeting people of many nationalities and his responsibility 'much exceeded what you could have reached nationally'. Upon his return, Andreas wanted to go abroad again but not without his family. Claudia agreed and Andreas secured a secondment with an international organisation, again receiving his salary plus a bonus for working abroad. When this secondment ended, after six years, Andreas took unpaid leave from his German job and obtained direct employment in France. He subsequently worked for various multi-national corporations and international organisations in multiple countries, before starting his current job at the UN in Nairobi.

From the outset, migration implied increased authority, pay and status for Andreas. His story shows that conflict and catastrophe produce a range of movement, some of it voluntary and privileged, associated with social mobility beyond what might have been possible at home. Nonetheless, Andreas' international career was not without difficulties and constraints, including fixed-term employment and being expected to move country on the behest of his employer. This evidences that also the exclusive international labour market spanning intergovernmental organisations, international non-governmental organisations and multinational corporations is governed by rules and norms that often tightly control the (migratory) lives of employees. Lavish salaries and benefits are often tied to temporary status – and together they produce specific forms of 'differential inclusion' of privileged migrant labour. In this context, accepting a job at the UN in Nairobi was partly a practical decision, for stability and security. The large number of UN agencies in Nairobi makes it easier to change laterally while staying put physically, plus a hefty salary increase allowed Andreas to build up his pension faster.

If, for Andreas, migration went along with career progression and social mobility far beyond what he could have achieved in Germany, his decision to migrate, opportunities, migratory experiences and career were never fully disconnected from Germany. Andreas never quit his job in Germany but instead took unpaid leave – a status he retains until today. While he was told that it would be better for his career in the German police to *not* go abroad, he was legally guaranteed a return to his old post, which he always saw as a bit of a 'safety net'. Andreas thus retained a 'latent' inclusion in Germany's relatively protected national labour market while navigating a far more lucrative and prestigious, yet 'hyper-flexible' global labour market. The possibility to return, not only to a wealthy and safe country but to a job, allowed Andreas autonomy and to take risks in pursuing his international career. Moreover, the symbolic, cultural and mobility capitals that come with being German, and European, opened up international opportunities for Andreas.

In comparison, the family's migration implied a different career trajectory for Claudia (Andres' wife). Claudia's story is, to some extent, typical of the 'trailing spouse' (Coles and Fechter, 2008). She prioritised her husband's career, (re)created a family home in several countries, raised children without a familial support network and had to craft a purposeful occupation around someone else's career. Claudia stepped into that role cautiously, initially keeping the door open to her former, professional life. Claudia was on parental leave from a managerial role at the local bank branch when they moved to France. Despite feeling uneasy about not speaking French, she agreed to the move because it was supposed to be temporary: they would return to Germany, and she to her job, when her maternity leave ended. Things were difficult at first but then Claudia started to enjoy her life abroad. Whenever they went back to Germany, 'it felt like nothing ever changed, time kind of stood still'. After three years, neither of them wanted to return and she quit her job. Andreas' salary could support the family and Claudia now looked after their children full-time: 'it was my job to raise the children and – just the family, be the family manager'.

In retrospect, migration implied a prolonged career break and career change, rather than an end to Claudia's working life. It closed some doors but arguably opened others. Claudia had always been a passionate horse rider and she brought her horse to France, where she continued her hobby and taught her children. When they first moved to Kenya, Claudia, then in her late thirties, gained a diploma and started to teach horse riding professionally. Another ten years on, her children have left home and Claudia now wants to fully focus on enjoying her career. She regularly travels across Kenya and internationally to take courses, teach and attend conferences. She half-jokes that the roles have changed now as her husband often has to watch house and dog and wait for her return. And while Andreas tells me he can imagine staying in Kenya past retirement, Claudia says that from a professional point of view, Kenya is not 'interesting enough' for her in the long run. It is thus possible that they will leave Kenya again, this time driven by Claudia's aspirations rather than those of Andreas. Yet Claudia's career is ultimately enabled by her husband's work and by living in Kenya; there is no need for her to contribute to the family income, domestic staff run their household, and she can afford to travel extensively for costly training and conferences. Further, her career, just like that of her husband, is greatly facilitated by having a passport that allows easy navigation of the world's increasing borders.

In Kenya, the Schmidts live a life they could have never afforded in Germany. They rent a large house with more bedrooms than they need, employ several domestic staff, and go on regular trips and holidays. They socialise with business elites, foreign ambassadors and Kenyan politicians, and their membership of the upmarket Muthaiga Country Club was arranged and paid for by Andreas' employer when they first moved to Kenya. Their privilege is not only socio-economic. Like Andreas, many foreign employees of big international organisations hold diplomatic status, which also means they are not accountable to the Kenyan police. Borders are 'transported into the middle of political space' (Balibar, 2004; cited in Mezzadra and Neilson, 2012: 63), also in the form of red licence plates and black passports. However, this – in a territorial and psychological sense – 'internalised' border produces a set of privileged foreigners rather than facilitating their marginalisation or exploitation. Accordingly, Anna (the elder child) recalls that many foreigners, including 'diplomat kids', felt 'invulnerable' and a class apart. This internalised border is also racialised, with whiteness often standing in for privileged foreignness. As Anna recounts, being white triggered differential and frequently preferential treatment by the Kenyan police, even in the absence of a diplomatic passport.

Claudia notes that their friends 'back home' say they are 'spoiled for life in Germany'. Some, she likes to think, thereby imply that their way of thinking has changed too much and their horizon expanded too far. However, she adds, others might simply be thinking about the 'luxurious life' they are now leading. Anna and Jonas have struggled with aspects of their privilege. They grew up blending in with the French middle class and both subsequently felt uneasy with their highly visible wealth in Kenya. Anna further relates, with some annoyance, that when she tries to explain where she is from, she is often labelled a 'diplomat kid' – a label loaded with assumptions about affluence and privilege. Yet she argues that while moving around has positive aspects it can also be difficult, and one can easily 'feel a bit lost'. At the same time, Anna and Jonas benefit from and enjoy their privileged lives. They were raised travelling extensively, speaking several languages and with a 'global conscious-ness' that is fast becoming a hallmark of the transnational elite and a potent form of cultural capital. Both Jonas and Anna now attend university, the first generation in their family to do so. As Anna tells me – further revealing the social mobility associated with the Schmidts' migration story – their parents did not attend university and it was not necessarily assumed as a given that Anna and Jonas would.

Shifting identifications and transnational geographies of belonging

The family members' narrations of identity and geographies of belonging further reveal shared experiences but also different life stages and positions within the family. For all of them, 'home' has become a messier construct. It is narrated along similar places ('Germany', 'France', 'Kenya') and with alike identity categories ('expat', 'German', 'third culture kid'). These, however, are signified and evaluated differently and organised into distinct constructs of being and belonging. This is exemplified by their varied relationship to the category 'expat'. Particularly in Kenya, the Schmidts are called expats – a flexible and contested category often linked to classed and racialised migratory privileges (Kunz, 2019). Yet, while all four Schmidts evoked the category expat, their interpretation and evaluation of this term differed.

Andreas embraces being an expat, a label he associates with his work and with continual mobility and cosmopolitanism. When he first heard about my research on expats, he immediately offered to take part: 'oh, you should come and look at me and my family, we have been on the move since 1997' (fieldnotes). Asked what being an expat means to him, he mentions the ability to live with and speak foreign languages, to immerse oneself in other cultures, and to interact with people of different backgrounds. He speaks about developing professionally in a way that does not represent a conventional career and distinguishes himself from those who only go abroad once, to 'tick a box'. Expats to him are 'nomads', those who get 'addicted, hooked … Germany then isn't enough anymore, or it is too provincial or restricted and then you go again and again'. Others, he notes, do not actually like moving around: they feel uprooted and 'homeless', their children have problems and partners are resentful about having to give up their career. This does not seem to apply to him. If Andreas struggles, it is not apparent. His career and family seem to provide all the continuity and rootedness he needs. He frequently and proudly speaks about 'expat life' and tells me that he 'loves Africa but might want to go to South America next, because he hasn't spent much time there so far' (fieldnotes). The world appears to be his oyster as he narrates a 'global life' with an ease and confidence that reflect his personal curiosity and drive, as well as a racialised and gendered sense of entitlement, and a career and citizenship that facilitate frictionless international mobility.

Less celebratory readings of the expat are evidenced by Claudia's conflicted relationship to the label, which she summons as well as rejects. Claudia speaks about the 'expat community' as a self-evident thing, which she can *choose* to be part of. She joined Facebook groups like 'Nairobi Expat Social' and *InterNations*, a social and professional network for expats. Yet, when I ask her if she self-identifies as an expat, she answers: 'Difficult question … in some ways yes, in others not: because, what I try, and so far, we have actually managed this in every country, we try to get as close as possible to the culture, without giving up our own identity.' For her, being an expat means to 'remain, as a guest, a little outside', to 'move to a foreign country but not let the foreignness get too close'. Claudia, and to some extent the rest of the family, frequently position themselves against the potent figure of this un-integrated and arrogant privileged foreigner often condensed in the label expat. Claudia repeatedly mentions friends 'outside the expat community' and emphasises that 'many of our Kenyan friends, if white or black, say the same, they say "you are not expats. You somehow belong here".' Claudia talks about appreciating local cultures, adopting local habits, learning local languages – and while she did not learn Kiswahili when they lived in Kenya before, she intends to do so now. Expatriate is evidently a tense term for Claudia, reflecting a range of anxieties related to her positionality as a privileged migrant.

In Nairobi, the label expat does work as a 'technology of everyday bordering' (Yuval-Davis et al., 2018) as it helps set apart a class of foreigners and establish their social status. Their socio-economic means, the way they chose to spend their money, and their whiteness render the Schmidts part of Nairobi's urban upper class, among which many are migrants. In this context, the category expat is highly productive in drawing socio-spatial boundaries, even as individuals reject it (Kunz, 2019). Accordingly, Claudia says that rather than as an expat, 'by now I see myself more like a world citizen with a German passport'. She explains: 'for me there is nothing more beautiful than to talk to so many people from different cultures, nations, religions. Just the other day we had a party and I enjoyed it so much suddenly seeing an Iranian, Iraqi and Israeli forget all problems, we talk, we just have fun.'

Yet, ultimately, Claudia's 'world citizen' also speaks from – and depends on – a position of privilege, where socio-cultural assimilation is not a requirement for socio-economic mobility and political conflict can be 'forgotten' – ignored – for the sake of having fun at a party. In this context, the debate about being or not being an expat not only reveals real anxieties and personal struggles; it can also deflect attention from shared privileges – and the systems that produce them – by accentuating personal differences between migrants of privilege and morally elevating some above others.

The Schmidts' journey reveals that migrant categories are highly contextual and bound up with broader histories, geopolitical power relations, and social inequalities. Indicatively, expat is much more salient in some contexts than others. It is not a common term in

Germany, and Claudia thinks she first encountered the label upon moving to Nairobi, where 'I then also had to, for myself, I think, find out what do they mean by "expat"'. While Claudia debates in Nairobi whether or not she is an expat – a decision she sees as largely dependent on personal attitudes and behaviours – she notes that the question never came up in France: 'In France we were Europeans in a European country. We weren't expats there, it was just about French or not French and if you speak French, you'll be closer to the French and if not, you're left out.' Similarly, Anna says she was not an expat in France: 'I was German-French, full stop. I am still annoyed that I did not have dual citizenship there, because I think that would have solved some of my identity problems back then.' She became an expat in Nairobi and also suggests that when they subsequently returned to Europe, she ceased being one, because 'I was again just like the others' – or at least not as visibly different as in Nairobi. Being an expat, then, is contextual and involves processes of socialisation, 'differential inclusion', into particular locales. The fact that, as white Germans, the Schmidts became expats in Nairobi, also has to do with Kenya's colonial history as well as with on-going international, political and economic inequalities and asymmetrical power relations.

Expat is a term that Jonas and Anna deploy habitually but also view critically, partly because of the different life stage at which they moved abroad. Anna notes that discussions with friends led her to critically reflect on the fact that expat is a term primarily used for white people. Moreover, Anna explains that she does not feel completely 'at home in' the term, because it implies a starting point, being *from somewhere*. This, she feels, does not apply to her, because she left Germany at such a young age. Anna therefore prefers 'third culture kid', which captures her feeling of 'being at home everywhere but then also not'. Anna does not comment on the fact that 'third culture kid' is arguably used similarly selectively as expat (Fechter and Korpela, 2016). Her unresolved struggle with terminology ultimately reveals an on-going struggle with who she is and where her home is – as well as an unease with privileges that she did not ask for but nevertheless accepts and enjoys.

While expat is a prevalent term in my conversations with the Schmidts, 'migrant' is not a term they mobilise, even when they recall the assimilatory pressure they felt in France. When I ask

Claudia whether she has ever seen herself as a migrant, or immigrant, she pauses to think before answering affirmatively – yes, she can relate to the category and she goes on to compare her 'world travels' to the 'great migration' of East Africa's wildebeests, who move from one pasture to the next. The category migrant, so widely used and politicised across Europe, has evidently not been applied much to her, either by herself or by others. This further reflects the very contextual yet consistently racialised constructions of nationhood and foreignness that render some people migrants in Europe – and others expats in Kenya.

Although no member of the Schmidt family relates to the term (im)migrant, Jonas and Anna's story began almost like the classic assimilationist 'immigrant tale'. Both were toddlers when the family moved to France. They went to a French school and had few German friends. While they spoke German at home, it became easier for them to speak in French – or in a mix of both languages incomprehensible to outsiders, as Jonas remembers. 'They were basically proper little French people', Andreas jokes and, indeed, for a long time Anna and Jonas almost felt more French than German. Yet there always remained a tension with their parents' German identity. At some point, Jonas recalls, Andreas and Claudia 'panicked' about their children's poor German skills and enrolled them at an international school. However, their German did not notably improve and they continued to associate Germany primarily with weeks of boredom during summer holidays, in a village where they only knew family, and nothing ever changed.

This immigrant tale was disrupted upon moving to Nairobi, where the Schmidts not only became expats, but where Germany became a more important presence in their everyday lives. In Nairobi, Anna and Jonas went to a German school for the first time, not without hesitation or difficulty. They spoke German fluently but struggled initially as they had never learned formal grammar rules. Further, because of the German school, they 'could not avoid' (Anna) meeting other Germans. The whole family strongly criticise fellow citizens in Nairobi who recreate their 'little Germany', only socialise with Germans, idealise Germany, and become 'more German than in Germany' (Claudia). Not being 'that kind of German' now became an important part of their identity. Andreas and Claudia repeatedly evoke Germany as a place of parochialism and racism, and Andreas argues they would not have been able to impart the same openness and worldliness to their children in Germany, because of its lack of 'racial' and cultural diversity. This statement arguably reveals as much about Germany – or at least the part of Germany they knew – as about their sense of self. Both construct their worldly and cosmopolitan identities, and chart their personal growth, against this 'Germany' they left behind. Also indicative of the latter is that Anna's construct of 'cliché Germanness' bears resemblance to her parents' life prior to emigrating: 'everything you want to achieve in life is my little house, my family and a Labrador'.

While Claudia mocks those Germans who idealise Germany, and situates herself as having outgrown the country, she also actively cultivates a German identity. When I ask her what she means by being 'a world citizen with a German passport' she replies, 'well, I lived in Germany for the first 30 years of my life and many things are still very German with me'. She also notes that her feelings about Germany changed after emigrating and recounts that encountering the strong patriotism displayed by her French friends 'taught' her to be 'proud' of being German, a feeling she would not have expressed previously, 'to not be put in that corner you don't want to be in'. She feels that:

> looking at it from the outside, we have a great country, not everything that shines is gold but altogether it is a great country and why shouldn't I say that I am proud to be German […] I like these aspects of being German, that I have kept, and I will safeguard those, and that is what I mean, where I say this is my German passport. Because of course there are many memories, many good friends, too.

Yet Claudia is adamant that she could not move back to Germany – and possibly Claudia's positive sense of Germany depends on her not doing so. What no-one speaks about, not even Claudia when she evokes her metaphorical German passport, is their retainment of German citizenship and the material privileges it affords. The cosmopolitan selves constructed by Claudia and Andreas, whether labelled expat or world citizen, focus on individualised practices and attitudes and on notions of culture divorced from socio-economic structures. This discursive individualisation eclipses and obscures the global inequalities that render the German passport privileged and position a decidedly particular form of cosmopolitanism as a universal ideal.

The Schmidts construct different 'Germanys', but for all of them this centrally functions to construct a migratory identity and to mark their personal development. Evidencing their ambiguous relationship to their country of origin and citizenship, Jonas recently moved to Germany to attend university but struggles with his parochial family there, while Anna, who had also considered moving back and even applied to join the German military, eventually decided against doing so, because: 'it felt as if I would forget all the years abroad just to become truly German [...] do I just want to assimilate and then finally feel like I fully belong somewhere? Not that I didn't feel comfortable abroad, but it was always like, okay, but really you're actually German.'

Then again, Anna goes on to argue, given that she only lived in Germany as a toddler, moving there would have been very much like moving to another foreign country. However, ultimately, it felt like 'too easy a solution' and 'like a step back'. Instead, Anna moved to New York, which feels like home now, *her* home, a place she chose and moved to without her parents. As she recounts with humour and some guilt, when her family recently came to visit, she felt defensive of the city as *her* space, thinking 'no, this is my home, mine!' Ultimately, for Anna and Jonas, their story of migration is also a story of coming of age and they narrate the different countries they lived in as representing stages of growing up. Migrating to another new, unmarked place is thus also a means for Anna to signify her transition into adulthood, with personal independence and autonomy being negotiated in and through space.

Conclusion

This chapter discusses how privileged migration might be understood through the lens of 'differential inclusion' and how doing so adds to our understanding of how inequality is produced, reproduced and sometimes contested in and through migration. I argue that partial inclusion, contingent status, and liminal belonging can root in privilege and aid its reproduction – as is the case for many privileged migrants labelled expatriate. This is the case, for instance, when mobility helps people negotiate a favourable 'partial inclusion' in several labour markets to pick the best of both worlds; or become socially and legally 'selectively incorporated' into a locale in a way that affords them preferential treatment, extra liberties and elevated status. We thus cannot equate (partial) inclusion/exclusion with subjugation or exploitation, and vice versa.

Further, also for privileged migrants, home and identity are elaborated through complex, sometimes tense emotional geographies stretched across borders and moulded by them. Rather than being neatly organised and hierarchically stacked, the places and social categories elaborated and arranged into a sense of self and belonging are contextual, relational and potentially contradictory; and as such, they often make for messy and precarious assemblages (see also Mhurchú, 2021). Finally, not only are relatively privileged migrants also 'differentially included' across multiple political, economic and cultural contexts, their experience is similarly structured by intersecting dimensions of social difference, by life-stage and familial relations. Home and identity are thus interpreted and experienced differentially within the same family. This further implies that migratory privilege needs to be analysed as an intersecting, relational and contextual construct with significant in-group tensions and fissures.

Moving beyond 'binaries of inclusion/exclusion' (Mezzadra and Neilson, 2012) when theorising migration is especially urgent as technologies of bordering are proliferating to produce new and ever more punitive forms of social differentiation, control and subjugation. To respond to this challenge, together with chapter 12, I urge further analysis into structurally interrelated but disparate mobilities and migrations. For instance, we can learn much about migration regimes as instruments of social differentiation, and the broader social inequalities they interact with, when we analyse, within one analytical framework, the mobilities of those who flee conflict and those who are tasked (like Andreas Schmidt) with mediating or ending it (see also Sheller, 2013). Further, the chapters suggest we explore what it means for a concept like 'differential inclusion' to move between analysing disempowered and privileged migrants, what analytical openings this affords, and what risks are associated with doing so.

Note

1 Names and personal details have been anonymised.

References

Coles, A., and Fechter, A. M., eds (2008). *Gender and Family among Transnational Professionals*. Abingdon: Routledge.

Croucher, S. (2012). Privileged mobility in an age of globality. *Societies*, 2(1), 1–13.

Fechter, A. M., and Korpela, M. (2016). Interrogating child migrants or 'Third Culture Kids' in Asia: an introduction. *Asian and Pacific Migration Journal*, 25(4), 422–8.

Fechter, A. M., and Walsh, K. (2010). Examining 'expatriate' continuities: postcolonial approaches to mobile professionals. *Journal of Ethnic and Migration Studies*, 36(8), 1197–210.

Klekowski von Koppenfels, A. (2014). *Migrants or Expatriates? Americans in Europe*. Basingstoke: Palgrave Macmillan.

Kunz, S. (2016). Privileged mobilities: locating the expatriate in migration scholarship. *Geography Compass*, 10(3), 89–101.

Kunz, S. (2019). Expatriate, migrant? The social life of migration categories and the polyvalent mobility of race. *Journal of Ethnic and Migration Studies*, 46(11), 2145–62.

Leonard, P., and Walsh, K., eds (2018). *British Migration: Privilege, Diversity and Vulnerability*. Abingdon: Routledge.

Mezzadra, S., and Neilson, B. (2012). Between Inclusion and exclusion: on the topology of global space and borders. *Theory, Culture and Society*, 29(4–5), 58–75.

Mhurchú, A. N. (2021). Intimately inhabiting borders: walking in-between belonging and otherness through constructions of home. *Geopolitics*, 26(2), 404–24.

Sheller, M. (2013). The islanding effect: Post-disaster mobility systems and humanitarian logistics in Haiti. *Cultural Geographies*, 20(2), 185–204.

Yuval-Davis, N. Wemyss, G., and Cassidy, K. (2018). Everyday bordering, belonging and the reorientation of British immigration legislation. *Sociology*, 52(2), 228–44.

12

'Milan doesn't want us to be comfortable': differential inclusion of refugees in Milan

Maurizio Artero

This chapter is concerned with the experience of a group of refugees in Milan and their feelings of belonging. By refugee, I mean a *status holder*, namely a person who has gone through the asylum application process and has received a residence permit. Drawing on 13 months of ethnographic fieldwork between 2017 and 2018,[1] this study addresses the changes to their everyday lives on obtaining their status and the perceived and real challenges they face living in Milan. During this period, I examined the 'asylum question' in Milan. Immersion in this field has made it possible to observe the relations that refugees have established within the city, its welfare system and socio-economic fabric. In particular, this analysis developed thanks to the participation of a subset of male refugees, mainly from Sub-Saharan Africa, whom I had the opportunity to get to know, listen to and interview. I focused on this population of refugees because they are one of the most prominent and highly 'visible minorities' and have been the subsequent focus of extensive public discussion in Italy in recent years.[2]

Italy has had consistent seaborne migration since 2011. Indeed, following the political upheavals that erupted in Northern Africa and the Middle East in late 2010 (i.e., the Arab Spring), about 800,000 people reached Italian shores by boat, and circa 500,000 applied for asylum.[3] In this context, growing negativity towards immigrant residents has impacted adversely on their receptivity (Ambrosini, 2018). Even in cities, a crucial backdrop for the immigration of this population, increasing stigmatisation of migrants, amidst hostility from host states, has meant that migrants can often experience marginality (e.g. Fontanari, 2016) or risk taking pathways of 'differential inclusion', which indicates 'how inclusion in a sphere or realm can be subject to varying degrees of subordination, rule, discrimination and segmentation' (Mezzadra and Neilson, 2012: 67). Often, this concept has been applied to so-called 'irregular migrants' (e.g. Könönen, 2018), and this group are a pertinent illustration of differential inclusion: included in the space of labour markets, but excluded in terms of aspects of their legal status and a wider set of rights. However, as shown here, even 'legitimate' migrants, such as refugees, may experience the absence of a sense of belonging.

In other words, holding refugee status grants access to civil and economic rights, and promises security and a sense of belonging, which is of critical importance for long-term refugees (Goldring and Landolt, 2011). Yet, without devaluing the significance of it, here it is noted how this entitlement does not equate to equal rights, since residents can still be differentially included according to diverse sets of attributes (e.g. gender, race, ethnicity; see Mezzadra and Neilson, 2012). Indeed, as argued by Mezzadra and Neilson (2012), the concept of differential inclusion points to a substitution of the binary conceptions of migrant legality versus 'illegality', to refer to a range of belongings. If lawful status, and the resulting permit of stay, is not a guarantor of rights or belonging, especially for those who are granted protection by the state after an extended period of careful consideration, then it is understandable that refugees may struggle to resolve their feelings of dislocation and marginality.

To this end, this chapter is structured into two main sections. The first section provides context on Milan and the presence of refugees. The second makes use of empirical material from the fieldwork. It illustrates the condition of refugees who are beneficiaries of protections in Milan by focusing on three aspects: refugees' experience of space, mediated by the network of charitable services; their representation of time, which is characterised by the repetitiveness and the lack of hope in the future; and the outcome of their interactions with discursive boundaries, which contribute to distancing refugees from native residents and place them at the margins of urban society.

In chapter 11, Kunz discusses the case of a family who emigrated from Germany and have since lived in various countries, including Kenya, where they are a part of a small contingent that 'manages' the movement of those seeking refuge. Together, we both demonstrate how war, conflict and economic hardship produce a range of human movements, and inequalities, which can be understood through the common lens of 'differential inclusion'. In particular, while Kunz focuses on forms of mobility that foster partial inclusion as well as social privileges, my contribution illustrates the dynamics of imperfect inclusion that affect, in the host society, those asylum seekers who were granted protection.

Milan: global connections and social dualisation

Located in the north-west of Italy, the municipality of Milan is Italy's economic and financial capital. This city represents an important industrial centre, which subsequently switched into a hub for the tertiary sector (Andreotti, Le Galès and Moreno-Fuentes, 2015). Nowadays, Milan is a global city region, at the centre of one of the most important and dynamic regions of Europe, particularly (but not exclusively) in economic terms. With its industrious province and its higher-than-average share of managers and intellectuals, Milan is a well-integrated node in the networks of global finance and capital (Andreotti, Le Galès and Moreno-Fuentes, 2015). At the same time, it has long been a popular destination for international migrants (see Barberis, Kazepov and Angelucci, 2014).

With the transition from Fordism to Post-Fordism, this once prosperous industrial city has shown a progressive trend toward 'social dualisation' (Cucca and Ranci, 2015). Particularly since the 1990s, the municipal government has adopted a market-oriented style of governance, which by privileging land valorisation, has reduced investments in social and educational policies (Cucca and Ranci, 2015). To cope with the disinvestment in welfare services directly provided by the municipality, local administrations encouraged a system based on the involvement of non-profit and private organisations, relying especially on what can be defined as a 'Catholic pillar' (Barberis, Kazepov and Angelucci, 2014). Consequently, Milan has mainly invested in big real estate development and flagship events with the aim of attracting financial investors in the city. As noted by González, 'this hyper-networked society […] creates global connections and local (dis)connections' (González, 2009: 33); a context where affluent inhabitants of skyscrapers, linked to global flows of capital through premium infrastructures, live side-by-side with a growing population that is economically deprived.

The recent economic crisis has partially worsened this scenario, with an increasing unemployment rate and the emergence of new forms of inequalities, especially in terms of labour market structure and spatial inequalities (Cucca and Ranci, 2015). Against this grim backdrop, the economic crisis seems to have worsened the condition of the most vulnerable inhabitants, who find themselves in conditions of severe social deprivation and without the protection of a strong welfare system, which is left to activism and the Third Sector.

An unavoidable node

In recent years, the economic crisis has coexisted alongside another 'crisis'. Since the mid-2010s, Europe has seen the arrival of significant numbers of refugees, a phenomenon that was referred to as a 'refugee crisis', but was rather a refugee *reception* crisis (Rea et al., 2019). Migration was concentrated in Milan, which represented a popular destination for asylum seekers and refugees, with the arrival of around 170,000 'transit migrants' between 2014 and 2017 in municipal reception centres, and up to 6,000 asylum seekers and refugees a day in different governmental centres (i.e. CAS and SPRAR) (Artero, 2019).

Despite all this, Milan (like many other Italian cities) has rarely been the intended final destination for refugees, but rather an important node within refugees' circulatory territories (Tarrius, 2014). With this expression, Tarrius describes territories which are woven by the circulation of migrants in recursive movements based on social and economic practices. These circulations produce and describe new routes of networks that cross and tie both urban and rural spaces, suggesting that cities can represent nodes of human mobility rather than 'fixed' territories (Tarrius, 2014). In the same vein, asylum seekers and refugees of Milan frequently move along circular networks of routes, mainly for economic reasons; in particular, those who do not possess a stable job in Milan go to work in the fields in rural areas in the summer and return to Milan in the autumn (see also Fontanari, 2016).

Although not always final destinations, however, large cities can be desirable stop-off points, where migrants can 'blend into the crowd', look for work, deal with the bureaucracy, and find their co-ethnic community (Fontanari, 2016). Moreover, in Milan, refugees could find a way to 'get by' and survive. The very limited role played by the municipality in the recent 'economic crisis' left the assistance of vulnerable people – in particular refugees – to Catholic and secular social service organisations (e.g. Caritas). The recent 'crises' have also provoked a new activism by parts of traditional social institutions (e.g. the Church, trade unions) as well as civil-society groups that fostered the expansion of a residual welfare for refugees and illegalised migrants. These actors have promoted the creation of a network of shelters, soup kitchens and facilities for the distribution of food. The networks are of the utmost importance for the most vulnerable migrants, especially those without refugee status, who are officially excluded from formal labour markets, housing markets and most welfare provisions (Ambrosini, 2018). It gives essential help to migrants in dire straits for their basic day-to-day survival, but at the same time, it risks fixing its user population into a 'circuit' which is difficult to escape, and which constitutes an important element of refugees' experience of space.

Space: the refugees' city and the 'hollowed-out' experience of space

This section focuses on the spatial dimension of refugees' daily life in Milan and its close connection with temporal representation and stigmatising discourses. A constituent of this spatial dimension is linked to the lack of adequate policies aimed at supporting refugees' long-term housing, particularly in the immediate aftermath of obtaining legal status and leaving the refugee camps. Indeed, in Italy, there is a longstanding weak relationship between legal standing and access to housing (Dell'Olio, 2004). At national and local levels, housing policies often limit themselves to simply ensuring that recognised refugees may remain in their reception centres for six extra months after the assessment of their asylum application has positively ended: a period that is deemed insufficient (Campomori and Feraco, 2018) and is not always ensured. What's more, rental discrimination represents a long-standing problem (see Baldini and Federici, 2011), and in Milan refugees are often forced to share small flats in substandard accommodation to afford higher rental prices. For many, the result is housing precarity and the lack of a proper home; for some, it means finding themselves completely homeless on the city streets.

Médecins Sans Frontières estimated that in Italy 10,000 beneficiaries of protection and asylum seekers live outside the state's institutions in camps with no access to basic services (MSF, 2018). Such situations exacerbate refugees' dependence on the above-mentioned residual welfare for refugees and illegalised migrants. Clothes distribution, shoe distribution, distribution of sustenance packages, soup kitchens, public showers, temp agencies and free medical clinics are all unavoidable focal points for many Milanese refugees, especially the most destitute ones, and constitute what we can call the *refugees'* city. This refugees' city exists in parallel to the 'mainstream city' (i.e. the city of native residents) without coming into contact with it: soup kitchens, help centres, medical clinics, and public toilets and showers stand side-by-side with elegant buildings near the city-centre, while their respective populations rarely interact.

Well known by the refugees, the inhabitants of this 'city' are often looked at as 'users', namely passive consumers of insufficient welfare services. In this city, daily life resembles a loop (see Fontanari, 2016), a circuit that mirrors, at the urban scale, the circulatory territories that refugees traverse (especially in summer). Within this circuit, refugees move in continual search of satisfaction for their basic needs, with the impression of being stuck and unable to escape (see also May, 2000). In this context, refugees often expressed a narrative of being entrapped. This feeling was also expressed as being stuck in 'circuits of thoughts' that make people 'sick', as expressed by Babacar,[4] a 24-year-old Senegalese man living in Italy since 2014:

> When you have 'pain' in your head [...] you think: how can I do this, how can I do that ... you get tired, you have many thoughts in your head, you become sick, you can even get crazy

The daily life of many refugees is thus characterised by a routine that revolves around the refugees' city, in which a day spent between soup kitchens and public toilets follows a bad night's sleep. This contributes to what May (2000: 747) termed 'a "hollowed-out" experience of place'. Babacar summarises the conditions in which he lives, stripped of his personhood:

> Milan doesn't want us to be comfortable, both the Municipality and the police [...] What wears me out is the lack of jobs, a good place to live [...] People think they're crazy, but they're not crazy [...] [You're yourself] if you live well, you have your private room, eat healthy, otherwise you're another person.

This feeling of resentment toward public authorities, expressed by Babacar, is common among the participants. These are refugees to whom the Italian state has recognised a form of protection and lawful residence, therefore they often feel that they earned the right to *belong* there. Nonetheless, this attribution of status often does not mark the start of their inclusion path, but their abandonment by public authorities.

In this regard, Kwame's story is emblematic. Kwame arrived in Italy from Libya in 2011 and obtained refugee status in 2014. The day after the attribution, he was discharged from the reception centre. His words first show the lack of commitment by the public authorities toward the housing situation of refugees; but also give voice to the sentiments of abandonment and betrayal that are shared among refugees in Milan, resulting from the mismatch between the expectations and the reality:

> My feeling for Italy is how can you let people sleep outside? Even in Africa, we don't sleep outside [...] Only in Italy, if they give document they say go [i.e. leave the reception centre]. To go to where? That's my question ... Where you should go? You gave me these documents and left me on the street [...] [but] the country must take care of you. It cannot treat you like a dog. We are human beings, but here we are living like animals!

Researchers have long underlined how crucial physical spaces are for people to develop their feeling of belonging to a context (e.g. see Boccagni, 2017). But both Babacar and Kwame illustrate how refugees experience Milan as an extraneous place, a space difficult to turn into a home, due to the lack of adequate policies aiming to support refugee housing. This experience marks them out as inhabitants *who do not belong* (Mezzadra and Neilson, 2012), and intertwines with two other dimensions of exclusion: the temporal experience, in which boredom and lack of control over the present situation are paramount, and the emergence of discursive boundaries.

Time: suspension and powerlessness

The temporal dimension plays a fundamental role in refugees' everyday life, constituting one of the main traits that characterise their experience of Milan. In this sense, Kabachnik, Regulska and Mitchneck, (2010) have illustrated how temporality is central in a displaced person's life. In their work, a refugee's time is dominated by nostalgia for their past and future, and their present is characterised by indefinite waiting. This literature, in addition, has often pointed out how asylum seekers and refugees experience time as temporarily paused, and how this often appears to be the consequence of their unpredictable legal status, which creates the deepest uncertainties (see Biehl, 2015). In effect, refugees' time experience is fraught with waiting and uncertainties associated with the determination and subsequent reconfirmation of their legal status. Indeed, according to the Italian legal system, both asylum seekers and beneficiaries of protection (e.g. 'humanitarian protection') need to undertake an evaluation of their application to determine their legal status, which can take from several months to several years.

However, in addition to this element – and connected with governments' ability to influence individuals and exert structural violence (see Artero and Fontanari, 2019) – there are dynamics that emerge at the urban level and that determine refugees' temporal experience as a time of waiting and emptiness. In this regard, during my fieldwork, it struck me that there was an immense sense of boredom which filled refugees' lives, due to the significant time they spent waiting: waiting for their lawyer to show up, in line for lunch or dinner, in the police station for renewing their documents, in the temp agency to hand in their CV, in help-desks' waiting rooms. To wait is an essential part of their everyday life. Indeed, beyond the more structural experience of waiting for their status, there is waiting time dictated by daily routines aimed at satisfying people's basic needs, especially within the above-mentioned refugees' city: e.g. in line for clothes distribution, lunch and dinner at the soup kitchen, the necessity to show up in time at the dormitory under penalty of exclusion. This daily routine often revolves around predetermined activities that keep repeating on a daily basis.

In this sense, if we analysed the urban rhythm (Lefebvre, 2004) of refugees, we might well end up concluding that refugees follow a repetitive and circular rhythm of time, which is perhaps not so very different from the circular shape of their movement within and beyond Milan. Also, in this case, the circularity is not the result of pure free choice but is influenced by welfare and bureaucratic agencies. Against this backdrop, many refugees express their aversion to a routine that has been imposed upon them. A case in point is Bamba. He preferred not to sleep in a dormitory in order not to follow its imposed schedule. He defends his decision to sleep rough on the basis of his distaste for imposed routines that in his view limit freedom:

> I know many people, many friends, that go to sleep in dorm houses. But, I know, there they tell you at 8 o'clock you go out [...] So I prefer to sleep outside, because I'm free! If I sleep outside I wake up any time, no problem, and nobody give me rules.

A refugee's rhythm is therefore often strictly organised from 'outside'. This situation is often lived by refugees as confirming their sense of powerlessness vis-a-vis their present situation. Moreover, it affects in a negative way their feeling of 'normalcy'. Goffman (2010 [1961]) observed that one of the ways to disrupt the sense of 'normalcy' in inpatients of psychiatric hospitals is to confer a particular measure to time, and to discipline and impose on individuals a daily routine that alienates them from their original way of life, with the result that time appears empty and out of their reach. In the case of refugees, the prearranged schedule to eat, sleep and wake up contributes to a sense of lack of control over their own time and increases refugees' dislocation vis-a-vis their new context. Consequently, present time is considered mostly as an 'in-between' time, as expressed by Kwame:

> I didn't come all the way to live like this but to have a normal life! [...] Of course, I can survive a hundred years like this ... Going to the soup kitchen and the drop-in centre ... But this is not normal life, the life that a person normally has and I want to have, with my family and friends.

Against this backdrop, while the present is a time of powerlessness and waste, a time of suspension from normalcy, the future takes the shape of a promised land. As advanced by Kabachin, Regulska and Mitchnek (2010), refugees frequently put their confidence in a future time in which their aspirations are fulfilled. In contrast, while they often perceive their future as full of promises, the present circumstance is a great cause for frustration. Similar to their experience of space, in which they feel stuck, refugees live a new experience of suspension of time in a recurring, circular and everlasting present that never makes space for a future of normalcy. Cheick, a refugee who arrived in Italy in 2014, utilised a metaphor to describe this condition:

> Being a foreigner here in Milan is like when somebody's cooking and you're hungry, they say: ok sit and wait. And you wait because they are cooking the food. But why, if they say wait here and there's no food?

Discourse: stigmatisation and relational boundaries

If the spatial dimensions of a refugee's life are filtered by their presence within the refugee city, and their temporal experience is characterised by feelings of boredom and lack of control over present circumstances, another pervasive experience concerns the drawing of discursive boundaries othering and externalising refugees. These boundaries limit refugees' relations with native residents. As illustrated by scholars (e.g. Yuval-Davis, Wemyss and Cassidy, 2018), nowadays we witness the proliferation of borders, which are not only physical but are also social, relational and symbolic. In this light, Kalir (2019) has noted that the present migration regime often justifies and perpetuates boundaries by portraying migrants in a dehumanising manner.

In effect, asylum seekers and refugees are often described in media discourses as threats to personal safety and socioeconomic prosperity. It is a stigmatisation mechanism, by which deviant conduct becomes associated with a whole population. The recent 'refugee crisis' appears to have worsened this scenario and turned refugees into specific discursive locations (Witteborn, 2011). In particular, such stigmatisation in Italy has crept into public opinion, and Italy has seen a deterioration of attitudes towards migrants. According to Eurobarometer data,[5] five of the ten most xenophobic European cities surveyed are in Italy: Turin, Rome, Bologna, Palermo and Naples. While not included in this list, Milan has also seen the emergence of anti-migrant movements. Here, anti-migrant attitude took on a variety of different expressions, ranging from residents on anti-migrant patrol in specific neighbourhoods[6] to the vocal opposition of residents and far-right parties to the opening of reception centres.

Therefore, it is no surprise that our refugee participants mentioned racist attitudes, together with some episodes of institutional discrimination, as recurrent incidents. For example, Omar said that he found some people 'racist, really racist' because of the way he is looked upon when walking down the street or sitting on the bus. In effect, together with not speaking much Italian and the fact of revolving around a refugees' city that is socially at the margins, this negative public discourse is a source of exclusion from social relations with other residents. In this sense, whereas verbal or physical attacks are infrequent events, the lack of meaningful relations and sympathy with Italian residents is a constant experience. Therefore, refugees rarely claim to have Italian friends. As Jerry, a refugee from Gambia, explained:

> The fact is that Italian people don't give us a chance [to be friends] ... I don't know, maybe some of them have a problem with people like me! But when you don't want to talk, when you don't show me dignity, I cannot make friends.

Indeed, stigmatisation mechanisms tend to reproduce separation, by creating an obstacle to social relations. The consequences of this attitude for refugees in this study were relevant and are related to their feeling of loneliness. This feeling can come to the point where migrants experience mental stress and '(dis)placement' (May, 2000). As Cheick expressed, it was not only his own state of mind, but a common feeling among refugees I interviewed:

> For the moment I feel nobody here. I have no family, I have no way to stay, I have no friends.

Conclusion

This chapter has focused on the experience of a group of refugees in Milan, highlighting the elements of differential inclusion they were subject to. The participants in this research are all refugees to whom the Italian state has awarded a form of protection and lawful residence. Nonetheless, unlike in chapter 11, their experience of differential inclusion has been one of abandonment and non-belonging. We have focused on three aspects that intertwine in the everyday life of the group of participant refugees. The first is their experience of space. This is marked by housing precarity and lack of a proper home. Unlike other countries, where legal status is, to a degree, strongly linked to housing benefits, in Italy there is a weak relationship between legal standing and access to housing, which represents an almost insuperable obstacle to overcome. This condition exacerbates refugees' dependence on what has been called the refugees' city, the network of charitable services made available to refugees in Milan.

This refugees' city is central also for the second aspect: a specific experience of temporality. Refugees' temporal representation of the present emerged as a time of waiting and emptiness. This is mainly due to the significant waiting time dictated by daily routines aimed at satisfying people's basic needs, especially within the above-mentioned refugees' city. Consequently, 'the present' is considered mostly as an in-between time for those who experience it, a great cause for frustration, while future takes the shape of a promised land.

Another relevant aspect concerns the drawing of discursive boundaries: 'othering' refugees. Nowadays, we witness the proliferation of stigmatisation mechanisms, by which refugees are turned into specific discursive locations (Witteborn, 2011). Racist attitudes and negative public discourses are sources of exclusion from social relations with other residents. In this sense, whereas verbal or physical attacks are infrequent events, the lack of meaningful relations and sympathy with Italian residents is a constant experience. Within this context, then, refugees' presence within the refugees' city of charitable services can add up to further stigma and limit interactions with the 'native' residents.

Ultimately, while having legal status is a crucial step for asylum seekers, this does not automatically spare refugees experiences of discrimination and subordination. The chapter can be situated within the debate on the processes of 'everyday borders' (e.g. Yuval-Davis, Wemyss and Cassidy, 2018) in urban settings. Cities are often depicted as having the potential to foster new forms of solidarity and social inclusion – one only needs to look at the rise of sanctuary cities in

North America and solidarity cities in Europe (Bauder and Gonzalez, 2018). In this research, we have taken as a point of reference a large European city, Milan, known for its progressive agenda toward migration (see Bazurli, 2019). Even in this case, we noted that urban contexts are still confronted with processes of differential inclusion that impact adversely on refugees' inclusion. Refugees in Milan make up a stratum of people equipped with access to rights which are granted formally but not in practice. Based on my observations, interviews and conversations with refugees, I found that this dynamic can place refugees on pathways toward limited integration in Italian cities. This can produce a subject that is never at home and always in discomfort – in tension between exclusion and inclusion.

Notes

1 In particular, this study has been developed within the PRIN 2017 project ASIT (Italian Ministry of University and Research. ASIT project (PRIN) Research, prot. 2017999JXZ).
2 See statistics: www.libertaciviliimmigrazione.dlci.interno.gov.it/it/documenta zione/statistica/i-numeri-dellasilo (accessed 11 October 2021).
3 Official statistics can be found at the following internet address: www.libertaciviliimmigrazione.dlci.interno.gov.it/it/documentazione/ statistica/i-numeri-dellasilo (accessed 11 October 2021).
4 All informants have been given a pseudonym to protect their identity.
5 See https://ec.europa.eu/regional_policy/en/information/publications/studies/ 2016/quality-of-life-in-european-cities-2015 (accessed 11 October 2021).
6 www.z3xmi.it/pagina.phtml?_id_articolo=6889-No-alle-ronde-private-a-Porta-Venezia.html (accessed 11 October 2021).

References

Ambrosini, M. (2018). *Irregular Immigration in Southern Europe.* Cham: Springer.
Andreotti, A., Le Galès, P., and Moreno-Fuentes, F. J. (2015). *Globalised Minds, Roots in the City: Urban Upper-middle Classes in Europe.* Chichester: John Wiley and Sons.
Artero, M., and Fontanari, E. (2019). Obstructing lives: local borders and their structural violence in the asylum field of post-2015 Europe. *Journal of Ethnic and Migration Studies*, 47(3), 631–48.

Artero M. (2019). Santuarios urbanos y el derecho al tránsito: migrantes en tránsito por Milán. *Revista CIDOB d'Afers Internacionals*, 123, 143–66.

Baldini, M., and Federici, M. (2011). Ethnic discrimination in the Italian rental housing market. *Journal of Housing Economics*, 20(1), 1–14.

Barberis, E., Kazepov, Y., and Angelucci, A. (2014). *Urban Policies on Diversity in Milan, Italy*. Urbino: DESP–University of Urbino Carlo Bo.

Bauder, H., and Gonzalez, D. A. (2018). Municipal responses to 'illegality': urban sanctuary across national contexts. *Social Inclusion*, 6(1), 124–34.

Bazurli, R. (2019). Local governments and social movements in the 'refugee crisis': Milan and Barcelona as 'cities of welcome'. *South European Society and Politics*, 24(3), 343–70.

Biehl, K. S. (2015). Governing through uncertainty: experiences of being a refugee in Turkey as a country for temporary asylum. *Social Analysis*, 59(1), 57–75.

Boccagni, P. (2017). *Migration and the Search for Home: Mapping Domestic Space in Migrants' Everyday Lives*. New York: Springer.

Campomori, F., and Feraco, M. (2018). Integrare i rifugiati dopo i percorsi di accoglienza: tra le lacune della politica e l'emergere di (fragili) pratiche socialmente innovative. *Rivista italiana di politiche pubbliche*, 13(1), 127–57.

Cucca, R., and Ranci, C. (2015). (Un)equal cities in Europe? The challenge of post-industrial transition in times of austerity. *RC21 The Ideal City: Between Myth and Reality*. Urbino (Italy), 27–29 August 2015.

Dell'Olio, F. (2004). Immigration and immigrant policy in Italy and the UK: is housing policy a barrier to a common approach towards immigration in the EU? *Journal of Ethnic and Migration Studies*, 30(1), 107–28.

Fontanari, E. (2016). Transiti (attra)verso Milano. In Pinelli B. e Ciabarri, L. *Dopo l'approdo. Un racconto per immagini e parole sui richiedenti asilo in Italia*. Firenze: Editpress, 184–95.

Goffman, E. (2010 [1961]). *Asylums*. Turin: Einaudi.

Goldring, L., and Landolt, P. (2011). Caught in the Work–citizenship matrix: the lasting effects of precarious legal status on work for Toronto immigrants. *Globalisations*, 8(3), 325–41.

González, S. (2009). (Dis)connecting Milan(ese): deterritorialised urbanism and disempowering politics in globalising cities. *Environment and Planning A*, 41(1), 31–47.

Kabachnik, P., Regulska, J., and Mitchneck, B. (2010). Where and when is home? The double displacement of Georgian IDPs from Abkhazia. *Journal of Refugee Studies*, 23(3), 315–36.

Kalir, B. (2019). Departheid: the draconian governance of illegalized migrants in western states. *Conflict and Society*, 5(1), 19–40.

Könönen, J. (2018). Differential inclusion of non-citizens in a universalistic welfare state. *Citizenship Studies*, 22(1), 53–69.

Lefebvre, H. (2004). *Rhythmanalysis: Space, Time and Everyday Life.* London: A. and C. Black.

May, J. (2000). Of nomads and vagrants: single homelessness and narratives of home as place. *Environment and Planning D: Society and Space*, 18(6), 737–59.

Mezzadra, S., and Neilson, B. (2012). Between inclusion and exclusion: on the topology of global space and borders. *Theory, Culture and Society*, 29(4–5), 58–75.

MSF (2018), *Informal Settlements: Social Marginality, Obstacles to Access to Healthcare and Basic Needs for Migrants, Asylum Seekers and Refugees.* 2nd edn. Médecins Sans Frontières.

Rea, A., Martiniello, M., Mazzola, A., and Meuleman, B., eds (2019). *The Refugee Reception Crisis in Europe: Polarized Opinions and Mobilisations.* Brussels: ULB Press.

Tarrius, A. (2014). Quand les territoires circulatoires des transmigrants traversent des quartiers enclavés de villes moyennes françaises. *Revue Européenne des Migrations Internationales*, 30(2), 169–92.

Witteborn, S. (2011). Constructing the forced migrant and the politics of space and place-making. *Journal of Communication*, 61(6), 1142–60.

Yuval-Davis, N., Wemyss, G., and Cassidy, K. (2018). Everyday bordering, belonging and the reorientation of British immigration legislation. *Sociology*, 52(2), 228–44.

Conclusion: highs and lows – breaching social and spatial boundaries

Rowland Atkinson

If the social sciences offer anything concrete to society at all it is surely the means by which we are better able to know ourselves. The development of sociology and its allied disciplines has been the history of techniques and ideas deployed to identify and chart social conditions, forces, connections and groups. Despite this valuable mandate and a slew of relevant and exciting studies, we now sit, after around a 150 years of the development of this new 'science', with little knowledge of those who are at the social apex (Hay and Muller, 2012). All too often the social sciences have focused on the poor, those without voice or recognition, and those excluded and discriminated against. On the face of it this is not a bad thing – surely the 'losers' in systems of oppression, alienation and exclusion are where we can and should start? In this sense social problems and 'problem people' remain the laudable mainstay of social scientific research and thinking.

Behind government attempts to address conditions by focusing single-mindedly on the poor, lies the question of whether others remain unexamined and uncharted by such efforts, who may be nevertheless linked to questions of poverty, violence, oppression and other social problems. Such connections may appear directly, in the form of extreme right violence, say, or in the obvious forms of classism inherent in school and university life. But the connection between privilege and poverty or exclusion is also formed of subtle methods and social forces (Therborn, 2012). This includes: the role of technology in pauperising swathes of the working poor; the aggregate effect of voting for political programmes which perpetuate the violent patrolling of national borders; or the socially devastating impacts of austerity programmes mounted in pursuit of financial prudence. These examples highlight how, in many ways, the central question of much social research should not simply be one of description or observed juxtaposition, but rather of the critical disentangling of interrelatedness. This volume represents an attempt to go to the heart of this question and to think across and between these forces and processes to offer ways into the debate about what and who our social sciences are for.

Fat cat sociology

There is no recording of Martin Nicolaus' incendiary speech to the American Sociological Association in 1968. It was here that he declaimed his academic fellows as offering one hand up to beg from government while looking down on the poor and the ostensibly dangerous citizens that he identified as the primary focus of their studies. We can only imagine hearing the pins drop and some mental machineries click as he described the tightly woven relationships of the social science machine to a surveillant, racist and classed system that helped to reproduce itself and its prejudices. Times have changed, in many ways dramatically. Yet the question of who social science is for remains a challenging one. The idea that the social sciences offer a panoptic survey of social conditions and problems has also been challenged, because we know that there are gaps and blind spots in our field of vision. Similarly there should be little room for complacency, or the view that social science has somehow progressed by leaps. In this regard progress is undermined by colonial legacies interwoven in our disciplinary assumptions (de Sousa Santos, 2017), the role of universities in reproducing privilege among the middle classes (Warikoo, 2016), and the forcing of increased relevance of publicly funded research to corporate needs (Holmwood, 2017). Despite such concerns, we also need to value and recognise universities as sites of critical, non-partisan and socially concerned knowledge production in which, for all the pressures and reforms of the past decades, faultfinding and critical research can still be conducted. The 'to and fro' of these concerns, critiques and counter-critiques can easily feel like a minefield or a kind of stasis, beyond which movement is challenging or impossible.

Incrementally perhaps, even despite all of this, progress of a kind is being made.

This book has highlighted the exciting possibilities of combining work on different aspects of social life in ways that illuminate its upper reaches as much as the necessary coverage of poverty and exclusion. In taking a leaf from Riis' work (2016 [1890]) on considering how the 'cheek by jowl' of urban life operated, the advantages of understanding disjuncture and adjacency are illustrated clearly. Here the pathway between high and low city, from male to female gaze, migrant to 'settled' resident, from estate to leafy terrace, and from violent actor to victim, can be seen as a more closely connected and interconnected series of conditions and stories. One of the most obvious questions that arises from these comparisons is the degree to which positive and negative outcomes and conditions might also be related – are these conditions inevitably part of some rich but unsettling social condition, or are they outcomes generated by interrelated forces and pressures in relation to each other (perhaps even by design or planning)? The sociologist will of course push for the latter, 'bigger' perspective, but it is also clear that careful and grounded study is required in order to allow such connections to be understood, and here the enduring tutor in such issues remains Mills (1959).

To return to Nicolaus, our empirical studies must and should encompass the high as well as the low city, the elite as well as the dispossessed. If this seems like an obvious point to make it is one that still requires making in the face of suggestions, often from within the academy, that studies of the middle-classes, elites and those in power are unnecessary and form a kind of frivolous diversion from the 'real business' of the social sciences. The most obvious point to make in response to these dismissals is that such problems exist precisely because of the wider structures of society, economy and politics – the poor do not try to impoverish themselves, the victims of white supremacist thinking do not stand as some incitement to their own abuse. In reality, is it not the case that elites and middle-class actors work as benign, rather than malicious, actors even while occupying positions that are often generative of widespread forms of social abjection, rejection, discrimination, poverty and violence? To accept this proposition is, I believe, the basis of a critical social science.

The social or spatial 'place' of problems and damaged lives are not simply some disconnected 'elsewhere' that operates according to some alternative set of physical laws, but rather one embedded within the wider social firmament of which they are a part. So it is in this sense of connection, of articulation and placing, that we begin to see the need to draw much larger rings around the object of social studies. The designation of a social problem is itself something that necessarily takes us to some other place or series of processes and forces that may be generative of, or linked to, the wasted, damaged or othered lives of those under examination (Rylko-Bauer and Farmer, 2016). Put more emphatically and in political terms, if we accept that much of what is studied by sociology and related disciplines is interconnected, then our sense of what or who a problem is becomes reversed or upended. Now we begin to see that the resolution or reform of conditions becomes something that invokes or takes in elites, managers, the wealthy, political systems of control and classification and so on. But we can in many ways have our cake and eat it too – we do not need to decide to study or work only for the excluded to the detriment of work that considers the role of power and elites. In the same way, it is possible and desirable to conduct work on the rich, on wealthy spaces and social institutions that are considered in relation to the 'outside' of those districts and networks.

Today the social sciences have undergone something of a rapid catch-up with Nicolaus' call to eschew what he called a fat cat sociology. In roughly a decade the marketisation of higher education and government itself have kicked away ideological and fiscal support for social scientific research. The result has been in part a public denigration of the value of expertise in general, and professed knowledge in the social sciences in particular. But this 'moment' has also arisen in newly mediated conditions which are both destabilis-ing in social terms (a new social order comprising tech elites, newly sorted forms of wealth as well as unsettled media environments that reflect and distort multiple realities) but also productively create new opportunities to hold power to account, through: data dumps of tax data; the expenses claim documents of politicians; the political connections of elites; the work of governing agencies and flows of information and networks that are less able to offer closure to the investigations of social scientists. This context has seen an emboldened and retooled social science that has generated new insights on tax and inequality (Saez and Zucman, 2019), on the influence of elites on the media (Bennett and Livingston, 2018), on the control of land and core resources in cities by elites (Atkinson, 2020) and the surveillance of ordinary and 'deviant' populations by governments and private agencies (Akhter, 2019). Taken as a whole this work begins to illuminate the 'peaks' and 'troughs' of our contemporary social condition. It also helps us as societies, albeit even as strained and increasing polarised bodies, to understand more about how opportunity and damage are unevenly distributed and reproduced.

Class, opportunity and privilege: new and old forms

Even with this observed step-change in social studies and new methodological advances, we may know more, yet perhaps still not enough, about social, economic and political elites of various kinds. Maybe more importantly, as this volume shows, we need not only to 'see' these privileged groups but also to be capable of mapping and connecting them to the unequal and damaging social conditions that afflict so many around them. The intrinsic nature of the life of the moneyed or the poor has little or no value unless it is set in its wider social context. In this sense we need explanation and connection as well as a sense of observing these conditions as though they were some kind of patchwork. Remarking on or describing inequality will get us some of the way, but it will not be sufficient in the face of a need to explain and highlight how groups, outcomes and injustices are linked, social phenomena.

In all of this the sense of the newly rich, older elites and masters, in political and corporate life, as captains of well-meaning and beneficent vessels, is increasingly questioned in academic work and indeed in investigative journalism (Shrubsole, 2019; Shaxson, 2018). To see profound wealth, as being 'self-made' requires enormous work to disembed and disentangle the lives and life-courses of the rich (Sayer, 2015). Such ideas are not only important to the defence and retention of abundance and opportunity by the very rich, but to the much larger social 'rump' of well-off asset holders who analysts increasingly see as forming the bedrock of class divisions today (Adkins et al., 2020). Privilege is in many ways all around us, but political ideology, as Piketty has observed, must not remain unchallenged for fear of upsetting a class whose contribution to tax and civic life must be defended. Yet such questions increasingly arise, and indeed compel attention, even by those on the political right who would prefer not to have to entertain them. As COVID-19 has cut away at human life and dignity, so has it torn a rug from under austerity governance that protected the wealth of middle-class and wealthy asset holders. Today taxes on wealth and property are a regular talking point. All of this highlights less a desire by government to infill the indefensible and yawning gaps between the hungry, vulnerable, deprived and the rich and more the need to maintain a system facing a significant crisis – if it didn't have to be done it wouldn't be.

Individualist notions of being self-made, without help or supporting hands of the state, community or family have been popularised within social conditions in which atomised individuals float freely (Tyler, 2013). In such social and economic conditions citizens and social actors are the author of their own fates and subject to the fickle winds of economic and technological change (Han, 2017). Social actors understand that the war is with themselves and their inadequacies as much as some sense of a social body that might lift them up or insure them against times of need or ill-health. What Nicholas Rose described as the 'death of the social' (1996) expressed a newly calculating mentality and operation of government, which prescribed markets, assessments of risk and self-governance as compensations for straining social budgets and state responsibilities. As Harvey (2007) would later pronounce, in reality the sharp practice of realpolitik is in fact a class war working in and through the auspices of neoliberal ideology. Here, there is a desire to find ideas that justify attempts at reinstating the project of gains and wealth for those who are already the richest and have seen their fortunes 'attacked' by settlements that needed to be funded by progressive taxation and contributions of wealthier groups.

Perhaps today even Rose's idea of community as a technology of government feels almost homely. With a mournful gaze to recent history we can see those years as an inflection point on a longer downward curve. That moment now appears to presage an increasing loss of social cohesion and mutual support, cleaved away by rising inequalities expressed around the axes of housing tenure (public and private renters and asset-rich homeowners), contracted and permanent labour, black and white, state and privately educated. Many of these problematiques were already in evidence; now they feel qualitatively and quantitatively of a different strength and magnitude. Now, the increasing application of market mechanisms and self-dismantling of the state has created more widespread precarity and the undermining of the state's connotation as a benign, provident and bridging space, replaced instead by multiple cuts to provision of support except for the affluent.

Breaching experiments

This discussion ties us back to the core aims of the book: to consider the dividing lines, the ups and downs, to acknowledge those living above and those below. To return again to Nicolaus for a moment we can see this ambition as novel and urgent: that social science can and should do more to fashion the lens through which we can see otherwise invisible lines that tie and bridge these conditions and outcomes. Often it has been only through the lens of the movie camera or in the lines of novels that we have been able to discern such connections. There is almost an identifiable form of such works that we might define as 'breaching', such as the highly successful South Korean film *Parasite* (minor spoilers to end of paragraph) which centres on the efforts of a basement-dwelling family (their rank signaled even by this below ground existence) down on their luck as they slowly inveigle their way into the service of a super-rich urbane family. The central technique of the film is to unsettle the elaborate deceits of the slowly intruding servant family by means of subtle contrast against the petty travails, shallowness and snobbery of their employers. *Parasite* (2019) is one of a number of films, such as Kurosawa's *High and Low* (1963), Lubitsch's *Trouble in Paradise* (1932) or *Elena* by Zvygentsev (2011) which use class boundary crossings to highlight their obvious strength and violence in everyday life. Some might argue that it is more through the arts that we have been granted particularly effective methods for charting the kind of symbolic violence and methods of social place setting that operate in daily contexts.

As is increasingly evident, the division between rich and poor is by no means the only boundary in many societies. In Raymond Williams' *Keywords* (1976) he discusses the meaning and origin of the idea of wealth, locating it in religious life and also the idea of welfare and well-being. Today it seems that welfare stands as an utterly stigmatised activity of the state while well-being is increasingly adopted as the mantra of the super-affluent in the pursuit of wellness and balance amidst 'overwhelming' professional lives. Against wealth Williams reminds us of its opposite, *illth*. Despite being slightly clumsy this term highlights how language itself operates to delimit or to close down effective discussion through the absence of commonly understood terms and concepts that help us to consider the range of experiences and divisions around us (akin to the lack of abusive terms for men when compared with the insults reserved for women, for example). Today we must push to generate new terms and forms of conceptualisation that allow us to see and locate forms of structural violence and interdependence of outcomes where much of politics seeks to deny such connections.

Intersection

Space, race, gender, class, sexuality, tenure all play a part in a kaleidoscope of configurations in which advantage and exclusion, violence, privilege and poverty can be witnessed. As this volume has shown, these divisions matter. But, of course, we can go further than this! We have long known, and social scientists profiled, the ways in which inequalities are shifting and growing (see for example, Dorling, 2019). We can also see clearly how those at the 'bottom' suffer and see their lives constrained or damaged by their conditions and how those with social power often seek to decry the poor and the neglected for their own 'condition' (Brown, 2021). But perhaps suddenly it also seems that the world of affluence and that of exclusion and poverty are very much more remote from each other than had originally been supposed, that the gulf between the haves and the have nots is less a question of income inequalities or simple class designations of working and middle class. Now, it is clear that we need to critically engage the long tail of the global distribution of fortunes: the property millionaires, the portfolio private landlords, wealthy citizens whose incomes come from shares or rent.

Today the sense of class division is increasingly moved to one of property and asset ownership versus those without. All of this is explored in detail in Adkins et al., *The Asset Economy* (2020), which suggests the need to highlight the profound role of property wealth among owners and landlords who enjoy access to what might be termed middle-class and secure lifestyles, while those who rent or who are precariously housed experience only transfers of their own income upward to landlords, with no chance of joining the game of circulation and advantage enjoyed by more privileged citizens. Similarly the work of Friedman and Laurison (2020) offers fascinating insights into the networks and connections that allow the privileged to reproduce their advantages alongside the harvesting and storage of surpluses, reputational goods and wealth that come with relative wealth.

The world of property wealth and the privileged is in many ways remote, inaccessible and remains underexplored. The methodological challenge of access and the epistemological challenge of knowing the 'high ground' of elite life, powerful actors and institutions presents real difficulties. Nevertheless, as this book has highlighted, promising work is all around us as doctoral students and the voices of other new researchers speak of the breaking of new conceptual and empirical ground to fill in many of the gaps and assumptions that operate around fortune, class and spatial divisions. We have seen how it is that the work of new, as well as more established, researchers is helping to map the contours and constitution of this territory. This agenda matters because the spaces and sociality of the affluent is not simply a co-present condition – in many complex ways it is fundamentally tied to the position of those who lack and who are weathered by the storm taking place within social conditions today.

As we have seen in this book, it is not possible to understand city life, eviction, dispossession, abuse, aggression and asymmetries around gender and sexuality without reference to its others and counterparts. Such ties operate through a diverse range of mechanisms, which include the partitioning and invisibility generated by class differences, and the spatial break between segregated areas of wealth and poverty, and of black and white urban zones. They also operate through the systemic emplacement of preferential tax regimes, and through the economic divisions focused around property and housing tenure, and around the life and spaces of minority and discriminated groups. The disconnect between high and low society is similarly expressed in patterns and priorities of policing, and in the regulation of the poor via subsistence welfare, as well as in penal conditions and workplace regulations that maintain a surplus population in sparse and bare ways.

Whereas social policy and sociological research tended to focus on the mad, the bad and the dangerous, and the areas and institutions they lived in, a more critical and strident tone has been struck in public conversations concerned with what should be done to create a fairer and more socially just society (Atkinson, et al., 2017). In this sense we continue to need to pay close attention to what goes on at the 'top'. This space can be defined in terms of economic elites, the apex of occupational structures, gender-based alpha masculinity, the membership of the top clubs and attendance at reputable schools, the best towns and neighbourhoods and indeed the 'best' universities that passport the progeny of the asset-rich into the winning jobs of the future. Instead of looking to the divide between the rewards of nurses and head teachers, the gulf instead, and its implications for resourcing social investments of all kinds, is to be found in the gap between the poor and the trillions in offshore wealth and massive capital holdings of the 0.001 per cent. We need to look less to the obvious scapegoat of 'bankers', and with more clarity at how it is that the owners of homes and the very rich above them have done so well, attended upon by a political system that has favoured property ownership as a means of getting rich, for themselves and their client electorates. The real treasure to be discovered at the end of such searches is deeper knowledge of the offshore gold, the unearned incomes on shares, the rewards of increased values that flow to homeowners and the possibility of locating, understanding and evaluating how such staggering wealth can be tapped to provide more of what so many others need right now.

Conclusion

As I write this conclusion, the COVID-19 pandemic is resurgent. Governments, appearing cash strapped, are considering how to fund an unavoidable bailout for workers and businesses whilst funding services for the homeless, the unemployed and other groups affected by the path that the virus has so cruelly cut through the conditions of the poorest and most vulnerable. The repeated call at this time is of how COVID-19 has 'revealed' or 'made clear' how much certain roles are worth, which have been denigrated or ignored in the past, or how much inequality and precarity exists all around us. This is, in reality, simply not true. The shelves of libraries, the terabytes of online research articles and the unending submission of evidence to governments by social researchers have carefully enumerated, measured, conceptualised and made proposals to address issues of child welfare, questions of disability and mental health, the chasms of various inequalities, the unjust treatment of minority ethnic citizens, the violence that has thrived in under-served communities and the problems of want and malnutrition. This research was in place well in advance of the first wave of damage wrought by austerity, brought in since the financial crisis. It spoke constructively and effectively of what needed to be done to heal divisions, prevent social harm and maintain more just social conditions. At the end of the 2010s – and those decades before in which deindustrialisation, the decline of many communities and the violence of neglect and inequality were manifestly clear – the sense of us and them, winners and losers, respectable and rough, rich and poor were all too clear.

By the time this chapter is in print it seems possible that the ravages of COVID-19 may have passed, lost to memory in the discovery of a vaccine or managed more effectively through technology, surveillance and treatment. At such a moment the intense social cost of the pandemic will nevertheless be a legacy, perhaps for generations. From one crisis to another the true cost is magnified by inequalities, borne most heavily by the pre-existing socially vulnerable. In that new set of social, economic and political conditions we will need a critical social science that hunts down the scale and root causes of manifold forms of inequality. We will also need the institutional settings of universities in which such work can be conducted and may hope for a less febrile political environment in which more constructive deliberations about how to resolve polarised conditions, inequalities and spatial divisions can be mended and healed. While speculation may seem an idle or error-filled pursuit it does at least drive energy toward efforts at heading-off the more regressive kinds of future we might imagine or come to live through.

To end this volume, we might look back in time to another commentator on social conditions, William Hogarth, whose pictures captured the inequalities, divisions and problems of city, politics and society. Of course many people know Hogarth's image of Gin Lane, complete with baby toppling from a drunken mother's arms and even the city around the near-crazed drinkers collapsing in apparent sympathy with the disorientation and moral decay of the street's inhabitants. Fewer people know the counterpart that Hogarth sketched, Beer Street, in which its happy, industrious imbibers of light ale (whose alcohol protected drinkers from germs) scurry around productively. These are distinct imaginaries, two entire social worlds that are to be found in two identifiable spaces. The sense of place is strong and the mapping of the social onto the spatial is clearly signalled here. A present-day Hogarth looking to highlight contemporary social evils might perhaps settle on 'Dodger's Island', complete with tanned ex-patriot tax evaders, set beside 'Diversity Row' in which people of a range of ethnicities, incomes, house types and inclusive street design measures show the possibilities of a more cohesive and egalitarian, even if not fully equal, society. The point of such comparative sketches, then and now, is to distil our feelings and ideas and consider where we can and should be going. But we need more than sketches and aphorisms and must work as social researchers to hone and refine our methods and measurements of a divided and polarised world for the benefit of all.

References

Adkins, L., Cooper, M., and Konings, M. (2020). *The Asset Economy*. London: John Wiley and Sons.

Akhter, M. (2019). The proliferation of peripheries: militarized drones and the reconfiguration of global space. *Progress in Human Geography*, 43(1), 64–80.

Atkinson, R. (2020). *Alpha City: How the Super-Rich Captured London*. London: Verso.

Atkinson, R., Mckenzie, L., and Winlow, S., eds (2017). *Building Better Societies: Promoting Social Justice in a World Falling Apart*. Bristol: Policy Press.

Bennett, W. L., and Livingston, S. (2018). The disinformation order: disruptive communication and the decline of democratic institutions. *European Journal of Communication*, 33(2), 122–39.

Brown, L. (2021). *The Black Butterfly: The Harmful Politics of Race and Space in America*. Baltimore: Johns Hopkins University Press.

de Sousa Santos, B. (2017). *Decolonising the University: The Challenge of Deep Cognitive Justice*. Newcastle: Cambridge Scholars.

Dorling, D. (2019). *Inequality and the 1%*. 2nd edn. London: Verso.

Friedman, S., and Laurison, D. (2020). *The Class Ceiling: Why it Pays to be Privileged*. Bristol: Policy Press.

Han, B. C. (2017). *Psychopolitics: Neoliberalism and new technologies of power*. London: Verso.

Harvey, D. (2007). *A Brief History of Neoliberalism*, Oxford: Oxford University Press.

Hay, I., and Muller, S. (2012). 'That tiny, stratospheric apex that owns most of the world': exploring geographies of the super-rich. *Geographical Research*, 50(1), 75–88.

Holmwood, J. (2017). The university, democracy and the public sphere. *British Journal of Sociology of Education*, 38(7), 927–42.

Mills, C. W. (1959). *The Sociological Imagination*, Oxford: Oxford University Press.

Riis, J. A. (2016 [1890]). *How the Other Half Lives: Studies Among the Tenements of New York*. Oxford: Benediction Classics.

Rose, N. (1996). The death of the social? Re-figuring the territory of government. *International Journal of Human Resource Management*, 25(3), 327–56.

Rylko-Bauer, B., and Farmer, P. (2016). Structural violence, poverty, and social suffering. In *The Oxford Handbook of the Social Science of Poverty*. Oxford: Oxford University Press. 47–74.

Saez, E., and Zucman, G. (2019). *The Triumph of Injustice: How the Rich Dodge Taxes and How to Make Them Pay*. New York: W. W. Norton.

Sayer, A. (2015). *Why we can't afford the rich*. Bristol: Policy Press.

Shaxson, N. (2018). *The Finance Curse: How Global Finance is Making us all Poorer*, New York: Random House.

Shrubsole, G. (2019). *Who Owns England? How We Lost Our Green and Pleasant Land, and How to Take it Back*. London: HarperCollins.

Therborn, G. (2012). The killing fields of inequality. *International Journal of Health Services*, 42(4), 579–89.

Tyler, D. I. (2013). *Revolting Subjects: Social Abjection and Resistance in Neoliberal Britain*. London: Zed Books.

Warikoo, N. K. (2016). *The diversity bargain: And other dilemmas of race, admissions, and meritocracy at elite universities*. Chicago: University of Chicago Press.

Williams, R. (1976). *Keywords: A Vocabulary of Culture and Society*. London: Fontana.

Index

EU authorised representative for GPSR:
Easy Access System Europe, Mustamäe tee 50,
10621 Tallinn, Estonia
gpsr.requests@easproject.com